T0046180

PRAISE FOR *PAUL AND JESUS*

"James Tabor is a meticulous historian who carefully and convincingly lays out the actual Jewish theology of earliest Christianity which lies shrouded in the New Testament. . . . Tabor's thorough yet succinct writing style brings a welcome new clarity to our understanding of the development of Christianity."

—The Rev. Jeffrey J. Bütz, S.T.M., adjunct professor of
Religious Studies, Penn State University, and author of
The Brother of Jesus and the Lost Teachings of Christianity

"A fresh, imaginative and insightful treatment of the original years of the Christian faith. It is not as we have been taught through the centuries. It is infinitely more complex and infinitely more exciting. James Tabor makes this clear."

—John Shelby Spong, author of
Re-Claiming the Bible for a Non-Religious World

"This superb, well written book carefully shows just how different Paul's religion was from that of Jesus and his first followers. . . . A fascinating book, packed with illuminating insights. Highly recommended."

—Barrie Wilson, Ph.D., Professor, Humanities and Religious Studies,
York University, and author of *How Jesus Became Christian*

"Tabor does a particularly fine job of explaining Paul's unique view of Jesus. . . . The crisp, clear writing gives readers much to consider—especially the fact that it is a Pauline Christianity that most Christians practice today. . . . The depth of his scholarship shows, but he also makes this an enjoyable read for those who want to know more about one of history's great mysteries."

—*Booklist* (starred review)

"Digging beneath the acceptable, scholars like Tabor . . . break through assumptions—even the sacred ones—and give rise to new perspectives and stories."

—Robert Orlando, *Huffington Post*

ALSO BY JAMES D. TABOR

*The Jesus Discovery: The New Archaeological Find
That Reveals the Birth of Christianity*
(with Simcha Jacobovici)

*The Jesus Dynasty: The Hidden History of Jesus,
His Royal Family, and the Birth of Christianity*

*Why Waco? Cults and the Battle for
Religious Freedom in America*
(with Eugene V. Gallagher)

*A Noble Death: Suicide and Martyrdom Among
Christians and Jews in Antiquity*
(with Arthur J. Droge)

*Things Unutterable: Paul's Ascent to Paradise in Its Greco-Roman,
Judaic, and Early Christian Contexts*

PAUL

AND

JESUS

HOW THE APOSTLE TRANSFORMED CHRISTIANITY

JAMES D. TABOR

SIMON & SCHUSTER PAPERBACKS
NEW YORK LONDON TORONTO SYDNEY NEW DELHI

Simon & Schuster Paperbacks
A Division of Simon & Schuster, Inc.
1230 Avenue of the Americas
New York, NY 10020

Copyright © 2012 by James D. Tabor

All rights reserved, including the right to reproduce this book or
portions thereof in any form whatsoever. For information address
Simon & Schuster Paperbacks Subsidary Rights Department,
1230 Avenue of the Americas, New York, NY 10020

First Simon & Schuster paperback edition November 2013

SIMON & SCHUSTER PAPERBACKS and colophon are
registered trademarks of Simon & Schuster, Inc.

For information about special discounts for bulk purchases,
please contact Simon & Schuster Special Sales at
1-866-506-1949 or business@simonandschuster.com.

The Simon & Schuster Speakers Bureau can bring authors
to your live event. For more information or to book an event,
contact the Simon & Schuster Speakers Bureau at
1-866-248-3049 or visit our website at www.simonspeakers.com.

Designed by Nancy Singer

Map by Paul Pugliese

Manufactured in the United States of America

10 9 8 7 6 5 4 3 2 1

The Library of Congress has cataloged the hardcover edition as follows:
Tabor, James D., date.
    Paul and Jesus : how the Apostle transformed Christianity / James D. Tabor.—
1st Simon & Schuster hardcover ed.
        p.   cm.
    Includes bibliographical references (p.   ) and index.
1. Christianity—Origin. 2. Paul, the Apostle, Saint. 3. Jesus Christ—Teachings. I.
Title.
    BS2653.T33 2012
    225.9′2—dc23   2011029549
ISBN 978-1-4391-2331-7
ISBN 978-1-4391-2332-4 (pbk)
ISBN 978-1-4391-3498-6 (ebook)

TO MY ESTEEMED TEACHER
JONATHAN Z. SMITH
WHO FIRST TAUGHT ME TO MAKE
THE FAMILIAR STRANGE
AND THE STRANGE FAMILIAR

CONTENTS

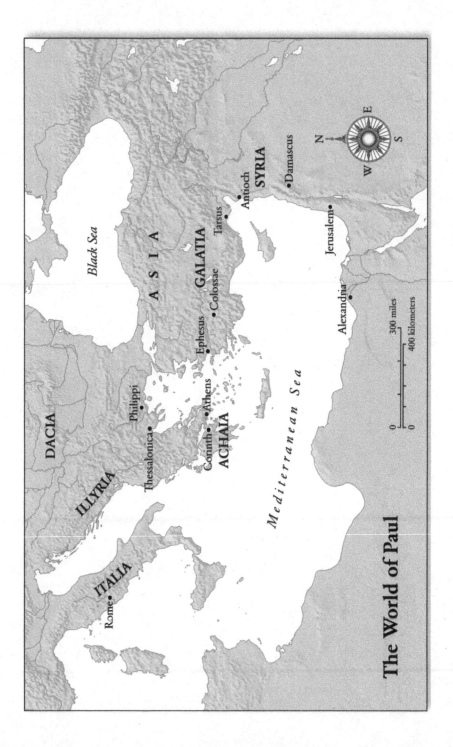

The World of Paul

Timeline of Major Events and Figures

63 B.C.	Roman conquest of Palestine by Pompey; Judea made a province
31 B.C.–A.D. 14	Rule of Augustus, 1st emperor of Rome
37–4 B.C.	Rule of Herod the Great, King of the Jews, over Palestine
4 B.C.	Death of Herod the Great and uprisings in Galilee and Judea
5 B.C.	Birth of John the Baptizer, Jesus, and Paul
4 B.C.–A.D. 39	Rule of Herod Antipas, son of Herod, over Galilee and Perea
A.D. 14–37	Rule of Tiberius, 2nd emperor of Rome
A.D. 29	Execution of John the Baptizer
A.D. 30	Execution of Jesus
A.D. 37	Conversion of Paul to the Nazarene movement
A.D. 37–41	Rule of Caligula, 3rd emperor of Rome
A.D. 41–54	Rule of Claudius, 4th emperor of Rome
A.D. 50	Jerusalem conference
A.D. 51–56	Paul preaches in Asia Minor and Greece, writes his early letters
A.D. 54	Rule of Nero, 5th emperor of Rome
A.D. 56	Paul's final trip to Jerusalem: confrontation with James
A.D. 62	Execution of James the brother of Jesus
A.D. 64–67	Paul's imprisonment in Rome and his execution
A.D. 69–79	Rule of Vespasian, 6th emperor of Rome; destruction of Jerusalem, A.D. 70

PAUL
AND
JESUS

DISCOVERING PAUL

I have spent my thirty-year career as a scholar of Christian origins investigating the silence between two back-to-back statements of the Apostles' Creed, namely that Jesus was *"Conceived by the Holy Ghost, Born of the Virgin Mary"* and that he *"Was crucified, died, and was buried, and on the third day He rose again from the dead."*[1]

Is it not striking that this oldest and most foundational Christian creed jumps from Jesus' birth to his death and resurrection, entirely skipping over his life?

How did it happen that the way Jesus came into the world, and how he left—Christmas and Easter—came to define Christianity itself? Here Catholics, mainstream Protestants, and Evangelicals all agree. To be a Christian is to believe in the virgin birth and resurrection of Christ, and thus to participate in the salvation Christ brought to the world as God-in-the-flesh. Where did this emphasis on the "entrance" and "exit" points of Jesus' heavenly existence come from, and how did it achieve such centrality—even above that of Jesus' life and teachings?

This book is a historical investigation of the origins of this particular way of defining and understanding Christianity. As we shall see, such an understanding of the Christian faith, confessed by millions each week in church services all over the world, originates from the experiences and ideas of one man—Saul of Tarsus, better known as the apostle Paul—*not* from Jesus himself, or from Peter, John, or James, or any of the original apostles that Jesus chose in his lifetime. And further, I maintain that there was a version of "Christianity before Paul," affirmed by both Jesus and his original followers, with tenets and affirmations quite opposite to these of Paul. This is the lost and forgotten Christianity of James the brother of Jesus, leader of the movement following Jesus' death, and the Christianity of Peter and all the apostles. In other words, the message of Paul, which created Christianity as we know it, and the message of the historical Jesus and his earliest followers, were not the same. In fact, they were sharply opposed to one another with little in common beyond the name Jesus itself. Discovering how such a state of affairs came about has been the quest, as well as the adventure, of my life.

I began my first serious encounter with the apostle Paul over forty-five years ago as a college student. I took a Greek reading course called "The Letters of Paul."[2] That course introduced me to Paul and his world in such a profound way that I was never the same. Day by day, phrase by phrase, we read through Paul's writings in the original Greek in a small seminar setting. We discussed every aspect of Paul's letters, their ideas, and their background. I became "hooked for life" on Paul and that college course marked the beginning of my lifelong spiritual and intellectual quest to understand Paul and his place in the formation of Christianity. Like Jacob wrestling the angel at the river Jabbok, I lay hold on Paul and swore that I would not let go until I understood his complex ideas and probed his mysterious depths. In this book I share with my readers what I have discovered over the past forty-five years.

I decided by my sophomore year in college that I wanted to pursue a professional career as a New Testament scholar with majors in Greek, Bible, and history. I had never encountered anything so fascinating, so alluring, as the historical investigation of the origins of Christianity. It was as if one were probing into the very foundations of our civilization in an effort to assay our most basic assumptions—what the Germans call our *Weltanschauung*. Philosophy, history, and literature all fascinated me, but it was this "history of ideas," and particularly these religious ideas, that became my intellectual passion.

Years later, at the University of Chicago, I wrote my Ph.D. dissertation on Paul, and my first book, *Things Unutterable*, dealt with Paul's mystical experiences and his unique message set in the context of the Hellenistic religions of his time.[3] Over the span of my academic career I have taught a course simply titled "Paul"—and I half-jokingly tell the students the first day that Paul is one of those people for whom a last name is not necessary, much like Elvis or Madonna. From my perspective, my class on Paul is the best of a half-dozen I regularly teach. I am sure the course is quite different today from when I first taught it, but each time I have begun the course I have introduced it with what I intend to be a startling assertion: *Paul is the most influential person in human history, and realize it or not, he has shaped practically all we think about everything.* I have in mind, of course, the West in particular, but since Christian culture has had such a global spread, I think my somewhat extravagant language about "human history" can be justified. As we will see in this book, the foundations of Western civilization—from our assumptions about reality to our societal and personal ethics—rest in a singular way upon the heavenly visions and apparitions of the apostle Paul. We are all cultural heirs of Paul, with the well-established doctrines and traditions of mainstream Christianity deeply entrenched in our culture. In contrast, Jesus as a historical figure, that is, a Jewish Messiah of his own time who sought to see the kingdom of God established on earth, has been largely lost to our culture.[4]

Visit any church service, whether Roman Catholic, Protestant, or Greek Orthodox, and it is Paul, and Paul's vision of Jesus, that are central—in the theological language of the hymns, the words of the creeds, the content of the sermons, the invocation and benediction, and of course, the rituals of baptism and the Holy Communion or Mass. Whether birth, baptism, confirmation, marriage, or death, it is predominantly Paul who is invoked to express meaning and significance.

The fundamental doctrinal tenets of Christianity, namely that Christ is God "born in the flesh," that his sacrificial death atones for the sins of humankind, and that his resurrection from the dead guarantees eternal life to all who believe, can be traced back to Paul, not Jesus.[5] Indeed, the spiritual union with Christ through baptism, as well as the "communion" with his body and blood through the sacred meal of bread and wine, also traces back to Paul. This is the Christianity familiar to us, the Christianity of the creeds and confessions that separated it from Judaism and put it on the road to becoming a new religion.

There is a late pseudonymous document in the New Testament known as 2 Peter that offers the cautionary warning that the letters of "our beloved brother Paul" contain "things hard to understand" (3:16), indicating that struggling with Paul was an experience we moderns share with the ancients.* Paul has often elicited passionately dichotomous reactions from his more engaged readers. He is loved and hated, praised and blamed, depending on one's evaluation of the validity of his claims about himself and his teachings, as well as one's view of orthodox Christianity. For many others, including many of my students, his writings are initially opaque, dense, and irrelevant to the modern world.

My challenge as a teacher, and now here as a writer, is to open up the fascinating world of the life, mission, and message of Paul

---

* Quotations from the Bible throughout this book are taken from the Revised Standard Version (Old Testament, 1962; New Testament, 1971, editions) with some modifications by the author based on the original Hebrew or Greek.

in a way that makes clear what we all owe to Paul, and what is at stake. I write for Christian believers as well as those of any religion, or no religion, who want to understand the deeper roots of our culture. Readers, whether familiar with Paul or not, should expect to be captivated, challenged, and surprised by the portrait of Paul that emerges. This is not the pious apostle of well-worn ecclesiastical tradition, Sunday school piety, or arcane theological discussions. What you will encounter here is Paul afresh, as he emerges in his own words, with his own voice, drawn exclusively from his earliest authentic letters. These are then set in the context of a critical reading of the New Testament and other ancient texts, some of which have come to light only in the last one hundred years.

The last week of May 2010, I traveled to Rome to carry out my final piece of research for this book. That trip in some ways was a culmination of my lifelong study of Paul. But for me the trip involved much more than research. It was very much a personal pilgrimage. My purpose was to visit the newly discovered tomb of Paul at the Basilica San Paolo, or St. Paul's Outside the Walls, one of the four major papal basilicas and the second largest, next to St. Peter's.[6]

Just before Christmas in 2006, Vatican archaeologists announced that they had unearthed an ancient stone sarcophagus, dated to the fourth century A.D., just below the central altar of the basilica and containing what they believed to be the skeletal remains of Paul.[7] It was inscribed *Paulo Apostolo Mart*, Latin for "to Paul Apostle Martyr." Tradition says that Paul was beheaded during the reign of the emperor Nero at the spot now identified as Tre Fontane, at the end of the Via Laurentina.[8] He was then buried two miles to the north, along the Ostian Way, the ancient road from Rome to the port of Ostia on the Mediterranean Sea. A necropolis just outside the basilica, dating from the first century B.C. to the fourth century A.D., has been partially excavated, indicating that the basilica was built over an ancient cemetery. There are references to this cemetery in the second century A.D.[9] In A.D. 324 the emperor Constantine built a small basilica at the site to receive pilgrims visiting Paul's tomb. On June 29, 2009, marking the traditional anniversary of Paul's death, Pope Benedict XVI announced that carbon-14 dating tests had been conducted on the skeletal remains inside the sarcophagus.[10] Vatican scientists had carried out their clandestine mission during the night to avoid arousing public attention. They drilled a small hole into the sarcophagus, allowing a tiny probe to be inserted to retrieve some small bone samples as well as fabric. The tests on the bones confirmed a date from the late first or early second century A.D.[11]

As an academic historian and scholar of Christian origins, I would not normally be drawn to a traditional Catholic site marking the tomb or relics of one of the saints, since the vast majority lack any historical authenticity. But this tomb of Paul seems different. It does indeed appear possible that these skeletal remains are those of Paul. For me that possibility cast this particular holy place in an entirely different light.

My visit to the tomb of Paul late that May afternoon was profoundly meaningful to me. I exited the B-line at the metro stop marked "Basilica San Paolo" and walked down the Via Ostiense, the modern street that traces the route of the ancient Roman road, with ancient ruins along the way visible between parks and modern apartment buildings. As I neared the cathedral grounds I felt an emotional quickening inside. A towering stone sculpture of Paul is at the main entrance. In his right hand is a sword and in his left a book. The cathedral is magnificent, absolutely breathtaking in its artistic and architectural beauty. A late afternoon Mass was in progress and the strains of Gregorian chants mixed with Latin prayers could not have been more appropriate for the setting. I stood briefly before the towering sculptures of Peter and Paul that guarded the way to the central altar, and gazed at the paintings and frescoes all around, but my focus was the area behind the central altar, now prepared for visitors to descend down a flight of steps, four and a half feet below the present floor level. There one can see the sides of the stone sarcophagus behind a modern brass grating, resting in its ancient crypt that had remained hidden from view for the past seventeen hundred years. Kneeling there in front of the tomb, surrounded by devoted pilgrims and curious visitors snapping photos, I was deeply moved. Somehow that physical proximity to what might likely be Paul's earthly remains marked a milestone to my forty-five-year search for the historical Paul. I felt I had come full circle. What follows are the startling but enlightening results of that quest.

May 31, 2010
Rome

PAUL
AND
JESUS

INTRODUCTION

PAUL AND JESUS

Paul never met Jesus. This book is an exploration of the startling implications of those four words. The chronological facts are undisputed. Jesus of Nazareth was crucified during the reign of Pontius Pilate, the Roman governor or *prefect* of Judea, in April, A.D. 30. As best we can determine it was not until seven years *after* Jesus' death, around A.D. 37, that Paul reported his initial apparition of "Christ," whom he identified with Jesus raised from the dead.[1] When challenged for his credentials he asks his followers: "Have I not *seen* Jesus our Lord?" equating his visionary experience with that of those who had known Jesus face-to-face (1 Corinthians 9:1). What this means is that Paul's claim to have "seen" Jesus, as well as the teachings he says he received directly from Jesus, came a significant number of years *after* Jesus' lifetime, and can be categorized as subjective visionary experiences (Galatians 1:12, 16; 2:2; 2 Corinthians 12:1–10). These "revelations" were not a one-time experience of "conversion," but a phenomenon that continued over the course of Paul's life, involving verbal exchanges with Jesus as well as extraordinary revelations of a nature Paul was convinced no other human in history had received. Paul confesses that he does not comprehend the nature of these ecstatic spiritual experiences, whether they were "in the body, or out of the body," but he believed that the voice he heard, the figure he saw, and the messages he received, were encounters with the *heavenly* Christ (2 Corinthians 12:2–3).

It was a full decade *after* Jesus' death that Paul first met Peter in Jerusalem (he calls Peter Cephas, his Aramaic name) and had a brief audience with James the brother of Jesus and leader of the Jesus movement (Galatians 1:18–23). Paul subsequently operated *independently* of the original apostles, preaching and teaching what he calls his "Gospel," in Asia Minor for another ten years before making a return trip to Jerusalem around A.D. 50. It was only then, *twenty* years after Jesus' death, that he encountered James and Peter again in Jerusalem and met for the first time the rest of the original apostles of Jesus (Galatians 2:1–9). This rather extraordinary chronological gap is a surprise to many. It is one of the key factors in understanding Paul and his message.

What this chronology means is that we must imagine a "Christianity before Paul," which existed independently of his influence or ideas for over twenty years, as well as a Christianity preached and developed by Paul, which developed independently of Jesus' original apostles and followers and with minimal contact with anyone who had known Jesus.

Many of the most important clues are hiding in plain sight. This is as true for a historian as it is for a detective, and I have experienced this numerous times in the course of working on this book, whether researching obscure texts in libraries, visiting the places connected to Paul, or just rereading Paul's letters in my Greek New Testament. So much depends on one's assumptions as to what is seen or unseen, what is noted or simply overlooked. This book is about the historical figure of Paul, but at the same time it uncovers a form of Christianity before Paul that has largely escaped our notice. The differences between these two "Christianities" are considerable and we shall explore both in some detail in the following chapters. When Paul is properly placed in this context, and within this world, a completely new and fascinating picture emerges. We are able to understand Paul in his own time and comprehend, for the first time, the passions that drove him.

The obvious place to begin is with Paul himself. His early letters are the first Christian documents of any kind in existence, written in the decade of the 50s A.D., and they are firsthand accounts. They are our best witnesses to the true state of affairs between Paul and the original apostles chosen by Jesus. For Paul this separation and independence, both from the "earthly" Jesus, as he calls him, and the apostles, was a point of pride and authenticity. He boasts that he has not derived the message he preaches "from men or through men," referring to James and the original apostles Jesus had directly chosen and instructed. Paul claimed that his access to Jesus has come through a revelation of the *heavenly* Christ (Galatians 1:11–12). He insisted that his second trip to Jerusalem, around A.D. 50, was not a summons from the leaders in Jerusalem, as if he were their inferior as some of his opponents had obviously claimed. He says he went there "by revelation," which is his way of saying Jesus told him to go. He refers to the three leaders of the Jerusalem church, James, Peter, and John, sarcastically as the "so-called pillars of the church" and "those of repute," but adds "what they are means nothing to me" (Galatians 2:6, 9).

Although he calls himself the least and the last, he is keen to make the point that his own revelations directly from the heavenly Christ are more significant than anything Jesus taught in his earthly life, and thus supersede the experiences of the other apostles (1 Corinthians 15:9–11; 2 Corinthians 5:16; 11:5). The force of this point has profound implications for our investigation of Paul and the gospel message he preached. He also boasts that he has "worked harder than any of them," referring to the other apostles who had known Jesus face-to-face (1 Corinthians 15:10). He refers to the period when people knew Jesus as "Jesus according to the flesh," and contrasts it with his own spiritual experiences, including the message he received from the heavenly Christ, which he asserts is far superior (2 Corinthians 5:16; Philippians 3:3).

Most readers of the New Testament have the impression that references to "the Gospel" are generally and evenly distributed throughout the various books. After all, Christians came to understand "the Gospel" as the singular message of Christianity—the Good News of salvation brought by Christ. In fact there are seventy-two occurrences of the term "the gospel" (*to euangelion*) in the entire New Testament, but they are not proportionately distributed. The letters of Paul account for sixty of the total, and Mark, who was heavily influenced by Paul, contains eight.[2] Paul refers to his message as "my Gospel," and it is clear that his usage is proprietary and exclusive (Romans 2:16; 16:25; Galatians 1:11–12). Rather than a generic term meaning "good news," Paul uses the term in the sense of "My Announcement"—a reference to a very specific message that he *alone* possessed.[3] The implications of this point are quite revolutionary: it means that the entire history of early Christianity, as commonly understood, has to be reconsidered.

The standard "Sunday school" or catechetical view of Christian origins goes something like the following: Jesus came to preach a new covenant gospel that superseded the Jewish understanding of God and his plan for the salvation of humankind. Jesus passed on the fundamentals of this new message to his chosen twelve apostles, who came to understand its full implications only after his death. Paul, who at first bitterly opposed the newly formed Christian Church, arresting Christians to be delivered up for execution, became the "Thirteenth Apostle," last but not least, chosen directly by Jesus Christ, who had ascended to heaven. Paul's mission was to preach the gospel message of salvation to the non-Jewish, or Gentile, world, while Peter, leader of the twelve apostles, led the mission to the Jews. Both Jew and Gentile were united in the one Christian Church, with *one single unified gospel message*. According to this mythology, despite a few initial issues that had to be worked out, Peter and Paul worked in supportive harmony. They were together in life and in death and they laid the foundations for a universal Christian faith that has continued through the centuries.

Historians of early Christianity question such a harmonizing view linking Jesus, his first apostles, and Paul. It serves theological dogma more than historical truth. To defend such a portrait requires one to ignore, downplay, or deny altogether the sharp tensions and the radically irreconcilable differences reflected within our New Testament documents, particularly in Paul's own letters.

"Christian origins," as an academic field of study, has been largely concerned with three issues: a quest for the historical Jesus; comparing him as he most likely was with what his first followers might have made of him in the interest of their own emerging Christian faith; and, finally, exploring the question of whether and to what degree Paul, who is a relative latecomer to the movement, operates in continuity or discontinuity with either the intentions of Jesus or those of his original apostles. There is also the related issue of whether Paul's "Gospel" represents the establishment of a new religion, wholly separate and apart from Judaism.

It is generally agreed that Jesus, who lived and died as a Jew, as well as his earliest followers, nearly all of whom were Jewish, continued to consider themselves as Jews, even with their conviction that Jesus was the promised Messiah. To identify someone as the Messiah was not uncommon in first-century Jewish-Roman Palestine. Josephus, the Jewish historian of that period, names half a dozen others, before and after Jesus, who made such a claim and gathered followers behind them.[4] Like Jesus, they all, without exception, were executed by the Jewish or Roman authorities.

What about Paul? Did he merely adapt his Jewish faith to his new faith in Christ or did he leave Judaism behind for what he saw as an entirely new revelation, given to him alone, that made the Torah of Moses obsolete?

Scholars are sharply divided on these complex questions, and the positions they take resist neat and easy categorization.[5] Some see Paul as extending and universalizing the essential teachings of Jesus and his early followers, so that differences are recognized but understood to be cultural and developmental. In this view Paul would be neither the apostle who betrayed the historical Jesus, nor the apostate who betrayed Judaism, but one who skillfully fashioned a version of Jesus' message for the wider non-Jewish world. Others recognize the sharp dichotomy between Jesus' proclamation that the kingdom of God was soon to be established on earth and Paul's message of a heavenly Christ, but nonetheless they imagine a practical functional harmony between Paul and the original apostles. In other words, Paul and the apostles agreed to disagree, recognizing that there was more that united them than divided them, particularly since Paul, in preaching to Gentiles, would have to tailor his message to fit the non-Jewish culture.

I go much further. Not only do I believe Paul should be seen as the "founder" of the Christianity that we know today, rather than Jesus and his original apostles, but I argue he made a decisive bitter break with those first apostles, promoting and preaching views they found to be utterly reprehensible. And conversely, I think the evidence shows that James, the brother of Jesus and leader of the Jerusalem church, as well as Peter and the other apostles, held to a Jewish version of the Christian faith that faded away and was forgotten due to the total triumph of Paul's version of Christianity. Paul's own letters contain bitterly sarcastic language directed even against the Jerusalem apostles. He puts forth a starkly different understanding of the message of Jesus—including a complete break from Judaism.

This viewpoint changes our understanding of early Christianity. But linking Peter and Paul in Christian tradition, history, and art is one of the bedrock foundations of the Christian Church in the past nineteen hundred years. How did this view come to prevail?

The answer seems as clear as it is surprising. Paul's triumph is almost wholly a *literary* victory, reinforced by an emerging theological orthodoxy backed by Roman political power after the time of the emperor Constantine (A.D. 306–37). This consolidation was not achieved in Paul's lifetime but it emerged by the dominance of pro-Pauline writings within the New Testament canon that became the standard of Christian orthodoxy. Even the order and arrangement of the New Testament books reflects the dominance of Paul's perspectives. Gradually alternative visions and voices faded, particularly those belonging to James and the early Jerusalem church. "Judaism" became a heresy, an obsolete religion replaced by a new covenant. Heresy became not simply an alternative opinion but a crime. We find the beginnings of this process in the letters of Paul and, surprisingly, even in the New Testament gospels that most people assume have little to do with Paul.

Paul's literary victory rested upon three pillars: 1) the gospel of Mark, our earliest narrative of the career and death of Jesus, is heavily Pauline in its theological content; 2) the two-volume work Luke-Acts vastly expanded Mark's story to culminate with a final scene of Paul preaching his gospel in Rome; and, 3) the six later letters written in Paul's name, but after Paul's lifetime offered a more domesticated Paul, which pleased the church and ensured the muting of his more radical message. (These six letters are Colossians, Ephesians, 2 Thessalonians, 1 and 2 Timothy, and Titus.)

The master narrative of Paul's literary triumph was the book of Acts. The author purposely hides his name and publishes his work anonymously—giving us our first signal that he wants us to think his work dates to an earlier time. He ends his story with Paul under house arrest in Rome. By not relating the story of Paul's death, which he surely knew, he leaves the impression that his book dates to the time of the emperor Nero, when Paul was executed. All this is a purposeful ploy.

Traditionally, the work was attributed to Luke, a companion of

Paul as well as a purported eyewitness to some of its main events. Paul mentions a certain Luke once in passing in a list of his fellow workers or assistants (Philemon 24). Presumably the same Luke, "the beloved physician," is named two additional times in later letters attributed to Paul but not written by him (Colossians 4:14; 2 Timothy 4:11). The final editors of the New Testament, in trying to support the tradition that Luke wrote both the gospel that bears his name and the book of Acts, likely added these references. The writer of 2 Timothy says that Luke was with Paul in prison and has Paul ask Timothy to "get Mark" and also bring his "books, and especially the parchments." The author's clear implication is that these purported gospel writers, Mark and Luke, were companions of Paul, eyewitnesses to many of the events in Acts, with access to documents they got from Paul.

Scholars have usually dated Luke-Acts to the 90s A.D., but a number of scholars have convincingly argued, more recently, for a date well into the second century A.D.[6]

The unabashed hero of the book of Acts is Paul, so much so that the work might be more properly named "The Acts of Paul," with a few preliminary remarks about the rest of the apostles. Peter and the others show up in the early chapters, but seldom again. The author's main intention is to glorify Paul as the apostle who brings the Christian message to Rome. Paul's enemies in Acts are the Jews, not the Romans or other non-Jews that he encounters. Acts is a remarkably pro-Roman book, and the author's implied context reflects a period many years after the destruction of the city of Jerusalem by the Romans in A.D. 70, with the crushing of Jewish national and messianic hopes and the scattering of the original Jerusalem church (Luke 19:41–44; 21:23–24).

This is not to say the book of Acts lacks historical value. For one thing it is all we have. It covers the critical period from the death of Jesus to Paul's journey to Rome (A.D. 30–60). As such, despite the author's strongly pro-Paul bias, it can serve as a source for a critical reconstruction of those missing "lost decades" of early Christianity. In fact it reveals much more than the author perhaps intended, once we factor in what we know from Paul's letters as well as some of our newly discovered other sources. The author apparently has access to some materials that go back to the days in the Jerusalem church, when James the brother of Jesus led the movement, even as he tries to mute influence of James. The cracks of his presentation show through since we have the other side of the story from Paul, and even a bit from James.

Unfortunately, Acts is seldom read critically. It is usually taken at face value and the portrait of Paul presented therein has become the dominant narrative. If people know anything about Paul, what they know is more than likely drawn from hearing about or reading the book of Acts.

Imagine the implications. Our primary source for the story of the origins of the Christian Church was written by an anonymous devotee of Paul decades removed from the events he purports to narrate. Some scholars have even called the book of Acts the great "cover-up" and as we will see, this language might be considered relatively mild.[7] Is it possible that this anonymous author has become, unwittingly, one of the most influential writers of the past two thousand years? Has he shaped our view of Jesus and early Christianity in ways that don't conform to the historical facts? As we will see, the author of Luke-Acts knew precisely what he was doing, and his *deliberate obscuring* of the original version of "Christianity before Paul" is one of our great cultural losses. So long as the portrait of Paul in Acts prevails, it obscures for us the Christianity of Jesus and his earliest followers.

Ironically, one need only go to Paul's own letters to recover a more authentic and reliable account of his relationship with James, Peter, and the Jerusalem church—what came to be called "Jewish Christianity" by later generations. Paul's seven earliest letters—1 Thessalonians, Galatians, 1 and 2 Corinthians, Romans,

Philippians, and Philemon, read carefully, tell the entire story, no holds barred. Most scholars consider these seven to be authentic and relatively free from later interpolations.[8] They occupy just fifty pages in a typical printed English New Testament totaling 275 pages, but implications of what they say are far-reaching. In this book I try to take Paul very much at his word. When he is allowed to speak for himself, without any predetermined assumptions about the essential unity of early Christianity, the results are clear and unambiguous, but also quite shocking and provocative.

It is also from these authentic letters of Paul that we can most reliably begin to reconstruct the bare biographical outlines of Paul's life. Paul calls himself a Hebrew or Israelite, stating that he was born a Jew and circumcised on the eighth day, of the Jewish tribe of Benjamin (Philippians 3:5; 2 Corinthians 11:22). He was once a member of the sect of the Pharisees. He states that he advanced in Judaism beyond many of his contemporaries, being extremely zealous for the traditions of his Jewish faith (Philippians 3:5; Galatians 1:14). He zealously persecuted the Jesus movement (Galatians 1:13; Philippians 3:6; 1 Corinthians 15:9). Sometime around A.D. 37 Paul had a visionary experience he describes as "seeing" Jesus and received from him his gospel message as well as his call to be an apostle to the non-Jewish world (1 Corinthians 9:2; Galatians 1:11–2:2). Paul was unmarried, at least during his career as an apostle (1 Corinthians 7:8, 15; 9:5; Philippians 3:8).[9] He worked as a manual laborer to support himself on his travels (1 Corinthians 4:12; 9:6, 12, 15; 1 Thessalonians 2:9). The book of Acts supplies many more biographical details, some of which might be historically reliable while others have been questioned by critical scholars. I address these issues in the appendix, "The Quest for the Historical Paul." In terms of method I have chosen to begin with what Paul says about himself, so that we get Paul, first and foremost, in his own words.

• • •

Based on Paul's authentic letters I have isolated six major elements in Paul's Christianity that shape the central contours of his thought—and thus my presentation in this book. Before considering each in detail it will be helpful to get an overview:

1. *A New Spiritual Body.* For Paul the belief that Jesus had been raised from the dead was a primary and essential component of the Christian faith. He states emphatically: "if Christ has not been raised, then our preaching is in vain and your faith is in vain" (1 Corinthians 15:14). His entire understanding of salvation hinged on what he understood to be a singular cosmic event, namely Jesus' resurrection from the dead. Paul's understanding of the resurrection of Jesus, however, is not what is commonly understood today. It had nothing to do with the resuscitation of a corpse. Paul must have assumed that Jesus was peacefully laid to rest in a tomb in Jerusalem according to the Jewish burial customs of the time. He even knows some tradition about that burial, though he offers no details (1 Corinthians 15:4).

   Paul understood Jesus' resurrection as the transformation—or to use his words—the *metamorphosis*, of a flesh-and-blood human being into what he calls a "life-giving spirit" (1 Corinthians 15:45). Such a change involved "putting off" the body like clothing, but not being left "naked," as in Greek thought, but "putting on" a new spiritual body with the old one left behind (2 Corinthians 5:1–5). So transformed, Jesus was, according to Paul, the first "Adam" of a new genus of Spirit-beings in the universe called "Children of God," of which many others were to follow.

   What is often overlooked is that Paul is our earliest witness, chronologically speaking, to claim to have "seen" Jesus after his death. And his is the *only* first-person claim we have. All the rest are late and secondhand. His letters were written decades earlier than Mark, the first written gospel. This means that Paul's view of Jesus' resurrection has profound implications for how we read the later gospel accounts—from the empty tomb to the "sightings" of Jesus reported in Matthew, Luke, and John. Most people read the New Testament "backwards," chronologically speaking, beginning with the gospels and then moving on to Paul, but Paul actually comes decades earlier and offers critical insight into what the earliest resurrection faith entailed. Once reexamined, the entire history of what happened "after the cross" is transformed and a new understanding emerges of what James, Peter, and the rest of the original apostles experienced and believed.

2. *A Cosmic Family and a Heavenly Kingdom.* According to Paul this new genus of Spirit-beings of which Jesus was the "firstborn" is part of an expanded cosmic family (Romans 8:29). Paul believed that Jesus was born of a woman as a flesh-and-blood human being, descended from the royal lineage of King David, so he could qualify as an "earthly" Messiah in Jewish thinking. But for Paul such physical Davidic lineage was nothing in comparison to the glorification of Jesus as the firstborn Son of God. Paul describes it thus: "The gospel concerning his Son, who was descended from David *according to the flesh* but appointed Son of God in power *according to the Spirit* of holiness through the resurrection of the dead" (Romans 1:4). What this means is that God, as Creator, has inaugurated a process through which he is *reproducing* himself—literally bringing to birth a "God-Family." Jesus, now transformed into the heavenly glorified Christ/Messiah, is the firstborn brother of an expanded group of divine offspring. Those who "belong to Christ" or are spiritually "in Christ," to use Paul's favorite expressions, have become impregnated by the Holy Spirit and like tiny spiritual embryos are growing and develop-

ing into the image of Christ until the time comes for their transformative "birth" from flesh and blood to life-giving Spirits. As Paul says, "He who is joined to the Lord becomes one spirit with him." Paul compares this union of "spirits" to that of a man and a woman when "the two shall become one flesh" (1 Corinthians 6:17).

The destiny of this cosmic heavenly family is to rule over the entire universe. Everything is to be put under their control, including things visible and invisible. At the center of the message of Jesus was the proclamation that the kingdom of God had drawn near. This kingdom, spoken of by the Hebrew Prophets, was envisioned as an era of peace and justice on earth for all humankind, inaugurated by a Messiah or descendant of the royal lineage of King David ruling over the nations of the world (Jeremiah 33:15; Isaiah 9:6–7). Jesus described it in clear and simple terms in the prayer he taught his disciples: "Let your Kingdom come, let your will be done, *on earth* as it is in Heaven" (Matthew 6:10). In anticipation of that reign Jesus had chosen the twelve apostles, whom he promised would rule over the regathered twelve tribes of Israel when the kingdom fully arrived (Matthew 19:28–29; Luke 22:30).

In Paul's view the kingdom of God would have nothing to do with the righteous reign of a human Messiah on earth, and the status of the Twelve or any other believers was to be determined only by Christ at the judgment. Paul understood the kingdom as a "cosmic takeover" of the entire universe by the newly born heavenly family—the many glorified children of God with Christ, as firstborn, at their head. Paul taught that when Christ returned in the clouds of heaven, this new race of Spirit-beings would experience its heavenly transformation, receiving the same inheritance, and thus the same level of power and glory, that Jesus had been given (Romans 8:17; Philippians 3:20–21). This instantaneous "mass apotheosis" would mark the end of the old age that began with Adam, and the beginning of a new creation inaugurated by Christ as a new or second Adam (Romans 8:21). This great event, the most significant in human history, would signal the arrival of the kingdom of God of which nothing flesh and blood could be a part (1 Corinthians 15:50). The group of divinized, glorified Spirit-beings would then participate corporately, with Christ, in the judgment of the world, even ruling over the angels (1 Corinthians 6:2–3).

3. *A Mystical Union with Christ.* Paul completely transformed the practice and understanding of baptism and the Eucharist to his Greek-speaking Gentile converts. Although rituals of water purification were common in Judaism, including the ceremonies of immersion practiced by John the Baptizer and Jesus as a sign of repentance, Paul's adaptation of baptism moved beyond ceremonial signification. Baptism brought about a mystical union with what Paul called the "spiritual body" of Christ, and was the act through which one received the impregnating Holy Spirit.

Sacred meals involving the blessings of bread and wine were also common in Judaism, and were thus part of the communal meals of the early followers of Jesus. Within apocalyptic groups, such as the Jesus movement and the sect that wrote the Dead Sea Scrolls, such sacred meals were considered anticipatory of the messianic age to come. When the Messiah arrived, his followers expected to gather around his table in fellowship, with Abraham, Moses, and the Prophets joining them. Paul's innovation, that one was thereby eating and drinking the body and blood of Christ in the form of bread and wine at the Eucharist or Holy Communion, has no parallels in any Jewish sources of the period. Three of our New Testament gospels record Jesus' Last Supper, in which he tells his disciples over bread and wine: "This is my body," and "This is my blood," and in the gospel of John, Jesus speaks of "eating my flesh" and "drinking my blood." These writers based their accounts of Jesus' final meal on Paul, directly quoting what he had written in his letters almost word for word (Mark 14:22–25; Matthew 26:26–29; Luke 22:15–20; John 6:52–56; 1 Corinthians 11:23–26). This is one of the strongest indications that the New Testament gospels are essentially Pauline documents, with underlying elements of the earlier Jesus tradition.

As a Jew living in a Jewish culture, Jesus would have considered this sort of language about eating flesh and drinking blood, even taken symbolically, as utterly reprehensible, akin to magic or ritual cannibalism. Despite what Paul asserts, it is extremely improbable that Jesus ever said these words. They are Paul's own interpretation of the meaning and significance of the Eucharist ceremony that he claims he received *from the heavenly Christ* by a revelation. For Paul eating bread and drinking wine was no simple memorial meal, but it was quite literally a "participation" in the spiritual body of the glorified heavenly Christ. This meal connected those who eat and drink through the Spirit with the embryonic nurturing life they needed as developing offspring of God (1 Corinthians 10:16). In contrast, as we will see, there is solid evidence that the Christians before Paul, and outside of his influence, celebrated a Eucharist with an entirely different understanding of the wine and the bread, one that reflects a practice much closer to what Jesus inaugurated at his Last Supper with his disciples. Fortunately, there are fragmented traces of this earlier view embedded in our New Testament gospels.

4. *Already but Not Yet.* Paul operated with a strongly apocalyptic perspective that influenced all he said or did. He was quite sure that he and his followers would live to see the return of Christ from heaven. Life in the world would go on, but not for long. Everything was soon to be transformed. At the same time there was a sense in which everything con-

tinued as it was. As Paul tried to work out the practical ethical and social implications of these ideas, he pressed hard
against the realities of time and history. Paul states emphatically that the "appointed time has grown very short," and
he advised his followers not to marry, begin a new business, or worry if they were slaves, since everything in the
world was about to be turned upside down and all social
relations were terminal. Right up until the end of his life
he expected to live to see the great event—what he called
the "Arrival" (Greek *parousia*)—the visible appearance of
the heavenly Christ in the clouds of heaven to usher in the
events of the final Judgment. He tried to inspire his followers to live *as if* the new spiritual transformation had already
arrived, all the time knowing that its full realization was
not yet. The tensions of life in the world, with its inarguable
realities of sex and marriage, birth and death, and ethnic
and social identities, were difficult to negotiate as if they no
longer were operative. It was one thing to say that *in Christ*
all such demarcations had passed, but it was quite another
to try to live one's life in a world that remained the same.

5. *Under the Torah of Christ.* As a Jew Paul decisively turned
   his back on the Torah revelation given to Moses on Mount
   Sinai, with all of its laws, customs, and traditions. In other
   words, Paul abandoned his Judaism. He would have never
   put it that way, though, since what he advocated he called
   a new and true Judaism, making the first version obsolete.
   He maintained that the Torah had now been replaced and
   superseded by the new Torah of Christ (Galatians 3:23–26).
   He never denied that the one God of Israel, who had sent
   Jesus and glorified him as Son of God, had once spoken
   through Moses and the Prophets. What he insisted upon
   was that alongside the one God of Israel was an exalted

heavenly Lord Jesus, to whom the whole cosmos would be in obeisance. He also believed that the new revelations he was receiving as the Thirteenth Apostle made anything that had gone before pale by contrast (2 Corinthians 3:7–9). For Paul there was no comparison between what the Torah of Moses promised the nation of Israel—physical blessings of prosperity, well-being, and peace—and the incomparable spiritual glory now promised to those destined to be part of the new cosmic heavenly family of glorified children of God. This process of cosmic birthing constituted a new spiritual "Israel," a new covenant, and a new Torah, replacing the old.

What Paul proposed as a replacement of the Torah of Moses he called the Torah of Christ. It was not a legal code, written in stone or on parchment, but a manifestation of the Christ-Spirit in those who had been united with Jesus through baptism, both Jews and non-Jews. It was this agency of the Spirit that defined the new Israel and enabled the select group to have both the motivation and the power to struggle against "the flesh." In contrast, the Law of Moses was powerless to actually deliver anyone from the power of sin that had its root in the flesh, since all it could do is define what was good. Paul put his own "life in the Spirit" forward as the model for his followers to imitate and was often disappointed in their seeming inability to "walk in the Spirit," since they failed to exhibit even the minimum standards of righteous behavior.

6. *The Battle of the Apostles.* Paul understood his own role as an apostle, "last but not least," as he put it, as the essential and pivotal element in God's cosmic plan to bring about the salvation of the world through Christ. Though he expressed grief over his former life as an opponent and persecutor of the Jesus movement, stressing that he was

unworthy even to be an apostle, he nonetheless believed that his call to be an apostle was a singular and extraordinary event (1 Corinthians 15:9–10). Unlike the other apostles, who had been chosen by Jesus at the beginning of his preaching in Galilee, Paul believed that he had been set apart and called *before he was even born*—while still in his mother's womb (Galatians 1:15). Given this perspective one might conclude that rather than being last, Paul was chosen *before* all the others. His "conversion," then, would just be a matter of God determining the time was right to reveal Paul as an apostle. As Paul puts it: God chose to "reveal his Son to me" (Galatians 1:16). This places him in a rather extraordinary position with reference to the original apostles, since he understood that his singular position as the "Thirteenth Apostle" was to take the message about Christ to the non-Jewish world. This special mission, he believed, was essential for him to complete before the end of the age could arrive. Just as Christ was sent to his own people, the Jewish nation, to confirm the promises given to the patriarchs, Paul, as a kind of "second Christ," was commissioned to go to the entire world (Romans 15:8–9). He believed that his specific role as an "apostle to the Gentiles" had been prophesied by Isaiah and that he, as a Suffering Servant, along with Christ, would also pour out his blood as an offering, and thus "fill up what is lacking in Christ's suffering" (Philippians 2:17; Colossians 1:24; Isaiah 49:1–6). Here Paul clearly believes that his own suffering, added to that of Jesus, was needed to fulfill God's universal plan.

Paul's relationship with the original apostles was sporadic and minimal. He is emphatic about this point, swearing with an oath to his followers that the gospel message he received directly from Christ came as a heavenly revelation and was not in any way de-

rived from consulting with, or receiving authority from, the original Jerusalem apostles (Galatians 1:16–18). Paul spoke of the
Jerusalem leadership sarcastically, referring to James, Peter, and
John as the "so-called pillars," and "those reputed to be somebody,"
but adds, "what they are means nothing to me" (Galatians 2:6, 9).
At the same time he insisted that they gave him the right hand of
fellowship and wished him well in his mission. It is possible that
the leaders in Jerusalem had initially reached some sort of "live
and let live" working agreement with Paul. His work, which was
almost exclusively with non-Jews, would not interfere with their
own preaching to Jews.

Sometime in the mid to late 50s A.D., Paul made a clear and
decisive break with the Jerusalem establishment. In one of his
last writings, an embedded fragment of a letter now found in 2
Corinthians, he declares "I am not the least inferior to these super-
apostles," and ends up calling them "false apostles, deceitful work-
men, disguising themselves as apostles of Christ" (2 Corinthians
11:5, 13). He had also become terribly bitter against his fellow
Jewish Christians who maintained their Jewish faith: "Look out for
the dogs, look out for the evil-workers, look out for those who mu-
tilate the flesh," sarcastically referring to the practice of circumcision (Philippians 3:2). Tradition has it that Paul ended up in prison
in Rome alone, with few supporters (2 Timothy 4:16).

Most scholars have interpreted this bitterly denunciatory language as directed against a group of unnamed Jewish opponents,
not the Jerusalem apostles. I think this is mistaken. The radical
nature of the break that took place between Paul and the original apostles is so threatening to our most basic assumptions about
Christian origins that it is easy to think that it just can't be true, but
the evidence is there. Unfortunately, outside of Paul's letters there
is little in the New Testament to document it further. After all, the
entire New Testament canon is largely a post-Paul and pro-Paul
production. But Paul himself provides his side of the story and that

is more than enough to reconstruct what happened. Fortunately a few additional sources outside the New Testament writings have survived that support what we can construct as the other side of the story. We will discuss these in the final chapter. They provide us with solid evidence of just how bitter and sharp the break between the Jerusalem apostles and Paul became.

If some of the elements of this brief overview of my analysis of Paul seem strange and unfamiliar to readers, that should be no surprise. Paul proved too radical, too apocalyptic, and too controversial even for the emerging Church in the second through the fourth centuries. He was domesticated, first by the author of Acts, as I have noted, but subsequently by letters written in his name, purporting to be from his hand, that are found in the New Testament. Paul was appropriated as a hero, a courageous preacher, and a martyr, who was responsible for taking the gospel beyond the Jewish world, but the radical content of his message, and his view of his unique calling and mission, were lost to subsequent generations of Christians. What Paul most expected to happen never came about and his grand vision of the imminent transformation of the world, and his pivotal role therein, utterly failed. The Paul who was appropriated over the centuries was a theological Paul, particularly as understood by Augustine and Luther. Paul was removed from his historical context and recast in terms of the great doctrines of Christianity, namely, predestination, justification by grace through faith, reconciliation, redemption, sanctification, and eternal life. The ethical teachings of Paul also had a practical and enduring legacy, from his incomparable celebration of the primacy of love in 1 Corinthians 13, to his views of women, sexuality and marriage, divorce, and other social issues. The thirteen letters attributed to Paul in the New Testament make up nearly one-quarter of the New Testament and they are the primary documents that have shaped the course of Catholic, Greek Orthodox, and Protestant Christianity.[10]

Jesus will always be the center of Christianity, but the "Jesus" who most influenced history was the "Jesus Christ" of Paul, not the historical figure of Jesus. There is a double irony here. Paul became the most influential defining figure for later Christianity, even beyond the historical Jesus, but he is also a man waiting to be discovered, even after nearly two thousand years. Paul transformed Jesus himself, with his message of a messianic kingdom of justice and peace on earth, to the symbol of a religion of otherworldly salvation in a heavenly world. Recovering the authentic Paul, as he was in his own time, and from his own words, is my task in this book. All of us, whether Christian or not, whether wittingly or unwittingly, are heirs of Paul, since the parameters of Christ and his heavenly kingdom created by Paul were what shaped Christian civilization.

ONE

CHRISTIANITY BEFORE PAUL

I grew up thinking that the "lost years" of early Christianity referred to Jesus' childhood and his early twenties. The gospels only record a single story from his youth.[1] I had no idea there was a much more significant gap of "missing years" in the history of early Christianity, much less a forgotten brother of Jesus.[2] Paul calls him "James the brother of the Lord," and it is James, not Peter, who takes over leadership of the movement following Jesus' death. Paul met James face-to-face, in Jerusalem, on at least three separate occasions.[3] In later tradition he is called "James the Just" to distinguish him from the other James, the Galilean fisherman, the son of Zebedee and brother of John, and one of the twelve apostles.[4]

Who was this James, the brother of Jesus, and why was he forgotten? And what kind of shape had the early Christian movement taken, under his leadership, before Paul even came on the scene? The Roman Catholic Church looks to Peter while the Protestants have focused on Paul, but James seems to have been deliberately marginalized, as we will see. The tradition most people know is that the apostle Peter took over leadership of the movement as head of the Twelve. Not long afterward the apostle Paul, newly "converted" to the Christian movement from Judaism, joined Peter's side. Together the apostles Peter and Paul became the twin "pillars" of the emerging Christian faith, preaching the gospel to the entire Roman world and dying gloriously, together under the emperor Nero, as martyrs in Rome—the new divinely appointed head-quarters of the Church. This view of things has been enshrined in Christian art through the ages and popularized in books and films. Indeed, Peter's primacy, as the first pope, has even become the cornerstone of Roman Catholic dogmatic teaching. We now know that things did not happen this way.

As we will see, the original apostolic Christianity that came be-fore Paul, and developed independently of him, by those who had known and spent time with Jesus, was in sharp contrast to Paul's version of the new faith. This lost Christianity held sway during Paul's lifetime, and only with the death of James in A.D. 62, fol-lowed by the brutal destruction of Jerusalem by the Romans in A.D. 70, did it begin to lose its influence as the center of the Jesus movement. Ironically, it was the production and final editing of the New Testament itself, in the early second century A.D., sup-porting Paul's version of Christianity, that ensured first the mar-ginalization, and subsequently the death of this original form of Christianity within Christian orthodoxy. By the fourth century A.D., the dominant Roman church classified surviving forms of this Jewish Christianity as heresy and Christians were forbidden under threat of penalties to follow any kind of Jewish observances.

One of my theses in this book is that the form of Christianity that subsequently developed as a thriving religion in the late Roman Empire was heavily based upon the ecstatic and visionary experiences of Paul. Christianity, as we came to know it, *is* Paul and Paul *is* Christianity. The bulk of the New Testament is dominated by his theological vision. Its main elements are: 1) the forgiveness of sins through the blood of Christ, God's divine Son, based on his sacrificial death on the cross; 2) receiving the Holy Spirit and the gift of eternal life guaranteed by faith in Jesus' resurrection from the dead; and 3) a glorified heavenly reign with Christ when he returns in the clouds of heaven. The mystical rites of baptism and the "Lord's Supper" function as experiential verification of this understanding of "salvation."

It is difficult for one to imagine a version of Christianity predating Paul with *none* of these seemingly essential elements. Yet that is precisely what our evidence indicates. The original apostles and followers of Jesus, led by James and assisted by Peter and John, continued to live as Jews, observing the Torah and worshipping in the Temple at Jerusalem, or in their local synagogues, while remembering and honoring Jesus as their martyred Teacher and Messiah. They neither worshipped nor divinized Jesus as the Son of God, or as a Dying-and-Rising Savior, who died for the sins of humankind. They practiced no ritual of baptism into Christ, nor did they celebrate a sacred meal equated with "eating the body and drinking the blood" of Christ as a guarantee of eternal life. Their message was wholly focused around their expectations that the kingdom of God had drawn near, as proclaimed by John the Baptizer and Jesus, and that very soon God would intervene in human history to bring about his righteous rule of peace and justice among all nations. In the meantime both Jews and non-Jews were urged to repent of their sins, turn to God, and live righteously before him in expectation of his kingdom.

But that takes us far ahead of our story. Let's begin with James the forgotten brother of Jesus. Since the late 1990s there have been over a dozen major scholarly studies of James published.[5] Prior to this, to my knowledge, not a single major scholarly study of James had ever been published. But these academic studies by and large did not reach the public.

Remarkably, on October 21, 2002, James made headline news around the world. Hershel Shanks, editor of the *Biblical Archaeology Review*, announced at a Washington, D.C., press conference that a first-century A.D. limestone burial box, or ossuary (literally "bone box"), inscribed in Aramaic "James, son of Joseph, brother of Jesus," had turned up in Jerusalem in the hands of a private collector. The news flashed around the globe. Experts involved in studying the artifact were convinced that it was genuine, that it most likely referred to James the brother of Jesus of Nazareth, and that it had once held his bones. As such, it would be our earliest archaeological reference to Jesus and to James.[6] Some scholars have since questioned the authenticity of various parts of the inscription and it has become part of a highly controversial ongoing criminal forgery case in Israel, but there is no question that the ossuary story gave James the brother of Jesus his fifteen minutes of fame, almost as if he had been resurrected from the dead after nineteen hundred years.[7]

Most people who read or heard the news story, even those claiming a fair knowledge of the New Testament, found themselves asking—James who? The fisherman James, one of the twelve apostles, might have been familiar, but who was this mysterious second James? And how could he have been a brother of Jesus, if Mary, Jesus' mother, remained a virgin throughout her life?

At least since the fourth century, Roman Catholics, represented by the church father Jerome, had claimed that the brothers of Jesus, mentioned and named in the New Testament, were cousins of Jesus, not literal brothers, since both Mary and Joseph remained virgins throughout their lives.[8] Eastern Catholics, represented by Epiphanius, held the view that they were stepbrothers, older than Jesus, and children of Joseph from a previous marriage.[9] According to Epiphanius, Joseph was a widower, over eighty years old, when he took Mary as his wife. Protestants tend to be divided, but many, particularly in modern times, accept that Joseph and Mary, following the virgin birth of Jesus, had other children together, so these would be half brothers of Jesus from his mother, Mary, since Jesus had no human father.[10]

Paul knows James as "the brother of the Lord," and he mentions the "brothers of the Lord" as a group as well (Galatians 1:19; 1

Corinthians 9:5). He distinguishes these brothers from Peter, from the Twelve, and from those called "apostles" in a more general sense (1 Corinthians 9:5; 15:5–7). When he mentions the name James without a descriptive tag, there is no doubt he refers to Jesus' brother James, as Paul is our earliest witness to James being the head of the Jerusalem church. According to Paul, James stands first, along with Peter and John, as the "pillars" of the movement (Galatians 2:9, 12).

Terminology can be quite tricky when it comes to James himself, as well as the movement he led for over thirty years. Before I take up the full story let me attempt some important clarifications and express some caveats.

First, the person we know as James the brother of Jesus, as well as the author of the letter of James that bears his name, tucked in the back of the New Testament, twentieth of twenty-seven documents making up the whole, needs a bit of explaining. *James* in English is the name *Iakobov* in Greek, consistent throughout the New Testament, which is in fact the name *Jacob* (*Yaaqov* in Hebrew). Thus it is the same name as that of the grandson of Abraham and the son of Isaac, used a total of 358 times throughout the Bible, including in the New Testament. So when Jesus says that "Abraham, Isaac, and Jacob" will be raised from the dead when the kingdom of God arrives, the Greek texts of our gospels use the word *Iakobov*, clearly and properly translated as *Jacob* (Mark 12:26). Yet the *same* word, when used of the fisherman apostle or the brother of Jesus, becomes James, not Jacob, in English. Imagine the reverse, if translators had put "Abraham, Isaac, and James." The effect would be quite jolting and most readers would have not the slightest idea of what might be going on.

The English name James is so rooted in our language it is not going to change. I can't imagine a time when we would speak of the King James Version of the Bible, or Jacob Dean, the late great movie star. But when we are translating the Greek New Testament this is a very different matter, since the English name James did not exist anciently, and the Greek name is plainly and clearly *Jacob* and so translated, so long as it does not refer to the apostle James or the James the brother of Jesus. It simply makes no linguistic sense.

Unfortunately, the effect is more than a matter of style. The name Jacob is clearly *Jewish*, not Greek or Latin, with deep roots in the Hebrew Bible and Jewish culture. To call Jesus' brother James, in English, dissociates and isolates him from his Jewish environment. But if one begins to use "Jacob" for "James," what tiny measure of familiarity anyone might have with James the brother of Jesus, given his obscurity and marginalization, will completely dissolve. So my first caveat is that I will continue to call Jesus' brother "James," even though it obscures his Jewish heritage.

It is also problematic in this period to use terms such as "Judaism," "Christianity," or even "Judaeo-Christian" to describe the emerging movement we come to know much later as Christianity. Neither Jesus nor his first followers understood themselves as part of a new religion called Christianity, and that goes for Paul as well. The word "Christianity" never appears in the entire New Testament and the word "Christian" never in any of Paul's writings. The early followers of Jesus were predominantly Jews, living within a Jewish culture that had as its main reference points Abraham, Moses, the Hebrew Prophets, and Israel as God's chosen people, with the world divided into "Jew" and "Gentile" rather than Judaism and Christianity. If the movement had any name it was most likely "Nazarene," taking its place among a diverse cluster of groups, sects, and movements that make up the variations of "Judaism" in this period.[11] Indeed, even talking about the "religion of Judaism" at this time is quite problematic, since those who identified themselves as part of Jewish culture were hardly monolithic or "orthodox" in their practices or their beliefs.[12] I have nonetheless, and quite purposely, chosen to use the anachronistic term "Christianity," or in some cases "Jewish Christianity," for these early stages of the Jesus movement, whether associated with James or Paul. I want to highlight the point that there were rival and competing versions of emerging "Christianity" during this period, each taking Jesus as their reference point, but with distinct and irreconcilable differences, even though in the end this dispute between Paul and the apostles is clearly a Jewish family feud.

REMEMBERING JAMES

As we have noted, it is Paul who gives us our earliest reference to James and his leadership over the Jerusalem-based movement following the death of Jesus (Galatians 1:18–19; 2:9). Paul's evidence here is invaluable since the author of the book of Acts only begrudgingly and obliquely acknowledges the leadership of James over the entire Jesus movement. Acts is our only early account of the history of early Christianity, and its prominent place in the New Testament, following the four gospels, ensured its dominance. It is the book of Acts that is largely responsible for the standard portrait of early Christianity in which Peter and Paul assume such a dominant role and James is largely marginalized or left out entirely. The presentation of Acts has become *the* story, even though its version of events is woefully one-sided and historically questionable. The author of Acts surely knew, but was not willing to state, that James took over the leadership of the movement after Jesus' death. In his early chapters he never even mentions James by name and casts Peter and John, the other two "pillars," as the undisputed leaders of Jesus' followers, effectively blurring out James entirely. His major agenda in the book as a whole is to promote the centrality of the mission and message of the apostle Paul. Although Acts has twenty-four chapters, once Paul is introduced in chapter 9 the rest of the book is wholly about Paul. Even Peter begins to drop out of the picture after chapter 12. Rather than "Acts of the Apostles" the book might better be named "The Acts of Paul." This suppression of James is systematic and deliberate, as we shall see.

According to Mark, our earliest gospel, the townspeople at Nazareth, where Jesus grew up, are amazed at his teachings and his miracles. They say to one another: "Is this not the carpenter, the son of Mary and *brother of James and Joses and Judas and Simon*, and are not his sisters here with us?" (Mark 6:3). Most scholars are convinced that the author of the gospel of Luke, who also wrote the book of Acts, used Mark as his main source. He has some independent material, as well as the Q source (which I will explain below), but his core story of Jesus is taken from Mark. Accordingly, he edits Mark freely, based on his own emphases and agenda. Here, for example, when he relates this scene in Nazareth, based on Mark, he *omits the names of the brothers* and has the people ask, "Is not this Joseph's son?" (Luke 4:22). His silence has nothing to do with the idea that Mary had no other children. His clear intention is to make the brothers, and James in particular, virtually anonymous. He continues this practice throughout his two-volume work of Luke-Acts.

When Mark describes Jesus' death on the cross he notes that "Mary the mother of James and Joses" was present.[13] Luke changes this to read "the *women* [unnamed] who had followed him from Galilee" (Luke 23:49). When Jesus is buried, Mark again notes that "Mary Magdalene and Mary the mother of Joses" were present at the tomb (Mark 15:47). Luke changes his account to read "the *women* [again unnamed] who had come with him from Galilee followed and saw the tomb" (Luke 23:55). In most cases Luke followed Mark rather closely as a source, much more so than did Matthew, who constantly adds his own editorial revisions. But this is not the case when it comes to the mother and brothers of Jesus. Such bold editing could not be accidental; there is something very important going on here. Since this editing runs through both volumes of this work, Luke and Acts, it is clearly part of the author's central agenda to recast the history of the early movement so that James and the family of Jesus are muted and Paul emerges as the ultimate hero who proclaims the true gospel to the world.

The author of Luke-Acts was also pro-Roman. Paul, according to Acts, was a Roman citizen. Luke wants his Gentile Roman readers to know and value that about Paul, and thus look with favor on the growing Gentile Christian movement. At the time he writes, in the first half of the second century A.D., after the bloody Jewish revolts against Rome, it was less and less popular to be Jewish or to be associated with Jewish causes—particularly anything that might be seen as messianic.[14] For example, in his account of the trial of Jesus, Luke goes far beyond Mark, his primary source, to emphasize that Pontius Pilate was a reasonable and just ruler who went to extraordinary lengths to get Jesus released. He removes the reference to Pilate having Jesus scourged and even omits the horrible mocking and abuse that Jesus suffered at the hands of Pilate's Roman Praetorium guard (Luke 23:25 compared with Mark 15:15–20). In Luke Jesus might not have been a friend of Rome, but he was surely treated fairly by his Roman captors, as is Paul throughout the book of Acts when he encounters Roman authorities.

For Luke there was *no* possibility that the followers of Jesus retreated to Galilee in sorrow and despair after Jesus' death. He puts *all* the "sightings" of Jesus in Jerusalem. He does not even mention Galilee and what might have happened there, and in Luke Jesus forbids the apostles to leave the city of Jerusalem. To him Galilee represents the native, indigenous, Jewish origins of Jesus and his family, where the leadership of James apparently took root following Jesus' death, and the influence of Mary his mother, Mary Magdalene, and Jesus' other brothers was strong. Galilee was also known, from the time of the Maccabees (c. 165 B.C.) as the center of political and religious unrest and ripe for messianic candidates such as Judas the Galilean, John the Baptizer, and Jesus of Nazareth.

These Jerusalem-based "sightings," according to Luke, happened on Sunday, the very day the empty tomb was discovered, so that any doubts the apostles must have had in response to the brutal and horrible death of their leader were immediately dispelled. Paul alone, who took the "Gospel" message all the way to Rome, would fulfill Jesus' last words, according to Luke:

> Thus it is written, that the Christ should suffer and on the third day rise from the dead, and that repentance and forgiveness of sins should be preached in his name *to all nations*, beginning from Jerusalem. (Luke 24:46–47)

According to this standard story, about forty days after Jesus' death the eleven apostles gathered together in Jerusalem in the upper room where they had had their last meal with Jesus. Their purpose was to choose a successor to Judas Iscariot, who had killed himself. Luke carefully lists the eleven by name: "Peter, and John, and James [the fisherman], and Andrew Philip and Thomas, Bartholomew and Matthew James son of Alphaeus, and Simon the Zealot, and Judas brother of James." Luke then adds this qualifying sentence, which has served to marginalize the Jesus family for the past nineteen hundred years: "All these [the Eleven] were constantly devoting themselves to prayer, together with certain women, including Mary the mother of Jesus as well as his brothers [unnamed]" (Acts 1:13–14). Luke effectively separates Jesus' family from the eleven apostles, associating his mother, Mary, with the group of unnamed women from Galilee, while making Jesus' brothers anonymous. Also, in listing the eleven apostles he places Peter and John first, giving them primacy, changing the order of his earlier list of the Twelve (Luke 6:14). He is quite aware the three pillars of the Jesus movement are James, Peter, and John, in that order—but who would ever imagine that James was actually installed as leader over the newly constituted council of the Twelve?[15] What Luke dared not do was to write the Jesus family out of his account entirely, knowing that later in his narrative he will have to reluctantly acknowledge that James was in charge of the entire movement.

This makes it all the more strange that the first time James is ever mentioned by name in Luke-Acts is when he mysteriously is presented as the undisputed *leader* at the Jerusalem council of A.D. 50—twenty years after the death of Jesus! At this meeting Paul and his assistant Barnabas appeared before the apostles and elders at Jerusalem to officially give account of the Christian message they were preaching to Greek-speaking non-Jews in Asia Minor. The main agenda was to deliberate the status of these non-Jews who had joined the Nazarene movement in response to Paul's preaching. At issue was whether Gentiles should be required to become Jewish through formal conversion, including male circumcision, and take on the obligations to follow Jewish laws and customs. Paul strongly opposed any such requirement and according to Acts, Peter supported him. Then suddenly, with no introduction, after everyone had spoken, James declared his "judgment" on the matter! (Acts 15:13–21) Luke does not even identify James as Jesus' brother. James just appears, suddenly, never mentioned by name before, and he is in charge of the entire movement, rendering a formal decision like a judge presiding over a Jewish court of law. James declares that converting to Judaism was not necessary for non-Jews in order to have a right relationship to God. James here echoed the position of the Pharisees toward the non-Jewish world. So long as one had shunned the worship of "idols," giving allegiance to the God of Israel alone, and was following the minimal ethical standards expected of all humankind, one could have the status of a "righteous Gentile" or "God-fearer." As the rabbis later put things, "The righteous of all nations have a place in the world to come."[16]

The book of Acts mentions James one other time, when Paul has returned to Jerusalem toward the end of the 50s A.D. The day after his arrival Paul went to "visit James and all the elders were present" (Acts 21:18). Once again it is clear that James is leader of the group and Paul knows he must account to him. There had been a serious charge raised against Paul, based on rumors that had circulated as to what he was preaching in Asia Minor and Greece. The claim was that Paul himself, as a Jew, had given up an observant Jewish life and that he was privately teaching other fellow Jews that they could do the same (Acts 21:17–26). Presumably this action might involve such things as dietary laws, observance of the Sabbath day and other Jewish holy days, and even the requirement of male circumcision (Galatians 4:10; Colossians 2:16–17). It is noteworthy that Luke, who wants to present a perfect picture of harmony and agreement between Paul and James, does not actually say that Paul denied this charge, but only that Paul allowed James and the other leaders in Jerusalem to think that it was not true.

Acts presents both of Paul's meetings with James and the Jerusalem apostles and elders as harmonious and positive. Fortunately we have Paul's side of the story in his letters and we know there was a diametrically opposite outcome. The irony of the Luke-Acts portrayal of James is quite amazing. James is mentioned only twice, both times in the book of Acts in an account that stretches over a thirty-year period. James is not even identified as Jesus' brother, yet those two scenes, separated by ten years, offer us the strongest kind of historical evidence that James presided over the Twelve as leader of the Christian movement.

To get the details of how James assumed this role of leadership, beyond what the letters of Paul indicate, we have to go to sources outside the New Testament. The *Gospel of Thomas* was discovered in upper Egypt in 1945 outside the little village of Nag Hammadi. Although the text itself dates to the third century, scholars have shown that it preserves, despite later theological embellishments, an original Aramaic document that comes to us from the early days of the Jerusalem church.[17] It provides us a rare glimpse into what scholars have called "Jewish Christianity," that is, the earliest followers of Jesus led by James. The *Gospel of Thomas* is not a narrative of the life of Jesus but rather a listing of 114 of his "sayings" or teachings. Saying 12 reads as follows:

> The disciples said to Jesus, "We know you will leave us. Who is going to be our leader then?" Jesus said to them, "No matter where you go you are to *go to James the Just*, for whose sake heaven and earth came into being."

Here we have an outright statement, placed in the mouth of Jesus, that he is handing over the leadership and spiritual direction of his movement to James. One should keep in mind that the *Gospel of Thomas* in its present form comes to us from a later period, when the matter of "who is going to be our leader" had become a critical one for the followers of Jesus, with many competing claims of authority and power. The phrase "no matter where you go" implies that the authority and leadership of James is not restricted to the Jerusalem church. According to this text, James had been put in charge over *all* of Jesus' followers. The phrase "for whose sake heaven and earth came into being" reflects a Jewish notion that the world, though wicked and unworthy of God's grace, is sustained because of the extraordinary virtues of a handful of righteous or "just" individuals.[18] James the brother of Jesus acquired the designation "James the Just" both to distinguish him from others named James and to honor him for his preeminent position.

Clement of Alexandria, who wrote in the late second century A.D., is another early source that confirms this succession of James. Clement writes: "Peter and James [the fisherman] and John after the Ascension of the Savior did not struggle for glory, because they had previously been given honor by the Savior, but chose James the Just as Overseer of Jerusalem."[19] In a subsequent passage Clement elaborated: "After the resurrection the Lord [Jesus] gave the tradition of knowledge to James the Just and John and Peter, these gave it to the other Apostles, and the other Apostles to the Seventy."[20] This passage preserves for us the *tiered structure* of the leadership that Jesus left behind: James the Just as successor; John and Peter as his left- and right-hand advisors; the rest of the Twelve; then the

Seventy, who are referred to in the book of Acts as the "elders." This council of Seventy is one that Jesus himself had established and appears to function as a kind of proto-Christian "Sanhedrin," the official governing body of the Jews at that time.

Eusebius, the early-fourth-century Christian historian, in commenting on this passage wrote, "James whom men of old had surnamed 'Just' for his excellence of virtue, is recorded to have been the first elected to the *throne* of the oversight of the church in Jerusalem."[21] The Greek term *thronos* refers to a "seat" or "chair" of authority and is the same term used for a king or ruler. In Eusebius's time the bishop of Rome had not yet achieved supremacy over bishops in other areas, so Eusebius seems to have no problem with presenting James as a kind of proto-pope in Jerusalem.

Eusebius also preserves the testimony of Hegesippus, a Jewish-Christian of the early second century, who he says is from the "generation after the Apostles":

> The succession of the church passed to James the brother of
> the Lord, together with the Apostles. He was called the "Just"
> by all men from the Lord's time until ours, since many are
> called James, but he was holy from his mother's womb.[22]

The Greek word that Hegesippus used here, "to succeed" (*diadexomai*), is regularly used for a royal blood line, for example, when Philip king of Macedon passes on his rule to his son Alexander the Great.[23]

We also have a recently recovered Syriac source, *The Ascents of James*, embedded in a later corpus known as the *Pseudo-Clementine Recognitions*, that reflects some of the earliest traditions related to the Jerusalem church under the leadership of James the Just.[24] It records events in Jerusalem seven years following the death of Jesus, when James is clearly at the helm: "The church in Jerusalem that was established by our Lord was increasing in numbers being ruled uprightly and firmly by James who was made Overseer over it by our Lord."[25] The Latin version of the *Recognitions* passes on the following admonition: "Wherefore observe the greatest caution, that you believe no teacher, unless he bring from Jerusalem the testimonial of James the Lord's brother, or of whosoever may come after him" (4:35). The *Second Apocalypse of James*, one of the texts found with the *Gospel of Thomas* at Nag Hammadi, stressed the intimate bond between Jesus and James, in keeping with the idea that James was the "beloved disciple." In this text Jesus and James were "nursed with the same milk" and Jesus kisses his brother James and says to him, "Behold I shall reveal to you everything my beloved" (50.15–22).

What is impressive about these sources is the way in which they speak with a single voice, yet come from various authors and time periods, confirming what the book of Acts never relates openly, but Paul states explicitly. The basic elements of the picture they preserve for us are amazingly consistent: Jesus passes to James his successor rule of the Church; James is widely known by the surname "the Just One" because of his reputation for righteousness both in his community and among the people; and Peter, John, and the rest of the Twelve, as well as Paul, look to James as their undisputed leader.

It is quite remarkable that the contemporary Jewish historian Josephus, who had no affiliation with the Christian movement, relates the death of James, not recorded in the New Testament, in some detail. Josephus reports that the Jewish people viewed James's death at the hand of the Jewish Sanhedrin, led by the high priest Ananus, with such disfavor that their protest caused Herod Agrippa, grandson of Herod the Great, to have Ananus removed from his priestly office after only three months.[26] Based on his account we can reliably date James's death to A.D. 62. The early Jewish-Christian writer Hegesippus preserves the bloody details, relating how James was thrown from the corner of the Temple enclosure into the Kidron valley, where he was stoned and beaten to death with a club.[27]

To think that the influence and importance of James has been all but forgotten by Christians through the ages is cause enough for wonder, but beyond the man is a message. What about the lost Christianity that Jesus, James, and the early followers of Jesus represented?

RECOVERING THE LOST CHRISTIANITY OF JESUS

Although James has been all but written out of our New Testament records he nonetheless remains our best and most direct link to the historical Jesus. However one evaluates Paul's "Gospel," it is nonetheless a fact that what Paul preached was wholly based upon his own visionary experiences, whereas James and the original apostles had spent extensive time with Jesus during his lifetime. Is there a reliable way to recover the Christianity of James and the early Jerusalem church?

The difficulty we face is that Paul's influence within our New Testament documents is permeating and all pervasive. It includes his thirteen letters, as well as the letter of Hebrews, sometimes even attributed to Paul, but much more. Even though tradition has it that the gospel of Mark was based on the tradition received from Peter, as I have already mentioned, most scholars today are convinced that Mark's story of Jesus is almost wholly Pauline in its theology, namely Jesus as the suffering Son of God who gave his life as an atonement for the sins of the world (Mark 8:31–36; 10:45; 14:22–25).[28] Matthew follows Mark in this regard. Luke-Acts, which comprises the standard story of early Christianity, with an emphasis on Paul, downplays James as we have seen. Even the gospel of John, in theology at least, also reflects Paul's essential understanding of Jesus. 1 Peter, a document one might expect to reflect an alternative perspective, is an unabashed presentation of Paul's ideas under the name of Peter. Paul's view of Christ as the divine, preexistent Son of God who took on human form, died on the cross for the sins of the world, and was resurrected to heavenly glory at God's right hand becomes *the* Christian message. In reading the New Testament one might assume this was the only message ever preached and there was no other gospel. But such was not the case. If we listen carefully we can still hear a muted original voice—every bit as "Christian" as that of Paul. It is the voice of James, echoing what he received from his brother Jesus.

The most neglected document in the entire New Testament is the letter written by James. It has become so marginalized that many Christians are not even aware of its existence. And yet it is part of every Christian Bible, tucked away well to the end of the New Testament. It was almost left out entirely. When the Christians began to canonize the New Testament in the fourth century, that is, to authoritatively determine which books would be included and which would not, the status of the letter of James was questioned. It was not included in the *Muratorian Fragment*, our earliest list of New Testament books that were accepted as scripture in Rome at the end of the second century.[29] The third-century A.D. Christian scholars Origen and Eusebius both listed it among the disputed books.[30] Even the great Western Christian scholars Jerome and Augustine accepted the letter only reluctantly. It was finally made part of the New Testament canon of sacred scripture not because its content pleased the later church theologians, but on the basis of it bearing the name of James, the brother of Jesus.

These early Christians who questioned the value of the letter of James were troubled that Jesus is mentioned just two times in passing and either reference could easily be removed without affecting the content of the letter or the points James was making (James

1:1; 2:1). In addition, the letter lacks any reference to Paul's view of Jesus as the divine Son of God, his atoning death on the cross, or his glorified resurrection. How could a New Testament document that lacked such teachings really be considered "Christian"? In fact, James directly disputed Paul's teaching of "salvation by faith" without deeds of righteousness. He does not mention Paul's name but the reference is unmistakable, given what we know from Paul's letters about faith in Christ alone being sufficient to bring salvation. James speaks positively of the enduring validity of the Jewish Torah, or Law of Moses, and insists that all its commandments are to be observed:

> What does it profit, my brothers, if a man says he has faith but has not works? Can his faith save him? . . . So faith by itself, if it has no works, is dead. (James 2:14, 17)

> For whoever looks into the perfect Torah, the Torah of liberty, and perseveres, being no hearer that forgets but a doer that acts, he shall be blessed in his doing. (James 1:25)

> For whoever keeps the whole Torah but fails in one point has become guilty of all of it. (James 2:10)

James addressed his letter to the "Twelve Tribes in the Dispersion" (1:1). The term "Dispersion" refers to the notion that large portions of the Israelite or Jewish people had been scattered widely among the nations and were no longer living in the homeland. James refers here directly to the scattered Twelve Tribes of Israel, over which Jesus had promised the twelve apostles would rule. As the presiding head of this newly constituted Israel, expected to emerge fully when the apocalyptic Day of the Lord arrived, James intends his letter to be a call to all Israel to prepare for the imminent Day of Judgment (James 5:7–9). The letter reflects an early Palestinian Jewish cultural context, perhaps in the 40s A.D., before there was a strict separation between the Nazarene followers of Jesus and other Jewish groups. For example, James referred to the local meeting or assembly of proto-Christians as a synagogue, not a church, reflecting his Jewish understanding of the Christian movement (James 2:2). Even though the letter is written in Greek, at least as we have it today, linguistically it reflects numerous Aramaic and Hebrew expressions and recent research has revealed its Palestinian Jewish milieu.[31]

What is particularly notable about the letter of James is that the ethical content of its teaching is directly parallel to the teachings of Jesus that we know from the Q source. The Q source is the earliest collection of the teachings and sayings of Jesus, which scholars date to around the year 50 A.D. It has not survived as an intact document but both Matthew and Luke use it extensively. By comparing Matthew and Luke and extracting the material they use in common but do not derive from their main source, which is Mark, we are able to come to a reasonable construction of this lost "gospel of Q." It consists of about 235 verses that are mostly but not entirely the "sayings" of Jesus. The Q source takes us back to the original teachings of Jesus minus much of the theological framework that the gospels subsequently added.[32] Perhaps the most striking characteristic of the Q source in terms of reconstructing Christian origins is that it has nothing of Paul's theology, particularly his Christology or view of Christ.

The most familiar parts of Q to most Bible readers are in Matthew's "Sermon on the Mount" (Matthew 5–7) and Luke's "Sermon on the Plain" (Luke 6). If one takes the letter of James, short as it is, there are no fewer than thirty direct references, echoes, and allusions to the teachings of Jesus found in the Q source! A few of the more striking parallels are the following:

JESUS' TEACHINGS IN THE Q SOURCE	TEACHINGS OF JAMES
Blessed are you who are poor, for yours is the kingdom of God. (Luke 6:20)	Has not God chosen the poor to be rich in faith and heirs of the kingdom. (2:5)
Whoever relaxes one of the least of these commandments . . . shall be [called] least in the kingdom. (Matthew 5:19)	Whoever keeps the whole Torah but fails in one point has become guilty of it all. (2:10)
Not everyone who says "Lord, Lord" shall enter the kingdom . . . but he who does the will of my Father. (Matthew 7:21)	Be doers of the word and not hearers only. (1:22)
How much more will your Father . . . give good gifts to those who ask him. (Matthew 7:11)	Every good gift . . . coming down from the Father. (1:17)
Woe to you that are rich, for you have received your consolation. (Luke 6:24)	Come now, you rich, weep and howl for the miseries that are coming upon you. (5:1)
Do not swear at all, either by heaven for it is the throne of God, or by earth for it is his footstool . . . let what you say be simply "Yes" or "No." (Matthew 5:34, 37)	Do not swear, either by heaven or by earth or with any other oath but let your yes be yes and your no be no. (5:12)

The letter of James has other important connections to the message of Jesus beyond these characteristic ethical teachings. James
knows about the practice of anointing the sick with oil, as Jesus
had practiced and taught his disciples (Mark 6:13; James 5:14).
Jesus had taught that one is forgiven of sins and "justified" before
God through repentance and prayer—that is, directly calling upon
God. James wrote that confession of sins and prayer were the way
to salvation (James 5:15–16). This is in keeping with Jesus' teaching
in the Q source. Jesus related a story in which two men were praying in the Temple, one who was proud of his righteousness and the
other who considered himself so unworthy he would not even lift
his eyes to heaven. The latter one struck his breast and cried out
"God be merciful to me a sinner." Jesus declared "this one went up
justified before God rather than the other" (Luke 18:14). This is
in keeping with the general Jewish understanding regarding forgiveness of sins. As the Psalms express: "Have mercy upon me O
God, according to your steadfast love, according to your abundant
mercy blot out all my transgressions and cleanse me from my sins"
(Psalm 51:1). Judaism does not teach "salvation" by human merit
as sometimes assumed, but rather that all human beings are "justified" by grace, finding forgiveness from their sins by repentance
and prayer—"calling upon the name of God" (Joel 2:32). Even the
animal sacrifices of the Jewish Temple were never understood to
atone for or cover sins unless one first turned in faith to God and
asked for grace and forgiveness (Psalm 51:16).

What we get in the letter of James is the most direct possible
link to the Jewish teachings of Jesus himself. James is quite sure
that the "Judge" is standing at the door, and that the kingdom of
God has drawn very near (James 5:9). He warns the rich and those
who oppress the weak that very soon the judgment of God will
strike. James seems to be directly echoing and affirming what he
had learned and passed on from his brother Jesus. It is important
to note that James did not directly quote Jesus or attribute any of

these teachings to Jesus by name—even though they are teaching of Jesus. For James the Christian message is not the person of Jesus but the message that Jesus proclaimed. *James's letter lacks a single teaching that is characteristic of the apostle Paul and it draws nothing at all from the traditions of Mark or John.* What is preserved in this precious document is a reflection of the original apocalyptic proclamation of Jesus—the "gospel of the kingdom of God" with its political and social implications.

If we move outside the New Testament, there is another major witness that has surfaced in recent times that allows us to trace more clearly the trajectory of this forgotten message through earliest Christianity. A text known as the *Didache* was discovered in 1873 in a library at Constantinople, quite by accident, by a Greek priest, Father Bryennios.[33] This document dates to the beginning of the second century A.D. or even earlier, making it as old as some of the books included in the New Testament canon. Indeed, among certain circles of early Christianity it had achieved near-canonical status.

The word *Didache* in Greek means "Teaching," and the document gets its name from its first line, which functions as a title: "The Teaching of the Lord through the Twelve Apostles to the Nations."[34] The work is divided into sixteen chapters and was intended to be a "handbook" for Christian converts. The first six chapters give a summary of Christian ethics based on the teachings of Jesus, divided into two parts: the way of life and the way of death. Much of the content is similar to what we have in the "Sermon on the Mount" and the "Sermon on the Plain," that is, the basic ethical teachings of Jesus drawn from the Q source. It begins with the two "great commandments," to love God and love one's neighbor as oneself, as well as a version of the Golden Rule: "And whatever you do not want to happen to you, do not do to another." It contains many familiar injunctions and exhortations, but often with additions not found in our Gospels:

> Bless those who curse you, pray for your enemies, and fast for those who persecute you. (1.3)

> If anyone slaps your right cheek, turn the other to him as well and you will be perfect. (1.4)

> Give to everyone who asks, and do not ask for anything back, for the Father wants everyone to be given something from the gracious gifts he himself provides. (1.5)

But it also contains many sayings and teachings not found in our New Testament gospels but that nonetheless are consistent with the tradition we know from Jesus and from his brother James:

> Let your gift to charity sweat in your hands until you know to whom to give it. (1.6)

> Do not be of two minds or speak from both sides of your mouth, for speaking from both sides of your mouth is a deadly trap. (2.4)

> Do not be one who reaches out your hands to receive but draws them back from giving. (4.5)

> Do not shun a person in need, but share all things with your brother and do not say that anything is your own. (4.8)

Following the ethical exhortations there are four chapters on baptism, fasting, prayer, the Eucharist, and the anointing with oil, which remind one very much of the kind of instruction one finds in the teachings of Jesus preserved in the Q source. The Eucharist is a simple thanksgiving meal of wine and bread with references to Jesus as the holy "vine of David." It ends with a prayer: "Hosanna to the God of David." The Davidic lineage of Jesus is thus emphasized. Absent is Paul's idea that the bread represented Jesus' flesh and the wine his blood, shed for the sins of the world.

There are final chapters on testing prophets and appointing worthy leaders. Again the instructions seem to reflect a Palestinian context, similar to that we see in the Q source, where wandering teachers and prophets are operating within the various communities. The last chapter contains warnings about the "last days," the coming of a final deceiving false prophet, and the resurrection of the righteous who have died. It ends with language similar to that used by the New Testament letter of Jude, the brother of Jesus and James. The key phrases are taken from Zechariah and Daniel: "The Lord will come and all of his holy ones with him" and "Then the world will see the Lord coming on the clouds of the sky." Both references to the "Lord" here are to Yahweh, the God of Israel.

The entire content and tone of the *Didache* reminds one strongly of the faith and piety we find in the letter of James, and teachings of Jesus in the Q source. The most amazing thing about the *Didache* in terms of the two types of Christian faith—that of Paul and that of Jesus—is that there is nothing in this document that corresponds to Paul's "Gospel"—no divinity of Jesus, no atonement through his body and blood, and not even any direct reference to Jesus' resurrection from the dead. In the *Didache* Jesus is the one who has brought the knowledge of life and faith, but there is no emphasis whatsoever upon the figure of Jesus apart from his message. Sacrifice and forgiveness of sins in the *Didache* come through good deeds and a consecrated life (4.6). What we have surviving in the *Didache* is an abiding witness to a form of the Christian faith that traces directly back to Jesus and was carried on and perpetuated by James, and the rest of the twelve apostles.

As we turn to Paul and begin to examine the elements of his understanding of the Christian message, it is important that we place him within this world of Jesus and the form of Christianity that he first encountered when he joined the movement. As we will see, Paul had his own fiercely independent "Gospel," which contrasted sharply to the Christianity of Jesus, James, and their earliest followers. Paul completely transformed everything from earth to heaven, and the largely untold story of how that happened is preserved in his own words within the New Testament itself.

Paul occupies a unique place historically in that he not only sets forth his own independent version of what he calls "the Gospel," but he is our earliest witness to faith in Jesus' resurrection from the dead. Since Paul's letters all date to the 50s A.D., and are thus our earliest Christian documents, they can provide us with some important historical clues as to how Christians might have understood Jesus' resurrection in the very earliest years of the movement—even before there were written gospels, and for that matter, even before Paul joined the movement. Before examining Paul's understanding of his own mission and message it makes sense to probe as far back as possible, using him as our earliest source, in trying to grasp what happened immediately after Jesus' death. As we will see, his view of Jesus' resurrection differs substantially from that of the later gospel accounts.

TWO

RETHINKING RESURRECTION OF THE DEAD

Since I was in college I have read every book on Jesus I could get my hands on, whether scholarly, popular, or even fiction. Irresistibly, like so many who were raised in the Christian faith, I found myself skipping to the end of a book to see just how the author handled the events following Jesus' crucifixion and death. No matter what else a writer might say about Jesus, the question of what happened "after the cross" was fascinating and critical in my mind. All four gospels report that Jesus' dead body was hastily laid in a rock-hewn cave tomb and blocked with a stone late in the afternoon on the day he was crucified but that the tomb was found empty by his followers on the following Sunday morning. New Testament scholars, historians, and even novelists seem incapable of offering a rational explanation as to what most likely happened that first Easter weekend. This seems to be the mystery of the ages when it comes to understanding Christian origins.

What happened to the body of Jesus? One recent historian wrote, after comprehensively surveying the historical and archaeological evidence: "The reality is that there is no historical explanation for the empty tomb, other than if we adopt a theological one, i.e., the resurrection. I leave it up to the reader to make up his own mind."[1]

What I had failed to consider in all those years of analyzing our New Testament gospel accounts was that the answer to this insoluble problem was found in the letters of Paul. I am convinced that there is a rational historical explanation for the resurrection of Jesus and the "appearances" to the disciples that can stand up to proper historical scrutiny, but if one reads the gospels alone, without using Paul as a key, everything remains a mystery. If we begin with Paul, suddenly everything becomes clear and we can sort through the gospels in a way that makes real historical sense.

It is easy to assume that the four New Testament gospels provided us with our earliest reports that Jesus' tomb was found empty, and that he was raised from the dead, whereas in fact they are our *latest* witnesses, ranging in date from A.D. 80 to 120 or even later.[2] Paul writes in the early 50s A.D., just twenty years after Jesus' crucifixion. That is not to say the gospels are without historical value. The problem is that they report a garbled mix of contradictory stories that have to be critically analyzed and sorted out chronologically. It is Paul's earlier testimony that provides us the insight to be able to do just that. Paul not only reports his own visionary experience but also passes along testimony he received from face-to-face contact with Peter, James, John, and the other apostles—interpreting for us what it meant to say Jesus was "seen" by this or that person following his burial.

Paul is the essential missing piece for understanding historically this most important cornerstone of the Christian faith. Ironically, evangelical Christian scholars often use Paul to make the point that he is our earliest source mentioning Jesus' resurrection, but then they promptly forget what Paul says when they turn to consider the subsequent gospel accounts.

In order to understand the historical background and context of Paul's language about Jesus' resurrection, and resurrection of the dead more generally, we need to diverge a bit from Paul's time and the Jewish culture of his day. It is essential that we first understand the views of afterlife among the Greeks, since Paul assumes that his readers, who were his contemporaries, shared a Greek cultural outlook. The Jews, on the other hand, represented to the Greeks a strange and naïve view of the matter of death and afterlife, one that the Greeks thought was patently absurd. In contrast the Jews had come to their view of resurrection from the dead from a completely different place.

I always begin my college course on Paul by assigning an article I published some years ago called "What the Bible Really Says About Death, Afterlife, and the Future."[3] Until one knows a bit about how the idea of resurrection of the dead developed and what was at stake in its unique view of the afterlife, there is no way to really comprehend Paul's "Gospel."

To put things succinctly: the notion of resurrection of the dead is a distinctly Jewish way of thinking about life after death. Even today people easily confuse the idea of resurrection with the notion of the immortality of the soul. They are two separate but related views of afterlife, both affirming what is commonly called eternal life, but there are important differences between them.[4] I want to begin with the Greek side of things.

GREEK DUALISM

The Greek idea of immortality of the soul presupposed a *dualistic* understanding of the human person as consisting of two separate components. The physical body, mortal and perishable, was viewed as a kind of "house" for the true self, which was the inner spirit or soul of the person and would never die. Death was not the end of the individual, but a release of the soul from the restrictions of the body. Plato, for example, likened the mortal physical body to a prison, from which the pure soul achieved release and moved to a more blessed place to continue on its path of spiritual development. The body, with its passions and sensual limitations, was seen as an obstacle to the soul's highest spiritual development. Detachment from the body was both the ideal and the goal of the higher spiritual life. According to Plato, "the soul of the philosopher greatly despises the body and avoids it and strives to be alone by itself."[5] Although one was not permitted to take one's own life, unless by necessity, nonetheless death was infinitely better than the imprisonment of the body, and philosophy, in essence, was "a training for death."[6]

In the classic Greek view the soul at death descended into Hades, the mythical realm of the dead, where it was judged, reborn to another human life in a cycle of reincarnation, and ideally, after eons of time, could ascend to the higher celestial realms wholly free from the restrictions, contaminations, and imperfections of the lower physical world. Ironically, given this perception of reality, death, which released the soul, was viewed as "life," while birth, which imprisoned the soul, was like a kind of "death."

In the second most famous death in Western history, that of Socrates, Plato relates how his master courageously, even cheerfully, drank the bowl of hemlock, choosing death over exile, all the while admonishing his disciples to weep for themselves, not for him, since his release from the body was at hand and he was departing to a better place. He presents an extended philosophical argument on the nature of the body and the soul as he lies dying, concluding, "it is perfectly certain that the soul is immortal and imperishable, and our souls will exist in Hades."[7]

Cicero's *Republic*, a text much closer to the time of Jesus and Paul, provides a concise précis of this philosophical dualism that was so popular in the Greco-Roman world:

> Strive on indeed, and be sure that it is not you that is mortal, but only your body. For that man whom your outward form

reveals is not yourself; the spirit is the true self, not that physical figure that can be pointed out by the finger. (6:24)[8]

Platonic body/soul dualism became the standard belief in Greco-Roman antiquity, even among some Hellenized first-century Jews such as Philo and Josephus.[9] The great early Christian theologians, Clement of Alexandria, Origen, and Augustine, considered Plato a kind of honorary "pre-Christian" and reshaped their exposition of the Christian faith almost wholly in Platonic categories.

As a result it is extremely difficult for people today, whether Christian, Jewish, or in any other Western spiritual tradition, to conceive of life after death other than in Platonic terms—the body perishes and the immortal soul passes on to an unseen realm of the spirit.

THE ANCIENT HEBREW VIEW OF DEATH

The Jewish concept of resurrection of the dead, adapted by the Christians and put at the center of their faith, insisted that the dead would live again at the "end of days," rising up from their graves in newly created bodies. This view of afterlife, unique to Jews and Christians, developed out of a distinctively different understanding of the human person, the nature of death, and the importance of a *body*. God "formed man of dust from the ground and breathed into his nostrils the breath of life; and man became a living being" (Genesis 2:7). The phrase in Hebrew, "living being," was translated in the King James Version and some older translations as "a living *soul*," which is quite misleading since it might imply some parallel to the Greek notion of the immortal soul. The Hebrew word (*nefesh*) simply means a "breathing creature" and the same phrase is used for the various animals that also have what is called the "breath of life" (Genesis 1:24; 7:15). When a human or an animal dies, the breath of life departs and the body returns to the ground, thus Adam is told, "You are dust, and to dust you shall return" (Genesis 3:19). So in Hebrew one can speak of a "dead" *nefesh* (Numbers 9:7). The book of Ecclesiastes, the most philosophical in the Hebrew Bible, or Old Testament, provides the starkest summary:

> For the fate of the sons of men and the fate of animals is the same; as one dies, so dies the other. They all have the same breath, and man has no advantage over the beasts; for all is vanity. All go to one place; all are from the dust, and all turn to dust again. (3:19–20)

Apparently the author has heard other views here and there, perhaps from Greek influence, but he skeptically concludes, "Who knows whether the spirit of man goes upward and the spirit of the beast goes down to the earth?" (Ecclesiastes 3:21).

Like the Greeks, the Hebrews had a concept of an underworld of the dead that they called Sheol, somewhat akin to Hades, but it was primarily a metaphor for the grave, and was often referred to as the "pit" (Psalm 30:3). Sheol is described as a land of silence and forgetfulness, a region gloomy, dark, and deep (Psalms 115:17; 6:5; 88:3-12; Isaiah 38:18). All the dead go down to Sheol, and there they make their bed together—whether good or evil, rich or poor, slave or free (Job 3:11–19). The dead in Sheol are mere shadows of their former embodied selves; lacking substance they are called "shades" (Psalm 88:10).[10] There is one "séance" story in the Hebrew Bible in which the infamous medium of Endor conjures up the "shade" of the dead prophet Samuel at the insistence of King Saul, who wants to communicate with him. When Samuel appears, rising up out of the earth, he asks Saul, "Why have you disturbed me by bringing me up?" (1 Samuel 28:8–15). But even Samuel must then return to Sheol. Death is a one-way street; it is the land of no return:

> But man dies, and is laid low; man breathes his last, and where
> is he? As waters fail from a lake, and a river wastes away and
> dries up, so man lies down and rises not again; till the heavens
> are no more he will not awake, or be aroused out of his sleep.
> (Job 14:10–12)

It is surprising to most people to realize that this starkly realistic view of death is consistent throughout the Hebrew Bible or
Christian Old Testament. Whether Abraham, Moses, or David,
one dies, is buried, and descends into Sheol. The body returns to
the dust, the life-breath or spirit returns to God, who gave it, and
the "soul" or shade of the former person rests in the underworld
(Ecclesiastes 12:7).

Nothing is ever said about any kind of a blessed or vital afterlife, much less the notion of an immortal soul leaving the body and
joining God in heaven.[11] The Hebrews understood the cosmos as
tripartite: the heavens were the spiritual realm of God and the angels; the earth was the domain of humans and all living creatures;
and below the earth was Sheol, the realm of the dead. For humans
the good earth was the designated place to be. They were forever
cut off and banished from the Tree of Life, in the middle of the
Garden of Eden, that would have allowed them to be like gods and
live forever (Genesis 3). Psalm 115 puts things succinctly:

> *The heavens are Yahweh's heavens,*
> *But the earth he has given to the sons of men.*
> *The dead do not praise Yahweh,*
> *nor do any that go down into silence.*
> *But we, the living, will bless Yahweh*
> *from this time forth and for evermore.* (verses 16–18)

The notion of resurrection of the dead has to do with a very obvious and simple question—will the dead, resting in Sheol, ever re-

turn to life? Death is death and life is life, but is it possible that one who has died and returned to dust might be raised up, escaping the grip of Sheol? And if so, in what sort of body would one come?

TWO IDEAS OF RESURRECTION OF THE DEAD

There are two related but separate concepts of resurrection of the dead in the Bible. The first involves the rare case where a prophet or holy man resuscitates the corpse of one who has recently died, so that the person has a reprieve on death, but eventually grows old and dies like anyone else. The other concept affirms that at the end of time those in Sheol, or Hades, will come forth, newly embodied in a transformed immortal form. Though both can be called "resurrection," these two concepts have little in common.

There are three such "resuscitation" stories in the Hebrew Bible. Elijah prays over the son of a widow who had fallen ill and stopped breathing and "the life-breath came into him again and he lived" (1 Kings 17:17–22). Elisha, his successor, performs a similar miracle for the dead son of a wealthy woman. He lies upon the corpse, literally mouth to mouth, until it becomes warm, and the child opens his eyes and gets up (2 Kings 4:32–37). Finally, after Elisha has died and been buried, another corpse is put into his grave and as soon as it touches the bones of Elisha, the man "lived and stood up." In the gospels Jesus performs three such miracles. He revives a twelve-year-old girl who had died, with the words "Little girl, I say to you arise." The child immediately gets up, walks about, and takes something to eat (Mark 5:41–43). On another occasion he halts a funeral procession, touches the bier, and speaks to the corpse of a young man who had died, "Young man, I say to you arise." The dead man sits up and begins to speak (Luke 7:11–17). Finally, when his friend Lazarus dies, and has already been buried for two days, Jesus goes to his tomb, asks that the stone be removed, prays, then shouts, "Lazarus, come out!" The dead man comes out with his hands and feet still bound in the burial cloths (John 11:43–44). The book of Acts records two such miracles: one by Peter, and the other by Paul. When a widow named Dorcas falls sick and dies, Peter is called in. He prays, then turns to the body and commands it to rise. Dorcas opens her eyes and gets up. Paul revives a young boy named Eutychus who fell from a third-story window and was presumed dead (Acts 20:9–12).

The descriptive language in each of these cases is noteworthy: "He lived," "she got up," "he sat up," or "he came out." These are verbal expressions of what took place, not conceptual terms about life after death more generally. In that sense the English term "resurrection from the dead" is misleading. In the Hebrew Bible there is no noun for "resurrection," just verbs describing the dead being revived. Even in the New Testament the Greek word *anastasis*, translated "resurrection," occurs forty-two times; it literally means "a standing up."

Most scholars agree that there is only one unambiguous reference to a general resurrection of the dead in the entire Hebrew Bible.[12] It is found in the book of Daniel, an uncharacteristically apocalyptic book, considered by scholars to have been written much later than the other books of the Prophets in the Hebrew Bible. Daniel receives a long visionary prophecy that purports to give him a glimpse into human history right up to the end of time. The revelation concludes with these words:

> And there shall be a time of trouble, such as never has been since there was a nation till that time; but at that time your people shall be delivered, everyone whose name shall be found written in the book. *And multitudes of those who sleep in the dust of the earth shall awake, some to everlasting life, and some to shame and everlasting contempt.* And those who are wise shall shine like the brightness of the firmament; and those who turn many to righteousness like the stars for ever and ever. (Daniel 12:1–3)

The metaphor of "sleeping in the dust of the earth" and then awakening captures precisely the core idea of resurrection of the dead in the context of the ancient Hebrew understanding of death. The dead come forth from Sheol and are judged at the end of time, receiving either everlasting life or shame and contempt. Their bodies have long ago decayed and turned to dust, so rather than a resuscitation of a corpse, their revival entails a transformed state of glorified immortal existence.

Daniel writes at a time, in the mid-second century B.C., when Jews had chosen to die at the hands of their Greek conquerors rather than give up the practice of their religion (1 Maccabees 1:41–64). Coinciding with these gruesome tales of martyrdom there are declarations from the mouths of those dying that God will restore to life those who have perished: "You accursed wretch, you dismiss us from this present life, but the King of the universe will raise us up to an everlasting renewal of life, because we have died for his laws" (2 Maccabees 7:9). Here we see emerging a new Jewish understanding of both life and death. The older idea, found in much of the Hebrew Bible, that God justly rewards good and punishes evil in this life, was beginning to unravel. The book of Job struggled mightily with this issue, with Job insisting that his suffering was undeserved and that God was obligated to adjudicate his case, even if it required that he be vindicated by some future interlocutor, long after his death (Job 19:23–27).[13] But if Daniel's vision of the future were true, then any question about God's justice would become moot, since the dead would be raised at the end of time and all would face final judgment.

As appealing as the notion of resurrection of the dead might be, it was sharply debated in Jewish circles for at least three centuries (200 B.C. to A.D. 100). Those who opposed the idea argued that since it was found only in the book of Daniel, a book whose authenticity some disputed, but nowhere else in the Hebrew scriptures, it represented an intrusive and unjustified addition to the teachings of Moses and the Prophets.

According to Josephus, the first-century A.D. Jewish historian, of the three major schools of Jewish thought, the Sadducees opposed the idea of resurrection of the dead while the Pharisees and the Essenes accepted it.[14] Josephus says the views of the Pharisees were accepted by the general populace, whereas the Sadducees tended to represent the aristocratic classes with decidedly "this worldly" interests in wealth and political power. The Essenes are most often identified with the sect that produced the Dead Sea Scrolls. Books like Daniel and Enoch, in which the idea of resurrection of the dead is pivotal, inspired their decidedly apocalyptic views. Both Jesus and Paul stood squarely with the Pharisees and the Essenes.

The Sadducees challenged Jesus on this point and in response he declared: "You are wrong, for you know neither the Scriptures nor the power of God," explaining his understanding of resurrection:

> Those who are accounted worthy to attain to that age and to the resurrection from the dead neither marry nor are given in marriage, for they cannot die any more, because they are equal to angels and are children of God, being children of the resurrection. (Mark 12:24–25; Luke 20:34–36)

Whether Jesus himself spoke these precise words or they were an elaboration by the gospel writers, what they show is that within the Jesus movement the resurrection of the dead at the end of the age was understood as the release of the dead from Sheol, or Hades, clothed in a new spiritual body no longer subject to death or decay. Resurrection involved transformation to a higher order of life, no longer differentiated as male and female, and thus no birth or death. The idea of resuscitating corpses or reassembling decayed flesh and bones long perished or turned to dust did not even enter the picture. Metaphorically one could speak of "those in the graves" coming forth, but since the "grave" ultimately referred to the underworld of Hades or Sheol, even those "buried" at sea come forth: "And the sea gave up the dead in it, Death and Hades gave up the dead in them, and all were judged by what they had done" (Revelation 20:13).

The Jewish notion of resurrection of the dead never means disembodied bliss, or even "life after death," but always a re-embodied life. This is quite different from the Greek idea of the immortal soul being freed from the mortal body and experiencing heavenly bliss. For Plato death is a friend, offering release from the prison of a mortal body, whereas for Jews and Christians death is an enemy that sends one to Sheol forever, until God intervenes and raises the dead in their new form.[15]

PAUL: FIRST AND BEST WITNESS

Paul was a Pharisee, one of the three major schools of thought among Jews of that time. He gives us our earliest and most extensive treatment of resurrection of the dead as understood, debated, and defended by his contemporaries (Philippians 3:5; cf. Acts 23:6). There are rabbinic traditions that discuss the Pharisaic view of resurrection of the dead, but they date much later, from the third to fifth centuries A.D. Josephus, our other first-century Jewish witness, offers little on this subject. Like Paul, he was a Pharisee, but he provides none of the expository detail that Paul provides, and he seems eager to cast the Pharisees and their views of afterlife in Greek dress: "Every soul, they maintain, is imperishable, but the soul of the good alone passes into another body, while the souls of the wicked suffer eternal punishment."[16] It is possible that his reference to "passing into another body" could refer to resurrection of the dead, but it could just as easily fit Plato's notion of reincarnation. Josephus was keen to slant things for his Roman audience, including the emperor Vespasian himself, who was his patron.

In contrast to Josephus, Paul addressed Plato directly, skillfully making use of the language of Greek dualism while maintaining a clear distinction between the Greek view of the immortality of the soul and the Jewish understanding of resurrection of the dead. Paul exhorts his followers at Corinth not to lose heart over persecutions:

> Though our outer nature is wasting away, our inner nature is being renewed every day . . . because we look not to the things that are seen, but to the things that are unseen; for the things that are seen are transient, but the things that are unseen are eternal. (2 Corinthians 4:16, 18)

One would be hard-pressed to find a more succinct expression of Platonic dualism. The body is obviously the outer perishing nature, which can be seen, while the unseen inner nature, which is eternal, is the soul. Paul is making use of standard Greek language but then he adds a most important twist.

According to Paul, we humans are "clothed" in a physical body, which we shed at death, but our desire is not to end up *naked* or *unclothed*—that is, stripped of the body, as Plato would have it—but to be *re*-clothed with a new eternal house that God will create (2 Corinthians 5:1–4). Paul draws upon a mixed set of metaphors here, contrasting a tent with a permanent dwelling and old clothing with new clothing. His meaning is subtle but clear. To die is to be in a naked state, unclothed, without a proper dwelling, whereas to be resurrected from the dead is to be reclothed, or rehoused, with a new spiritual body.

We can draw two very important conclusions. First, in contrast to Plato, Paul has no interest in the "naked" or disembodied soul. Second, the old clothing or the tent, that is, the physical body, perishes and is of no concern to him. This is Paul's view of resurrection of the dead and it is consistent in all his letters.

1 Corinthians 15 is often called Paul's "resurrection chapter."

There he clearly expresses his view of what resurrection of the dead involves, both for Jesus and those who have died and who he believes will be raised from the dead when Jesus returns. Apparently he had gotten a report that some in the Corinthian congregation were maintaining that "there is no resurrection of the dead" (1 Corinthians 15:13). Presumably they had accepted Paul's gospel message that Christ had been raised, but they saw no need for any future resurrection for those who had died. Their objection was likely based upon the influence of Greek thinking, in which the notion of the dead coming bodily out of their graves was absurd and unnecessary. If the dead were now free of their bodies, were they not closer to God than those yet imprisoned in the mortal body?

This Greek objection to resurrection of the dead appears in the book of Acts when the Stoics and Epicureans in Athens mock Paul as soon as he mentions the idea of resurrection (Acts 17:32). Celsus, a second-century Greek philosopher who wrote a treatise against Christianity, charged that Christians "believe in the absurd theory that the corporeal body will be raised and reconstituted by God, and that somehow they will actually see God with their mortal eyes and hear him with their ears and be able to touch him with their hands."[17] This is not at all what Jews and Christians believed about resurrection, as we have seen, but their position was easy to caricature in this way. Why would God, who is pure Spirit, have any interest in rotting corpses or dried bones? But even more to the point, *how* could God possibly raise the dead with bodies turned to dust, burnt to ashes, or lost at sea?

Paul's Corinthian opponents challenged him directly with these very questions: "How are the dead raised? With what kind of body do they come?" (1 Corinthians 15:35). They found the very idea absurd. Paul calls them fools who limit the capacities of God as Creator. If God created our physical world with all of its variety of "bodies," or outward forms, for various plants and animals, surely he can provide spiritual bodies for those whom he raises from the dead in the new creation (1 Corinthians 15:36–38). Paul thinks of a body as a *mode of being*, whether in a physical creation or in the new spiritual creation that God would fashion in the future.

Paul uses the resurrection of Christ as his illustrative example, viewing Jesus as the prototype of what will take place in the future for all the dead who will be raised at Jesus' coming. Just as God created Adam "from the dust" with a physical body, Christ, through his resurrection from the dead, became a new heavenly Adam, with a spiritual body. Paul expresses this with five contrasting couplets and a conclusion:

1. If there is a physical body, there is also a spiritual body.[18]
2. The first man Adam became a living being; the last Adam [Christ] became a life-giving spirit.
3. It is not the spiritual that is first but the physical, and then the spiritual.
4. The first man was from the earth, a man of dust; the second man is from heaven.
5. Just as we have borne the image of the man of dust, we shall also bear the image of the man of heaven. (1 Corinthians 15:45–49)

   Conclusion: Flesh and blood cannot inherit the kingdom of God, nor does the perishable inherit the imperishable (verse 50).

As a Pharisee Paul must have had some general notion of resurrection of the dead as involving a reembodied spiritual self, but as a Christian he has developed his understanding much further. He is convinced that Jesus' resurrection is actually the proof that this new cosmic process of transforming physical beings into a higher spiritual form is underway. He argues, "For as by a man [Adam] came death, by a man [Christ] has come also the resurrection of the dead." This is not something Jews in general, or Pharisees and

Essenes in particular, would say, since the hope that God would raise the dead would have no necessary connection to Jesus' being raised. But for Paul the two are inseparable: Christ's resurrection as a life-giving spirit inaugurates the process of the new creation.

THE BODY IN QUESTION

Paul's understanding of Jesus' resurrection allows us to approach with a new perspective the question of what happened to Jesus' body after he was taken from the cross. Paul begins his "resurrection chapter" with a formula-like recitation of what he calls "the Gospel":

> For I delivered to you as of first importance what I also received, that Christ died for our sins in accordance with the scriptures, that he was buried, and that he was raised on the third day in accordance with the scriptures. (1 Corinthians 15:3–4)

Paul is writing this around twenty-five years after Jesus' crucifixion and since he was not a witness to the death, burial, and resurrection on the third day, he passes along something he has "received" to the Corinthians. Most scholars take this to mean he is passing on a formal early Christian creed that he got from the Jerusalem apostles, or perhaps from Christians at Antioch. Although this is possible, I don't think it is at all certain, since Paul swears so adamantly that the gospel he "received" was not through men or from men, but by a direct revelation of Christ (Galatians 1:11–12). Earlier in 1 Corinthians he writes that he "*received* from the Lord" (same Greek verb, *paradidomi*), meaning from Jesus, his tradition about the Last Supper. Either way, whether by tradition or revelation, Paul offers his testimony of what he preaches.

Paul then lists a series of "sightings" (Greek *ophthe*) of the risen

Christ to various people, including Peter, James, and the twelve apostles, and finally his own experience of having "seen" Jesus.[19]

Two conclusions seem to follow from Paul's formulaic testimony. First, since Paul emphatically makes the point in 1 Corinthians that the resurrected Christ dwells in a spiritual body as a *life-giving Spirit*, we can say with assurance that the Christ that Paul claimed to have "seen" was not Jesus' physical corpse revivified. According to Paul, the "Lord," that is Jesus, *is* the "Spirit" (2 Corinthians 3:17–18). Second, since Paul equates his experience of "seeing" Christ with the experiences of the Jerusalem apostles who were before him, we can conclude that, at least in Paul's view of the matter, their experiences were identical—they all saw the same risen Christ in his glorified spiritual body. Since Paul explicitly says that Christ died *and was buried* but was subsequently "raised from the dead," he most likely believed that Jesus' physical body returned to the dust, and like a change of old clothing, had nothing to do with the new spiritual body Jesus received. His reference to Jesus' *burial* was to make the point that he was truly dead.

Paul clearly believes in a bodily resurrection, or more properly, an *embodied* resurrection. It is one thing to say the dead will be raised *bodily* and it is quite another to insist that the *same* bodies, long ago turned to dust and ashes, or buried at sea, must somehow be reconstituted in order to experience resurrection. The latter was the absurdity that Greeks objected to in offering naïve objections to the Jewish idea of the resurrection of the dead.

Resurrection is not the transformation of the physical *into* the spiritual, for given the corruption of the body there is nothing left to transform. Resurrection is rather the reclothing or "reincorporation" of the essential self with a new immortal body that frees it from the Hadean state of death.

A good illustration of this point is the case of John the Baptizer. The gospel of Mark, as well as Josephus, records John's brutal death at the hands of Herod Antipas, who had him beheaded.[20] Mark says that John's disciples, hearing of his death, were allowed to take his body and lay it in a tomb. Sometime later Herod received reports of the miraculous activities of Jesus. He was so impressed that he said "John the baptizer has been raised from the dead," thinking that what was reported of Jesus could only be explained if John had somehow returned from the dead (Mark 6:14). Yet there is no indication that Herod had John's tomb checked to see if it was empty. He was not thinking about a beheaded corpse being revived but he still considered the possibility that John might have returned to life. This account illustrates how the Jewish culture of the time could imagine someone being resurrected and reclothed in a new body, their former body left in the tomb.

If we take Paul seriously as our earliest witness to Jesus' resurrection, leaving aside for the moment the later reports in the gospels about an empty tomb, or stories of Jesus appearing after death as flesh and bones, we end up with an entirely different perspective on the resurrection. Paul's position is clear. He concludes his lengthy exposition on resurrection with the emphatic declaration that "flesh and blood will not inherit the kingdom of God" (1 Corinthians 15:50).

THE GABRIEL REVELATION

Recently an exciting new text was published that sheds significant light on this entire discussion.[21] It was found around the year 2000 in Jordan, near the eastern shore of the Dead Sea. It is now in the hands of a private collector in Europe. This ancient Hebrew text contains eighty-seven lines written in ink on a stone tablet. Experts date it to the end of the first century B.C., so it is definitely pre-Christian. The text purports to be a revelation of the angel Gabriel about the final apocalyptic battle between the forces of good and evil. We have various texts from this period dealing with this theme, including some of the Dead Sea Scrolls, but the second half of the text contains something entirely new. According to Israel Knohl of Hebrew University, the final section of the text focuses on the death and resurrection of a messianic leader, most likely Simon of Perea, who led a revolt in Judea in 4 B.C. following the death of Herod the Great.[22] Josephus reports that Simon's followers crowned him, a tall and handsome figure, as king of the Jews. He ravaged the countryside for a time, burning down the royal palace at Jericho. Gratus, Herod's military commander, pursued Simon and caught up with him in Transjordan and beheaded him.[23] What is fascinating and new about this text is that the slain leader, who has, according to the text, become "dung of the rocky crevices," his body decayed in the desert heat, is nonetheless addressed by the angel Gabriel: "I command you, prince of princes in three days you shall live!"

Since the text is pre-Christian, the parallels with Jesus are all the more amazing. Not only do we have reference here to a "slain" Messiah, an idea many have argued originated only with the unexpected crucifixion of Jesus, but also the reference to Simon being raised from the dead after three days. Since Paul is our earliest source for the tradition that Jesus was raised "on the third day," one has to ask whether this tradition of a slain Messiah being raised after three days was one that he appropriated and applied to Jesus.

What is all the more striking about this text is that it affirms Simon's resurrection from the dead even though his mutilated body had turned to "dung" in the hot Jordanian desert. Clearly the person composing the text, who surely believed that Gabriel's divine decree had been fulfilled, was not concerned with the decaying remains of Simon's beheaded body. Whoever wrote this text, most likely a follower of Simon, believed that God had vindicated him by raising him from the dead. Unfortunately, other than this text and Josephus's account of Simon's death, we have no way of knowing anything about the followers of Simon and what they might have done after his death. Simon apparently had no "Peter" or

"Paul" to carry on his messianic mission, but nonetheless the faith his followers had in his death and resurrection after three days was written down in a text. It provides us with significant new evidence about how the concept of resurrection of the dead was understood among Jewish messianic groups precisely from Jesus' time. It is our closest contemporary parallel to the resurrection faith.

By taking our clues from Paul's reports of "seeing" Jesus, and factoring in Paul's understanding of resurrection of the dead as a contemporary Jew of that time, we are now in a position to understand and interpret the gospel accounts in their proper historical contexts. What emerges is a consistent and coherent story of how Christian faith in Jesus' resurrection developed before it changed over time, allowing us to reconstruct what Jesus' earliest followers likely believed versus the later understanding of the resurrection that came from Paul.

THREE

READING THE GOSPELS IN THE LIGHT OF PAUL

It makes perfect sense to read the New Testament in its current order. The four gospels, Matthew, Mark, Luke, and John, introduce us to the life, death, and resurrection of Jesus. The book of Acts gives us the early history of Christianity, ending with the career of Paul. The letters of Paul and the other apostles, Peter, John, James, and Jude, come next, and the mysterious book of Revelation provides a climactic finale to the whole. It all makes perfect sense—unless one is a historian.

Historians read the New Testament *backward*. Over the last hundred and fifty years they have made a significant discovery. If the New Testament writings are ordered chronologically, according to the dates the various books were written, a wholly different picture emerges, with radical and far-reaching implications. Historians disassemble these various sources in an attempt to understand them in chronological order. They focus on a precise set of questions: Where do we find our oldest and most authentic materials? How and when were they passed along, edited, and embellished? Who was involved in this process and what theological motivations were operating? As it turns out, this seemingly destructive process of "disassembly" yields positive and fascinating results.

I want to return to the question of what happened following the death of Jesus. Now that we have Paul as our master key, when we attempt to analyze the four New Testament gospels with their narratives of the empty tomb, an entirely different perspective opens up. Understanding Paul turns out to be fundamental to understanding what the earliest followers of Jesus most likely experienced, and the central affirmation of Paul's message and apostleship—that he had "seen" Jesus raised from the dead—can be placed in its proper historical light.

In looking at the gospels, chronology turns out to be a remarkably fruitful starting point. There is no absolute guarantee that what is early is more accurate than what came after, but unless we begin the process of disassembly and comparison we have no way of even approaching our questions.

Evangelical Christian scholars, both Protestant and Catholic, believe that the only possible explanation for the empty tomb is that God raised Jesus bodily from the dead and that he emerged from the tomb fully and miraculously restored to health. They maintain that there is no other logical explanation for all the facts as reported and are quite keen to uphold Jesus' resurrection as the solid, demonstrable bedrock of Christian faith.[1] Their thinking runs something like the following.

The disciples were in great despair over Jesus' death, having lost all hope that he could be the Messiah. After all, a dead Messiah is a failed Messiah. None of them was expecting Jesus to die, much less rise from the dead, so how were they suddenly transformed from disappointed hopelessness to dynamic faith? Rather than wither away, the Jesus movement began to mushroom, gaining strength and numbers as the apostles proclaimed all over Jerusalem that they had seen Jesus alive and his tomb was empty. How can such a dramatic change, three days after Jesus' death, be explained any other way? Why were the apostles willing to face persecution and even death if they were spreading a story they knew to be false?

There are a limited number of nonsupernatural explanations to explain what might have happened. The oldest explanation, that the disciples stole the body to deliberately promote the fraudulent claim that Jesus had been raised from the dead, is mentioned in the gospel of Matthew as a rumor that was spread among the Jewish population (Matthew 28:13–15). A second explanation, that some unknown person with no connection to the disciples, usually said to be a gardener, removed the body, also shows up in some later Jewish texts. The earliest source for this story is Tertullian, a late-third-century Christian apologist. He writes that some Jews were claiming that a gardener, upset that crowds visiting Jesus' tomb were trampling his vegetables, reburied the body elsewhere, never revealing the location.[2] In more recent times, the so-called Swoon Theory, popularized by Hugh Schonfield's 1965 bestseller, *The Passover Plot*, suggested that Jesus was not really dead but unconscious, either through a drug or from the trauma of crucifixion, and that he revived in the tomb.[3] The most common explanation among biblical scholars is that Mark, our earliest gospel writer, invented the entire burial and empty tomb story to bolster faith in the resurrection of Jesus. It is Mark's invention, lacking any historical basis.[4] I find this last explanation highly unlikely since it is hard to imagine the early followers of Jesus relating his death on the cross, but then saying nothing about what happened to his body. It would essentially be a story with no ending. But perhaps more to the point, Paul, our earliest source, written decades before the gospels, knows the tradition that Jesus was at least buried. I think Mark does his share of inventive mythmaking—but not regarding the fact of Jesus' burial, or even that his tomb was found empty on Sunday morning by his followers. That seems to me to be at the minimal core of what we can responsibly say about what happened after the cross.

Geza Vermes, in a recent work, *The Resurrection: History and*

Myth, surveys these various alternative explanations and concludes that none of them "stands up to stringent scrutiny," despite our need for some rational, scientific explanation.[5] Like so many others he concludes that historical investigation, given our limited evidence, has reached a dead end, given the contradictory and mythological nature of our evidence—namely the texts of the New Testament. Is there a way through this impasse?

Since the earliest surviving Christian texts are seven letters of Paul (1 Thessalonians, Galatians, 1 and 2 Corinthians, Romans, Philippians, and Philemon), dating to the early 50s A.D., twenty years after Jesus' death, it makes sense to give them priority, particularly in our attempting to solve the mystery of what happened after the cross. Not only are these letters the earliest evidence we have, but they come to us firsthand, as first-person testimony from one who had direct dealings with Peter, James, and the other apostles.

If gospels were written a generation or more later, when Paul, Peter, and James were dead, and the Romans had shattered the original Jerusalem church following the destruction of the city in A.D. 70, they should be considered as secondary evidence. It comes as a surprise to many people familiar with the names Matthew, Mark, Luke, and John to learn that all four are anonymous productions, written in the generation after the apostles, and based on a complex mix of sources and theological editing. Scholars are agreed that none of the gospels is an eyewitness account and the names associated with them are assigned by tradition, not by any explicit claim by their authors. In other words, the names themselves are added as titles to each book but are not embedded in the texts of the works themselves. Each gospel writer had his own motives and purposes in telling the Jesus story in a way that supported his particular perspectives. None of them is writing history but all four can rightly be called theologians. From a distance their differences might seem minimal, but once carefully examined they are quite significant, revealing a process of mythmaking that went on within decades of Jesus' death.

Of the four gospels, Mark, not Matthew, comes first, written sometime around A.D. 80 or later. Mark gives no account of Jesus' birth at all, miraculous or otherwise, and most strikingly, in his original version, as we will see, there are no post-resurrection appearances of Jesus to the disciples! This fact alone provides us with an important key to unraveling the mystery surrounding the empty tomb. The author of Mark preserves for us a stage of history when the Jesus story is being told with an entirely different ending.

Matthew was written at least a decade or more later and the author uses Mark as his main source. He does not start from scratch and he obviously does not have his own independent account to offer. Matthew incorporates 90 percent of Mark but he edits Mark's material rather freely, embellishing and expanding the story as fits his purposes. That is why most readers of the New Testament who begin with Matthew, and then come to Mark, have the strange sense that they have already read the story before. They actually have, but in Matthew's edited version. The result is that Mark is almost always read as a cut-down version of the more complete story in Matthew.

Matthew's embellishments are many but most particularly he finds Mark's beginning and ending wholly unsatisfactory. How could one possibly write a gospel of Jesus Christ with no birth story of Jesus and no appearances of Jesus to the disciples after the resurrection?

What this means is that for several decades, when there were no other gospels but Mark in circulation, Christians were relating the Jesus story without the two elements that later came to be considered foundational for the Christian faith—Jesus' virgin birth and his Easter morning appearances.

Matthew's gospel represents a watershed moment in Christian history. He composes the first account of the miraculous virgin birth of Jesus, and he creates a spectacular scene of resurrection:

And behold, there was a great earthquake; for an angel of the Lord descended from heaven and came and rolled back the stone, and sat upon it. His appearance was like lightning, and his raiment white as snow. And for fear of him the guards trembled and became like dead men. (Matthew 28:2–4)

Mark has none of this. In his account there is no angel but a young man sitting inside Jesus' tomb and no miraculous intervention from heaven. Matthew ends his story with a dramatic scene of the resurrected Jesus meeting the apostles on a mountain and giving the so-called Great Commission, to preach the gospel to all nations and baptize them in the name of the Father, Son, and Holy Spirit (Matthew 28:18–20). Luke was written several decades after Matthew, perhaps at the end of the first century or the beginning of the second, and the author expands and embellishes the core Mark story even further than Matthew had done. Luke adds multiple appearances of Jesus to various individuals as well as to all the apostles, and like Matthew, he also provides his own version of a birth story.

Even with these later embellishments Luke and Matthew nonetheless provide us with an unexpected surprise, discovered by scholars over a hundred and fifty years ago. In addition to Mark, both writers had access to the Q source. This early collection of the sayings of Jesus, probably compiled around A.D. 50, was apparently not known to Mark. It can be extracted and reconstructed with some degree of certainty, but as I mentioned in an earlier chapter, we don't have an independent copy of Q itself, only its reconstruction from Matthew and Luke. I mention it again here because one of its most important features is that in the Q source Jesus never speaks of his resurrection from the dead, whereas in Mark, who comes later, Jesus refers several times to being "raised on the third day." This is one more example of how putting our

sources in proper chronological order might enable us to reconstruct the ways in which faith in Jesus' resurrection developed in
the first few decades of the movement.

Most scholars place the gospel of John as the latest of the four
gospels and certainly it is the most theologically embellished in
terms of its view of Jesus as the divine, preexistent Son of God.
So far as the empty tomb and resurrection of Jesus are concerned,
John, like Luke, recounts multiple appearances of Jesus to his disciples in Jerusalem, as well as an appended final chapter in which
Jesus also appears to several of them on the Sea of Galilee (John 21).

All of this disassembly, sorting, and sifting might suggest historians are just picking and choosing at random whatever suits them
to support a preconceived theory, but there is definitely a method
to this critical historical investigation. Historians of any period
have a similar challenge in evaluating the reliability of multiple
sources. What is required is that one be explicit and clear about
one's methods with careful arguments as to why this or that bit of
evidence is given whatever weight. What is needed is a synthesis of
our best evidence, incorporating the essential clues that Paul provides for probing a series of related questions:

Why was Jesus' tomb found empty?
What happened to the body of Jesus?
How did his earliest followers understand his resurrection?

A Rushed Burial and an Empty Tomb

Jesus died in the year A.D. 30 in the late afternoon, just hours before
the Jewish Passover meal was to begin in the evening.[6] Mark says
it was "the day of preparation, that is, the day before the Sabbath"
(Mark 15:42). The rush was to remove the bodies of Jesus and the
two others crucified that day from their crosses before sundown,
when these holy days would begin, since both Jewish law and custom forbade the corpses of executed criminals to be left hanging

past sunset, much less through a holiday (Deuteronomy 21:22–23). Josephus, the contemporary Jewish historian, explicitly mentions this practice, asserting that the Jews "took down those who were condemned and crucified and buried them before the going down of the sun."[7]

This rush to bury provides us with our first insight into why Jesus' tomb was found empty. Mark tells us that Joseph of Arimathea, a respected member of the Sanhedrin, the governing council of the Jews, obtained permission directly from the Roman governor, Pontius Pilate, to remove Jesus' body from the cross and take charge of his burial (Mark 15:42–46). Apparently Joseph had sympathies toward Jesus and his followers since he shows up suddenly in Mark's story and voluntarily exercises his influence to facilitate Jesus' burial. Given the impending festival that began at sunset, there was no time for full and proper Jewish rites of burial that would involve washing the body and anointing it with oil and spices. The women of Jesus' family, who had followed him from Galilee, had plans to carry out these duties but had to defer them until after the Passover and the Sabbath (Mark 16:1). There is no indication that they were in communication with Joseph of Arimathea at the time he took Jesus' body or through the Passover holiday. The followers of Jesus had mostly fled in fear and were in hiding (John 20:19). One gets the idea that the women watched from a distance, surely a bit frightened themselves, but wanting to know where the body was taken (Mark 15:47; Luke 23:55). The burial was in the hands of Joseph, but they hoped he would allow them, as Jewish custom prescribed, to carry out the traditional rites of burial and mourning.

Mark says that Joseph of Arimathea wrapped Jesus in a linen shroud and laid him in a rock-hewn tomb, blocking the entrance with a sealing stone. There are hundreds of these hewn-out cave tombs of this type in the Jerusalem area, some of which have been excavated, so what Mark describes is quite familiar to us. They typically have a small squared entrance that can be blocked up with a stone cut to fit. They are of various sizes but are intended for family burials. Mark says nothing about where this tomb was or how or why it was chosen. It is the gospel of John that provides a key missing detail:

> Now in the place where he was crucified there was a garden, and in the garden a new tomb, where no one had ever been laid. So because of the Jewish day of Preparation, as the tomb was *close at hand,* they laid Jesus there. (John 19:41–42)

People assume that the tomb into which Joseph of Arimathea placed the body of Jesus belonged to him but here we see that such was not the case.[8] It was a newly hewn tomb with no one buried inside that just happened to be close by. Jesus' body was laid inside, but only temporarily. He was not really buried there, since full and formal burial involved the preparation rites and mourning rituals carried out by the family over a seven-day period (Mark 16:1; John 20:1). That is why the women show up early Sunday morning at the tomb, expecting to initiate the burial process with Joseph's cooperation.

Jesus' corpse would have been badly mutilated with bruises, wounds, and dried blood. Preparing it for proper burial would require quite a bit of time and effort. The body could not be left exposed over the holidays, and the empty unused tomb with its blocking stone would provide protection from predators. Joseph's actions were practical temporary emergency measures.

We have to assume, since Joseph had taken responsibility for Jesus' proper burial, that his intention was to fulfill this obligation as soon as possible after the Passover. When the Sabbath was over, on Saturday night, he would have his first opportunity to properly bury the body and presumably returned to the temporary unused tomb to remove Jesus' body for permanent burial—hence the empty tomb. As a man of means, and a member of the highest Jewish judicial body, the Sanhedrin, this makes perfect sense. Based on Jewish law, he would not have placed Jesus in his own family tomb, but would have provided a separate tomb for Jesus.[9]

What Mark knows is that very early Sunday morning, just as the sun was rising, Mary Magdalene, Mary the mother of Jesus, and Salome, most likely Jesus' sister, came to the tomb with the intent of washing the body and anointing it with oil and spices.[10] When they arrived the large blocking stone had already been removed but the tomb was empty, the body gone. This was precisely what one might expect given the circumstances of Joseph's intentions and activities. But it was a total surprise to the women. They arrived fully expecting to be involved in the rites of a proper and final burying. That is why they arrived so early, so as not to miss Joseph, who they expected would return at first light Sunday morning—but they arrived twelve hours too late! What they did not consider is that Joseph had returned to the tomb the instant the Passover Sabbath day was over at sundown.

Mark says that when the women looked into the empty tomb they saw a young man sitting inside, who told them:

> Do not be amazed; you seek Jesus of Nazareth, who was crucified. He has risen, he is not here; see the place where they laid him. But go tell his disciples and Peter that he is going before you to Galilee; there you will see him, as he told you. (Mark 16:6–7)

Here the line between history and theology is clearly drawn. That the tomb was empty fits what we know of the circumstances of Jesus' temporary "burial" by Joseph of Arimathea, but that the women were told that Jesus would meet his disciples in Galilee is clearly a theological embellishment. It is Mark's attempt to connect the empty tomb with subsequent appearances of Jesus. The link is quite weak, since Mark knows of no specifics of any appearances

of the risen Jesus to the disciples in Galilee; otherwise he surely
would have related them to round out the ending to his gospel. I
think we have to assume that Mark tells us all he knows but what
Mark knows he gets from Paul. Mark is following Paul here, since
it is Paul who reports that Jesus first appears to Peter and the disciples, and in Mark's account the young man sitting in the tomb
specifies Peter by name (1 Corinthians 15:5).

Mark relates next that the women fled the tomb in fear and
amazement and that they said nothing to anyone (Mark 16:8). The
oldest, most authentic copies of Mark end abruptly here, at verse 8.
The additions found in most translations of the Bible, where Jesus appears to various people mentioned in Matthew, Luke, and John, were
interpolations added to later manuscripts of Mark by editors who
could not imagine a gospel ending without appearances of Jesus.[11]

Mark also knows an old tradition, not mentioned specifically
by Paul, that the first time Peter and the disciples saw Jesus was in
Galilee, in the north, not in Jerusalem the week of Passover. This
is not a minor difference from Luke and John, as we will see. It is a
blatant counter-story.

If we put Mark and Paul together we get the earliest and most
reliable tradition—faith in Jesus' resurrection began in Galilee
with Peter and the apostles as the first to claim they had seen him.

Matthew and Luke, using Mark as their source, follow closely
his account of the women finding Jesus' tomb empty, though
Matthew adds all sorts of supernatural elements, as noted previously. Both flatly contradict Mark's statement that the women said
nothing to anyone; in Matthew and Luke they run to tell the disciples (Matthew 28:8; Luke 24:9). All seem to agree, however, that
the discovery of the empty tomb by the women that Sunday morning did not inspire anyone to believe that Jesus had been raised
from the dead. The assumption of everyone was that someone had
removed the body.

The gospel of John offers an alternative empty tomb story that is not based on Mark, and although John is our latest gospel, this particular story seems to offer us a less theological account of the story, leading some historians to conclude it might represent a much earlier independent tradition:[12]

> Now on the first day of the week Mary Magdalene came to the tomb early, while it was still dark, and saw that the stone had been taken away from the tomb. So she ran and went to Simon Peter and the other disciple, the one whom Jesus loved, and said to them, *"They have taken the Lord out of the tomb, and we do not know where they have laid him."* So Peter went out with the other disciple, and they were going toward the tomb. Both of them were running together, but the other disciple outran Peter and reached the tomb first. And stooping to look in, he saw the linen cloths lying there, but he did not go in. Then Simon Peter came, following him, and went into the tomb. He saw the linen cloths lying there, and the face cloth, which had been on his head, not lying with the linen cloths but folded up in a place by itself. Then the other disciple, who had reached the tomb first, also went in, and he saw and believed; for as yet they did not understand the Scripture, that he must rise from the dead. Then the disciples went back to their homes. (John 20:1–10)

John, of course, gives other stories following his account of the empty tomb in which Jesus appears to Mary Magdalene and to the disciples as a group, including Thomas, the famous doubter. But this account of the empty tomb stands out.

There is no young man or angelic interpreter in the tomb to proclaim the resurrection. Instead, Mary is quite sure the body has been taken elsewhere for burial: "They have taken the Lord out of the tomb, and we do not know where they have laid him" (John 20:2). One has to ask, who is the "they" Mary Magdalene has in mind? Based on the hasty burial of Jesus' body in this temporary tomb, it seems obvious that she is referring to Joseph of Arimathea and his assistants. After all, just a few verses earlier it is John who tells us that the tomb was a temporary one (John 19:41). Peter and the other disciple race to the tomb to verify that it was empty. What they "believe" is not that Jesus has been raised from the dead, as John clarifies, but that the body of Jesus has been removed and reburied—presumably the night before. This fits precisely what we have reconstructed above, based on all our sources.

I argued a version of this "reburial" scenario in my book *The Jesus Dynasty*,[13] and one response in particular, from an esteemed academic colleague, seemed to sum up some possible objections to my thesis quite well:

> You say that the body of Jesus was removed from its temporary resting place to a permanent tomb. This is not at all impossible. Extreme improbability sets in only when you invite us to assume that this group, who knew perfectly well what had actually happened to the body of Jesus, permitted their co-religionists to proclaim, not that he was still alive (immortality of the soul, well attested in Judaism) but that he was risen from the dead. This, of course, is against the background of what "resurrection" meant for first-century Jews. In order for me to take your "evidence" seriously, you would have to explain why the family and/or disciples based their future lives on what they knew to be a falsehood, namely that the body had been raised, and finally to justify how the secret was preserved in one of the gabbiest societies in ancient history.[14]

In my judgment there are several incorrect assumptions embedded in this objection. I showed in the previous chapter that, according to Paul, the resurrection of Jesus, and resurrection more generally, was understood as the reembodiment of one who has died, not the resuscitation of a corpse.

The gospels, written decades after Jesus' death, begin to connect the empty tomb and the disappearance of Jesus' body to subsequent and immediate appearances of Jesus to his followers, even the same day, in Jerusalem, proving that he had been raised from the dead. But as we will see, these are late expansions of earlier tradition. What Mark only implies ("you will see him in Galilee") is lavishly embellished by Luke, and John, but is now set in Jerusalem, on the Sunday after the crucifixion. Jesus walks around, wounds and all, eating meals and claiming he is still flesh and bones—directly contradicting Paul's emphatic assertion that Jesus has become a "life-giving spirit"—embodied, yes, but not physical or material. It is a mistake to allow these later texts to frame our objections and take priority over earlier materials.

Whether the family and followers of Jesus knew immediately where Jesus had been reburied, or learned of the location later, they were not running around Jerusalem in that first week following Jesus' death proclaiming he had been raised. In fact, a critical reading of our sources will show that there were no sightings of Jesus in Jerusalem at all, but only in Galilee, other than perhaps the single experience of Mary Magdalene (John 20:11–18; Matthew 28:9–10).[15] The matter of a first appearance to Mary Magdalene is always possible but she is not included in the list of first witnesses that Paul relates—perhaps since appealing to the testimony of a woman was considered less than convincing, as we will see below.

SORTING THROUGH THE SIGHTINGS OF JESUS

Sometimes clues show up from the most unexpected quarters. In 1886 a fragmentary eighth-century A.D. copy of the lost *Gospel of Peter* was found buried in the grave of a monk in Egypt. Eusebius, a fourth-century church historian, had mentioned its existence but regarded it with disfavor.[16] It is written in the first person, claiming to be by Peter, but scholars generally place it in the late second century A.D. It narrates Jesus' death and resurrection and scholars have debated without resolution whether it is dependent on our New Testament gospels or represents an independent tradition. It has a highly legendary flavor to it, with quite a few fantastic embellishments, so whether it has much historical value is debatable. At the end of the text the author seems to retell his empty tomb story in a much more straightforward way, for a second time in the text, but this time almost identical to Mark. It is as if he is passing along two versions, one highly fantastic and legendary, and the other more sober and realistic. In this second version Mary Magdalene and the other women arrive at Jesus' tomb, finding it empty, and as in Mark, they encounter a young man who tells them Jesus is risen, and they flee the tomb frightened. The critical final lines of the text, before it breaks off, read:

> Now it was the last day of unleavened bread and many went to their homes because the feast was at an end. But we, the twelve disciples of the Lord, wept and mourned and each one, grieving for what had happened, returned to his own home. But I, Simon Peter, and my brother Andrew took our nets and went to the sea. And there was with us Levi, the son of Alphaeus, whom the Lord . . . [17]

This text is a bombshell in its implications. The Passover festival lasts for eight days and according to this text, rather than running around Jerusalem celebrating various appearances of Jesus, Peter and the rest of the disciples spent that week in Jerusalem weeping and mourning. At the end of the eight-day feast they returned home, to Galilee, still grieving for what had happened. Each went to his home, and Peter, with his brother Andrew, returned to their fishing business. This evidence—that the followers of Jesus returned home to Galilee in despair and mourning, and even went back to their businesses, and only sometime later, in Galilee, began to have faith that Jesus had been raised from the dead—rings true with the rest of our evidence when put in proper chronological order. The body of Jesus, resting in a tomb in Jerusalem, was no threat to their faith that Jesus, though dead, had been vindicated by God and was indeed the Messiah they had hoped for.

That we even have such a text, running so counter to the reports of appearances of Jesus in Jerusalem the week following his death, given the subsequent embellishments of the gospels with multiple appearances of Jesus, is quite remarkable. The text also fits in with Mark, who mentions no appearances of Jesus, but also relates the tradition that the disciples returned to Galilee. It is more than likely that the *Gospel of Peter*, after this abrupt break, goes on to narrate a "sighting" of Jesus by Peter, Andrew, and the others on the Sea of Galilee, after they had returned to their fishing and given up hope.

Strangely, we have a version of this story tacked on to the end of the gospel of John—an extra chapter, 21, like an appendix, after the original text had clearly ended with chapter 20. It has been edited to read as if Jesus had already been appearing to the disciples in Jerusalem and now just showed up in Galilee. But it is clear that it reflects an entirely independent source, preserving a story very similar to the ending of the *Gospel of Peter*. Peter has returned to the Sea of Galilee with a few others and he has gone back to fishing. They are out in the boat when they think they see Jesus, distantly on the shore. The way the story is related, even though the author of John has elaborated and embellished it, shows that this tradition of a return to Galilee, and a resuming of the fishing business, was a persistent one.

Matthew follows Mark with his emphasis on Galilee as the place where the disciples first saw Jesus. What he relates is quite telling:

> Now the eleven disciples went to Galilee, to the mountain to
> which Jesus had directed them. And when they saw him they
> worshiped him; but some doubted. (Matthew 28:16–17)

Presumably Matthew is associating a specific mountain as a place
of visionary experience, much like his account in chapter 17
where Jesus appears as a transfigured shining being with Moses
and Elijah. Many scholars have suggested that the account of the
transfiguration, related also in Mark 9, is a misplaced resurrection
story.[18] But whether that is the case or not, what we learn here is
that Matthew only knows a single story of Jesus appearing to his
disciples. It takes place in Galilee—a "misty mountain" visionary
experience—and some doubted!

If we put all our "sighting" evidence together in chronological
order from all our sources, including the evidence we have surveyed
from Paul, we get an interesting breakdown, and one can clearly see
how the stories expand and develop. What follows is a basic summary.

Paul had his revelation of Christ approximately seven years
after Jesus' crucifixion. He claimed that he saw Jesus in a glorious
heavenly body. Twice in his letter 1 Corinthians he equates his own
experience with that of those who had seen Jesus earlier, based on
traditions he had received: namely, Peter (Cephas), the Twelve, a
group of five hundred at once, James, and the rest of the apostles:

> Last of all, as to one untimely born, he was seen also by me. (15:8)

> Am I not an apostle? Have I not seen Jesus our Lord? (9:1)

He does not say when or where these earlier "sightings" by the others took place but since he mentions "the Twelve," he might be referring to a time when Judas Iscariot, who was dead, had been
replaced, which would mean several weeks had passed since the
crucifixion of Jesus.[19]

Mark has no accounts of anyone seeing Jesus but the young man who meets the women at the tomb and tells them explicitly to go tell the disciples they will see Jesus in Galilee.

Matthew relates that the women who first went to the tomb are told by an angel to go tell the disciples they will see Jesus in Galilee. As they run to convey this message they meet Jesus, who repeats the message, even more explicitly, "Tell my brothers to go to Galilee and there they will see me" (Matthew 28:10). Matthew closes his gospel with the scene on a mountain in Galilee, clearly somewhat later, in which the eleven disciples see him, though he mentions that some of them doubted it was Jesus.

Luke writes that later on that first Sunday two men who were walking on a road outside Jerusalem met Jesus and shared a meal with him, at first not recognizing him. Subsequently he says that Peter then saw Jesus, but no details are given, only the report. That evening Jesus appears in the room where the eleven disciples are gathered and eats with them, showing them his physical body of flesh and bones and convincing them he is not a ghost or spirit.

John says that Jesus first appears to Mary Magdalene, outside the tomb on Sunday morning. Later that evening he appears to the rest of the disciples, showing them his wounds, but Thomas is not present. Eight days later he appears again, where they are staying, and Thomas is able to see and even touch his wounds, which convinces Thomas he is not seeing a ghost.

The *Appendix* to John (chapter 21) relates a separate story, unconnected to the main narrative and taking place in Galilee, where Peter and the other disciples have returned to their fishing but see Jesus on the shore from a distance. They come to land and he is cooking fish on a charcoal fire and they eat together.

The *Gospel of Peter* ends with the disciples leaving Jerusalem a week after the crucifixion and returning to Galilee. Even though Mary Magdalene and the women have found the tomb empty, the disciples have no faith that Jesus is alive. They are in despair, mourning the death of Jesus, and they return to their fishing business. Unfortunately the text breaks off at that point.

Two important observations emerge from this breakdown of sources.

1. The earlier texts (Mark, Matthew) agree that the disciples encountered Jesus only in Galilee sometime after the empty tomb was discovered. They are actually told to *go* to Galilee, where they will see him. Since they would not have left Jerusalem until after the eight-day Passover festival ended, their experiences would have been several weeks after Jesus' death. Matthew's account indicates that whatever encounter they had, it was more visionary in nature, and subject to doubt. As a kind of addendum to the Galilee tradition, even though they come later chronologically, the *Gospel of Peter* and the Appendix to John indicate that Peter and the others returned to their homes in Galilee and that Peter and his brother Andrew resumed their fishing business.

2. The later accounts (Luke and John) put Jesus' appearances in Jerusalem as immediate, on the same day as the tomb is discovered empty. Jesus appears as a flesh-and-blood human being, shows his wounds, and eats meals to demonstrate that he is not a ghost or spirit. The strong impression one gets is that the empty tomb is directly tied to Jesus appearing and one is dealing here with the idea of resurrection as the literal resuscitation of a corpse.

These dichotomies are quite striking: Where: Galilee or Jerusalem? When: immediately on the day the tomb was discovered or weeks thereafter? And what: visionary-like experiences or resuscitation of a physical corpse? The internal evidence is decidedly in favor of the Mark/Matthew tradition. To even imagine that the kinds of stories that Luke and John relate, set in Jerusalem, were circulating when Mark wrote his gospel is highly improbable. That Mark could publish the first gospel in Christian history and include no appearances of Jesus, with the focus on Galilee, not Jerusalem, pushes our evidence decidedly in favor of the Galilee option. It is also hard to imagine a text like the ending of the *Gospel of Peter* even existing unless it were related to a strong tradition of remembering the despair and sorrow of the disciples following Jesus' death, as they returned to their vocations in Galilee, giving up hope. It is not an edifying story, but it is a realistic one, and it fits our earlier evidence.

Some have argued that these differences in our gospel accounts are the expected result of reports from a variety of witnesses but all testify to the same essential fact—Jesus was raised from the dead. Sometimes the analogy of an automobile accident is suggested. When eyewitnesses report what they saw, each reflects a particular perspective, and there are always differences in details, but the essential facts related to the accident are usually the same. Such an analogy fails in the case of the gospels. First, there are *no* eyewitness accounts at all. Second, the reports we have don't even agree on where the sightings of Jesus took place—Galilee or Jerusalem? What we have is a series of theologically motivated traditions written decades after the event, removed from both place and time, battling out competing stories of what happened after Jesus died. They cannot be harmonized. Luke even has Jesus telling the eleven apostles that they are not to leave Jerusalem, which closes the door on even the possibility of subsequent appearances of Jesus in Galilee as alluded to in Mark and recorded in Matthew (Luke 24:49; Acts 1:3–4).

Paul is a decisive witness for this reason. He does claim to have seen something firsthand, and he equates his "sighting" experiences with those of Peter, James, and the rest of the apostles, based on his personal acquaintance with them. Given his view of resurrection of the dead, as being reclothed in a glorious heavenly body, he would have found the emphasis on flesh and bones meaningless. When Paul says Jesus was "buried" he is indicating that he knows the tradition of Jesus' body being put in a tomb (1 Corinthians 15:4). His point is to emphasize that Jesus truly was dead and buried. What was then "raised on the third day," just as in the Gabriel Revelation, was not the perishable mortal body but a new spiritual body, no longer "flesh and blood," the old body having been shed like discarded clothing (1 Corinthians 15:42–50; 52–54).

Jesus' own teaching about resurrection, preserved in the Q source, as we have seen, emphasizes an angelic-like transformation in which even the sexual distinctions between male and female are obsolete (Luke 20:34–36). This parallels precisely Paul's view of resurrection.

So why does this shift from Galilee to Jerusalem come about in Luke and John? And why their insistence on connecting the empty tomb with the literal appearances of Jesus as revived from the dead in the resuscitated corpse that had been buried? I think we can assume that the reasons were largely apologetic. These texts come late in the first century and even in the early second century. Sophisticated Greek critics of Christianity such as Lucian, Trypho, and Celsus were on the horizon.[20] Their common charge was that Christianity thrived only among the ignorant, simple-minded, and gullible classes of society, who were led astray by the foolish tales of deluded women and hallucinations passed off as "visions."[21] There were also similar, rival tales of other "divine men" circulating, such as Apollonius of Tyana, a Pythagorean wonder worker, born about the same time as Jesus in Asia Minor, who traveled throughout the eastern Mediterranean world. According to his followers, Zeus fathered Apollonius, so he, like Jesus, was a "Son of God." According to his biographies or "gospels," he healed the sick, raised the dead, and ascended bodily into heaven.[22] Various versions of Apollonius's death were passed along, including one where he was arrested by persecutors, set himself free, and was taken up from the earth into heaven. According to another story he appeared mysteriously to a doubtful follower after his death and convinced him of the doctrine of immortality. A fascinating stone inscription containing the following epigram has turned up in Asia Minor not far from Tarsus, where Paul grew up:

> *This man, named after Apollo and shining forth Tyana,*
> *Extinguished the fault of men.*
> *The tomb in Tyana (received) his body,*
> *But in truth heaven received him*
> *So he might drive out the pains from men.*[23]

As with Jesus there were debates among his devotees as to whether his body remained in a tomb or whether he was assumed bodily into heaven. The early-third-century Roman emperor Caracalla built a shrine to Apollonius, and Caracalla's successor, the emperor Alexander Severus, is alleged to have had a private shrine in which the images of Abraham, Orpheus, Christ, and Apollonius were given divine honors.[24]

If Jesus' followers came to believe in his resurrection only after a period of despair, and in Galilee, far removed from the empty tomb in Jerusalem, based on visionary experiences, they were surely open to the charge that the entire phenomenon was mass hallucination. That Matthew, who gives us our first and earliest account of such a group appearance, says it took place on a mountain but that some of the eleven disciples doubted, while others believed, was clearly quite problematic for Luke and for John, writing a generation later (Matthew 28:17).

That is also why Luke, alone of our four gospels records a scene in which Jesus ascends bodily from the earth, taken away in a cloud from the Mount of Olives, just east of Jerusalem, as the eleven apostles stand gazing into the sky (Acts 1:9–10). To leave him bodily on earth, eating and drinking, in his physical form, simply would not do, since one would presume that like others "raised from the dead" by Jesus, he would have eventually died again as he grew older. And John, although he has no ascension scene per se, records that Jesus said that he was "ascending to where he was before" (John 6:62).

These New Testament gospels and the book of Acts take us decades beyond Paul, into a time and place that he never lived to see. It is deeply ironic that Paul is in some ways the shadow behind all four of our gospels, yet to understand Paul we need to put the gospels aside, which means, at least in terms of sources, to learn to read the New Testament backward. If we can resist making assumptions and pick up Paul's letters with fresh eyes, we will capture an amazing moment in time, for which he is our only firsthand source. We will learn how Paul transformed the original Christianity into a new religion that claimed to abrogate and supersede the "old" by moving everything from earth to heaven.

FOUR

LAST BUT NOT LEAST

Paul believed that God had selected him before his birth for a singular and pivotal mission that would determine the future of the cosmos. Though Jesus had directly chosen the twelve apostles, and in that order of things Paul came after them, God's choosing him before birth would actually make Paul the *first* apostle. Paul was further convinced that his specific role in God's plan of salvation was predicted in various prophecies of the Hebrew Bible, just as was the role of Christ. Although Jesus had instructed the twelve apostles over a period of three years, Paul did not believe that he had disclosed to them the hidden *mystery* of God's secret plan, nor revealed to them "the Announcement" that Paul referred to as "my Gospel." That came later, when God chose to reveal his Son, the heavenly glorified Christ, to Paul and to Paul alone:

> But when he who had set me apart before I was born, and had called me through his grace, was pleased to reveal his Son to me, in order that I might preach him among the Gentiles, I did not confer with flesh and blood, nor did I go up to Jerusalem to those who were apostles before me, *but I went away into Arabia.* (Galatians 1:15–17)

Arabia, as Paul uses the term here, refers to the desert area south of the Land of Israel, where Mount Sinai was located (Galatians 4:25). This rather extraordinary decision of Paul, to go to Arabia, is not mentioned at all in the book of Acts, where Paul heads up to Jerusalem right after his Damascus road revelation and even meets the apostles—something Paul swears was absolutely *not the case* (Acts 9:26–28). Either the author of Acts knows nothing about the Arabian sojourn, or he is so keen to have Paul linked with the Jerusalem apostles that he purposely ignores it. So why did Paul go to Arabia?

Mount Sinai, also known as Mount Horeb, is called the "mountain of God" in the Torah. It was the sacred place, the "holy ground" where God first spoke to Moses in a burning bush, giving him his critical mission to gather the people of Israel and bring them into the Promised Land. It was also on this mountain, over a forty-day period, that God delivered to Moses the revelation of the Torah (Exodus 3:1–6; 34:27–28). When Moses came down from the mountain the skin of his face was glowing, because he had been talking directly with God, exposed to God's glory (Exodus 34:29). As a result of this revelation Moses made a covenant between God and the people of Israel. The covenant and the giving of the Torah became the foundational pillars of Judaism, as Paul points out (Romans 9:4). Mount Sinai was also the place to which the prophet Elijah retreated, and it was there, in a cave in the same mountain, that he had his own extraordinary encounter with God, speaking with him face-to-face and also witnessing God's glory (1 Kings 19:1–18).

It was neither accident nor arbitrary choice that drove Paul into the Arabian desert immediately after he received his initial vision of Christ. Paul traveled to that desolate area not to confer with any human being, but to hear directly from Jesus Christ: "For I would have you know brethren, that the Gospel which was preached by me is not man's gospel. For I did not receive it from a man, nor

was I taught it, but it came through a revelation of Jesus Christ"
(Galatians 1:12). Paul doesn't say how long he stayed in Arabia, but
he does note that it was three years *after* his vision of Christ when
he finally went up to Jerusalem to meet Peter and James (Galatians
1:18). That visit appears to have been a clandestine one, in that he
swears he did not meet any of the other apostles, only these two
leaders. One must assume he wanted to convey to them his own
experience of seeing Christ and to gain, if possible, some measure
of acceptance from them.

It is certainly not far-fetched to imagine that Paul spent his
time in Arabia in isolation, perhaps at one of the mountains that he
identified as Sinai, praying, meditating, and trying to sort through
his dramatic experiences. Like the Twelve he had his own "three
years" with Jesus—but now as the glorified heavenly Christ!

In 2 Corinthians 12 Paul mentions an ecstatic experience that
he had "fourteen years ago" in which he was taken up into the
heavenly realms, and even entered paradise, seeing and hearing
things that were so extraordinary he was not permitted to reveal
them. He uses the third person, for irony's sake, but in the context
he is obviously talking about himself:

> I know a man in Christ who fourteen years ago was caught
> up to the third heaven—whether in the body or out of the
> body I do not know, God knows. And I know that this man
> was caught up into paradise—whether in the body or out of
> the body I do not know, God knows—and he heard things
> that cannot be told, which man may not utter. (2 Corinthians
> 12:2–4)

The idea of ascending to the third, or highest, level of heaven
and gazing upon the glory of God was viewed within the mystical Jewish circles of Paul's day as the highest and most extraordinary experience a human could have.[1] Moses alone had been

allowed to ascend Mount Sinai and communicate directly with
God and Elijah had been taken up to heaven in a fiery heavenly
chariot (Exodus 24:15–18; 2 Kings 2:11–12). In the two centuries
before Paul's time, texts like the *Similitudes of Enoch*, 2 (*Slavonic*)
Enoch, and the *Ascension of Isaiah*, in which Enoch and Isaiah ascend to the highest heaven, gaze upon God's throne, and experience a transformed glorification, were widely circulated.

We don't know the precise year Paul writes this report in this
section of 2 Corinthians, but it falls into the general range of his
time in Arabia.[2] One should not imagine Paul's "conversion" as
necessarily a sudden one-time event on a single day, as reported in
the book of Acts. What he calls his "revelation of Jesus Christ" was
something he was "taught," which implies a period of heavenly tu-
toring that would have involved multiple "visions and revelations
of the Lord" (Galatians 1:12; 2 Corinthians 12:1). This particular
ascent experience was one of *many* visions and revelations he had
received, and his experiences were so extraordinary that there was
some danger that he would fall victim to pride—knowing that he
among all human beings had been allowed to see and hear such
forbidden mysteries. Consequently, Christ allowed a messenger
(Greek *angelos*) of Satan to harass Paul with some kind of physical
affliction he describes:

> And to keep me from being too elated by the abundance of
> revelations, *a thorn was given me in the flesh*, a messenger of
> Satan, to harass me, to keep me from being too elated. Three
> times I besought the Lord about this, that it should leave me;
> but he said to me, "My grace is sufficient for you, for my pow-
> er is made perfect in weakness." (2 Corinthians 12:8–9)

Presumably Paul refers to some kind of physical disability, and
speculations as to its nature read like the multiple entries in a med-
ical encyclopedia—epilepsy, stuttering, extreme nearsightedness,

migraine headaches, and colic, to name a few.[3] Since Paul explicitly says the thorn in the flesh *was* an "angel" of Satan, it is more likely that he refers to a demonic attack of some type—perhaps causing him to be tempted in some way.[4]

This extraordinary experience of being taken to heaven and presumably seeing both the glory of God as well as Jesus Christ in his *glorified* state put Paul among a select privileged few in the history of ancient Israel and in his mind this experience superseded anything Peter, James, and the rest of the apostles had experienced with Jesus on earth. One could safely say that Paul would have seen this privileged experience as surpassing anything any human being had ever received. In effect, Paul had tasted in a proleptic way the *glorification* that would be revealed at the second coming of Jesus in the clouds of heaven.

Moses and Elijah at Mount Sinai

What makes it all the more likely that Paul's choice of going away into Arabia had to do with Moses and Elijah is that he discusses the Mount Sinai revelations of both of them in his letters (2 Corinthians 3:4–11; Romans 11:2–5). These are not passing references that merely indicate Paul's familiarity with biblical narratives. He draws specific parallels between the *message* and *mission* that he received by revelation from Christ and the roles of Moses and Elijah in their own times. Pairing these two particular figures is not accidental. They were considered the two greatest prophets of Israel's past, and the work of each was to be repeated in some fashion in the Last Days. There are prophecies in the Hebrew Bible about a "Prophet like Moses" appearing once again, as well as a second "Elijah," who would restore the people of Israel just before the final Day of Judgment (Deuteronomy 18:15–18; Malachi 4:5–6). Various Jewish apocalyptic groups in the time of Jesus expected both Moses- and Elijah-like figures to manifest themselves in the Last Days.[5]

The gospel of Mark reports an extraordinary experience in the life of Jesus when he and three of his disciples, Peter, James, and John, are "on a high mountain." They see Jesus "transfigured" before their eyes, so that his body and clothing are gleaming white, and standing beside him are Moses and Elijah—indicating that the Last Days had indeed arrived (Mark 9:2–8).

By tracing the journeys of Moses and Elijah to the Arabian area of the Sinai desert, quite literally, Paul was paralleling his own extraordinary revelations with those of the two greatest Hebrew prophets. He is quite specific about this point.

Moses saw the extraordinary glory of God at Mount Sinai, he received the revelation of the Torah, and he inaugurated the covenant between God and the nation of Israel. Paul likewise believed that he saw the glory of God—in the face of Christ, that he received the Torah of Christ, and that he became the administrator of God's *new covenant* with a *new spiritual* Israel. In view of the new, all that was old was now fading and passing away. Paul refers to the covenant that Moses brought as the "dispensation of death," contrasting it to the *new covenant* that he calls the "dispensation of the Spirit": "Now if the dispensation of death, carved in letters on stone, came with such splendor that the Israelites could not look at Moses's face because of its brightness, fading as this was, will not the dispensation of the Spirit be attended with greater splendor?" (2 Corinthians 3:7–8). Indeed, this "greater splendor" of the new covenant is so much more brilliant that "once it comes, what once had splendor has come to have *no splendor at all*, because of the splendor that surpasses it" (2 Corinthians 3:10). Paul then makes the startling assertion that God has hardened the minds of the Jewish people so that when they "hear Moses read," the reading of the Torah actually becomes a veil to keep them from seeing the splendor of Christ! (2 Corinthians 3:14–15).

One has to appreciate how utterly alien this idea is within Judaism. The reading and study of the Torah was considered the *central* duty and occupation of every faithful Jew:

Rabbi Hillel said: Be of the disciples of Aaron, loving peace and pursuing peace, loving your fellow creatures and bringing them close to the Torah. (*Pirke Avot* 1:12)

Rabbi Shammai said: Make your study of the Torah a fixed habit. Say little and do much, and receive all men with a cheerful face. (*Pirke Avot* 1:15)[6]

According to the New Testament, Josephus, Philo, and other contemporary sources, the Torah was read regularly in synagogues throughout the Roman world and both Jesus and his Jerusalem apostles participated in these activities in the homeland, as did the apostles in the Diaspora—the term for Jews who were living outside the Land of Israel.[7]

According to Paul, this listening to Moses is the very problem at the root of Jewish unbelief in Jesus. If one lays aside the Torah and turns to Christ, the veil is suddenly removed and those who were blinded by the Torah of Moses can see the true glory of God in the face of Christ: "And we all, with unveiled face, beholding the glory of the Lord, are being changed into his likeness from one degree of glory to another; for this comes from the Lord, who is the Spirit" (2 Corinthians 3:18). Paul links the Spirit of Christ, the glory of Christ made in the image of God, and the ongoing transformation of those who are *in Christ* from one degree of glory to another. This cluster of ideas is consistent in all Paul's letters, as we have seen. Paul's Gospel is the revelation of the hidden mystery that God is creating a family of glorified Spirit-beings. That message necessitates a new covenant or Torah of Christ and a newly formed people of Israel—now defined by the Spirit and no longer by the "flesh."

Elijah's Sinai revelation came much later than Moses's. The nation as a whole had turned to idolatry during the reign of the infamous and wicked king Ahab and his wife, Jezebel. Elijah was deeply discouraged and had reached the point of thinking that he alone was left as a devoted worshipper of God. His journey to Sinai was not a casual one, but a panicked flight to escape arrest and execution by the king. His intention was to encounter God at the mountain, as Moses had once done, and lay before him his desperate plight (1 Kings 19).

Paul quotes Elijah's complaint as well as God's revelations to him and draws a startling parallel to his own Gospel message and mission:

> Do you not know what the scripture says of Elijah, how he pleads with God against Israel? "Lord, they have killed your prophets, they have demolished your altars, and I alone am left, and they seek my life." But what is God's reply to him? "I have kept for myself seven thousand men who have not bowed the knee to Baal." So too *at the present time there is a remnant, chosen by grace.* (Romans 11:2–4)

Paul makes use of this Elijah story to address one of the most obvious questions arising from his contention that his new covenant Gospel has superseded the Sinai revelation given to Moses. What about God's promises to the nation of Israel? What about the great majority of the Jewish people who had not "turned to Christ" but were living their lives based on the Torah revelation of Moses at Sinai? Since God had chosen them, given them the Torah, and made a covenant with them, had he suddenly changed course and rejected his own people? At issue was the faithfulness of God.

Paul states unequivocally that God has not rejected the Jewish people. He insists that the promises made to them are irrevocable (Romans 11:1, 29). But then he adds, based on the Elijah story, that the great majority of Jews, whom he calls "Israel according to the flesh," have been broken off like unfruitful branches of an olive tree because of their "unbelief," just as in the days of Elijah, leaving only a tiny "remnant" that God has "chosen by grace."

The catch here is the word "unbelief." Paul does not mean that those "broken off" had rejected God and disregarded the Torah, as had those idolatrous Israelites in the days of Elijah. Their "transgression," as Paul calls it, was that they did not believe in Christ! God had purposely hardened their hearts in order that their failure could open the way for the salvation to come to the Gentiles (Romans 11:7–12). Paul compares these Gentiles to "wild olive branches" who had no connection to the tree of Israel but could be grafted in through their faith in Christ (Romans 11:17). This new covenant nation of Israel is constituted wholly of those who are *united* with Christ through his Spirit, having nothing to do with physical pedigree.

Once again, Paul's view is utterly alien to contemporary Jewish interpretations of Israel's future. The only reference to a "new covenant" in the entire Hebrew Bible is from the prophet Jeremiah. The term is perhaps more properly translated as a "*re*-newed" covenant, as it certainly does not imply any repudiation of the Torah of Moses or of the Jewish people, but quite the opposite. What Jeremiah envisions is a renewal of the Torah of Moses with the reconstituted nation of Israel when all twelve tribes return to the Land of Israel in the messianic age (Jeremiah 31:31–37). This is the idea we see reflected in the Dead Sea Scrolls, as well as in the teachings of Jesus preserved in the Q source, where he appoints the twelve apostles to sit on thrones, one over each of the tribes of a re-gathered people of Israel.[8] There is a place for Gentiles in this prophetic view of the age of the Messiah, not as replacements for the Jewish people, but as God-fearers who stand in partnership with Israel. The vision is that God's house will be a "house of prayer for all peoples" (Isaiah 56:6–7).

We have no sure way of knowing what Paul experienced in his sojourn in Arabia, but the connections with Moses and Elijah seem too direct to ignore. There is a sense in which Paul, fortified with the extraordinary revelations he says he received from Christ, thinks of *himself* as fulfilling the roles of a new Moses and a new Elijah. Like a Moses figure, he became the mediator of a new covenant, drawing together a new nation of Israel defined by faith in Christ and under the Torah of Christ. Like an Elijah figure, Paul believed that his proclamation of his gospel would draw together the remnant group that God was choosing in the Last Days.

Paul's Moses- and Elijah-like experiences in Arabia were foundational as he began his work as an apostle, but he came to believe, based on his continued experiences and his further revelations, that he had been chosen from birth for something far greater. Much like a "second Christ," he had been appointed by God to fill the key role that would usher in the return of Christ. Unless and until Paul fulfilled his special role as an apostle, those Israelites who had rejected Christ would remain in unbelief, and the end of the age would not arrive.

A SECOND "CHRIST"

Paul calls himself "an apostle of the Gentiles" and this unique role was one that he believed gave him a special and essential place in the plan of God (Romans 11:13). It was the reason he was born and it was for this mission that he had been chosen by God:

> But when he who had set me apart before I was born, and had called me through his grace, was pleased to reveal his Son to me, *in order that I might preach him among the Gentiles,* I did not confer with flesh and blood. (Galatians 1:15–16)

Paul says that he was "called to be an apostle, set apart for the Gospel of God" in order to "bring about the obedience of faith for the sake of his name *among all the Gentiles*" (Romans 1:1–5). He defines his gospel as the revelation of the mystery that was kept secret for long ages but is now being made known *to the Gentiles* to bring about the obedience of faith (Romans 16:25–26). When Paul finally did have his official public audience before James, Peter, and the Jerusalem apostles fourteen years after he had already begun his work as an apostle, he was keen to get their agreement that he alone would be entrusted with the mission to the Gentiles (Galatians 2:7–8). This was no mere practical division of labor, at least in Paul's mind. He was convinced that his role was foretold in the Hebrew Prophets, and like the role of Christ, was essential to God's plan of salvation for humankind.

Paul understood the mission of Christ, and by extension that of James and the twelve apostles, in a very particular way, intimately paired with that of his own calling as an apostle to the Gentiles. God, in sending his Son to the world, had inaugurated a *two-stage* plan. Stage one was fulfilled by Jesus, but stage two had been laid at the feet of Paul.

Jesus had been "born of a woman, born under the Law, to redeem those who were under the Law"—Paul's terms for the Jews or Israelites (Galatians 4:4–5). Jesus was an Israelite of the tribe of Judah of the lineage of David and he was sent to the Jewish people: "For I tell you that *Christ became a servant to the circumcised* to show God's truthfulness, in order to confirm the promises given to the patriarchs, *so that the Gentiles might glorify God for his mercy*" (Romans 15:8–9). This is a surprising declaration. Paul says here that Jesus was sent to the Jews to fulfill God's promises about sending the Messiah, but that God's ultimate plan *was that the Gentiles would come to glorify God*. That second stage Christ would also fulfill, but only *through* the apostle Paul as his chosen "instrument."

Paul follows this statement with a string of quotations from the Hebrew Scriptures that foresee the role of the Messiah as reaching the Gentiles and causing them to turn in praise to the One God of Israel. He includes a verse from Isaiah 11 that is particularly straightforward: "The root of Jesse shall come, *he who rises to rule the Gentiles*; in him shall the Gentiles hope" (Romans 15:12).

The "root of Jesse" is a reference to the Messiah of the line of King David, whose father's name was Jesse. Notice, this Messiah actually *rises* to rule the Gentiles, who come to hope in him—their resurrected Lord! This is what Paul regularly refers to as "the obedience of faith" among the nations (Romans 16:26). But Jesus never went to the Gentiles, having been sent as a "servant to the circumcised." Even though Jesus did on occasion deal with non-Jews who showed extraordinary faith, we have no record of Jesus leading any movement to reach Gentiles. In fact, there are several strands of gospel tradition in which he explicitly avoids such a mission (Mark 7:27; Matthew 10:5; 15:24). Jesus' twelve apostles were commissioned to extend Jesus' work to reach those Israelites scattered throughout the world. The letter we have in the New Testament from James is addressed "to the Twelve tribes of the Diaspora" (James 1:1). Peter's first letter is likewise addressed to "the exiles of the Diaspora."

It is here that Paul finds his unique and pivotal role. Paul understands his mission as extending and advancing the work that Jesus inaugurated in his lifetime, but never completed. If the Messiah's ultimate purpose is to rule over the Gentiles, what Paul calls the "reconciliation of the world," causing them to turn to God, how can this goal ever be accomplished? Peter and the Twelve had already agreed with Paul that they would go "to the circumcision"—so what about the rest of the world?

As Paul fulfills this messianic mission he understands himself to be performing the work of Christ. In that sense Paul is an extension of Christ, finishing up the main task of the Messiah as a kind of "second Christ." He explains this complicated dynamic in the following way: "[God gave me grace] to be a servant of Christ Jesus *to the Gentiles* in the *priestly service* of the gospel of God, so that *the offering of the Gentiles* may be acceptable, sanctified by the Holy Spirit" (Romans 15:16). Here Paul is acting in behalf of Christ and his mission is to function like a priest who brings an offering to God—in this case the offering is the "obedience of the Gentiles," which fulfills the messianic mission of Jesus. Paul says he will not boast of anything in this regard "except what Christ has *worked through me*, to win obedience from the Gentiles" (Romans 15:18). In Paul's mind his work is really Christ's work and whatever he does is as an extension of Christ, now acting in the world through him. In the same way he can tell the Corinthians to expel the man living with his stepmother in a gathering at which *his* Spirit would be present—everything that Paul did he attributed to Christ *working through* him, and his commands were thus the "commands of the Lord" (1 Corinthians 14:37).

Paul believed that his calling and his mission to the Gentiles were witnessed in the Hebrew Prophets, long before his birth (Romans 15:9–12). His was a destined role, backed up by the scriptures and his own visionary experiences. There are various passages in the Hebrew Bible that indicate a time when the Gentiles will turn to the God of Israel (Isaiah 11:10). Notice these lines in particular from one of Isaiah's passages about a "Servant" of Yahweh who will serve as an agent to bring light to the Gentiles:

Listen to me you coastlands,
and hearken you Gentiles
After a long time it will happen.
From my mother's womb he has called my name.
He has made my mouth a sharp sword,
and he has hidden me under the shadow of his hand;
He has made me a chosen shaft . . .
Behold I have given you for the covenant of a race,
for a light to the Gentiles,
That you should be for salvation
to the end of the earth. (Isaiah 49:1–6)

The personal way in which this passage addresses one who would specifically be designated from his mother's womb to preach a message that would bring light to the Gentiles and result in the salvation of the earth likely drew Paul's attention. He quotes the passage directly in 2 Corinthians 6:2 (Isaiah 49:1–2, 6) in justifying his special "ministry." Apparently some at Corinth had questioned his authority, suggesting that he needed "letters of recommendation," presumably from James or the Jerusalem apostles, to vouch for his claims (2 Corinthians 3:1–3). His response was that their Spirit-led lives are his "letters" and his sufferings and hardships are his commendation, including beatings, imprisonments, poverty, and hunger (2 Corinthians 6:4–9). This also fits well with Isaiah 49, where this servant who goes to the Gentiles is "deeply despised, abhorred by the Gentiles," but nonetheless becomes a "covenant to the Gentiles" (Isaiah 49:7–8).[9]

What Paul expected was that his priestly service of turning thousands of Gentiles to the God of Israel would cause some of those Israelites who rejected Christ to be jealous:

> Now I am speaking to you Gentiles. Inasmuch then as I am an apostle to the Gentiles, I magnify my ministry in order to make my fellow Jews jealous, and thus save some of them. For if their rejection means the reconciliation of the world, what will their acceptance mean but life from the dead? (Romans 11:13–15)

According to Paul, God had purposely "hardened" the majority of the Jewish people so that they would temporarily reject Christ, so that he, Paul, could then take his gospel message to the Gentile world—thus reconciling the world to God and completing the work of Christ. According to Paul, this was God's secret plan: "Lest you be wise in your own conceits, I want you to understand this *mystery*, brethren: a hardening has come upon part of Israel, until the full number of the Gentiles come in, and so all Israel will be saved" (Romans 11:25). This was Paul's way of accounting for the fact that the Jewish people as a whole had not accepted Jesus as Messiah but were continuing to practice the Torah of Moses. He had come to believe that everything depended on him and thus he set his travel itinerary to travel west, to Rome and finally even to Spain—so that he could literally say that he had reached to the ends of the earth, fulfilling Isaiah's prophecy (Romans 15:23–29).

Paul saw his suffering in the world as an extension of the redemptive suffering of Christ, who was God's Suffering Servant to the Israelites. At one point, when pressed hard by some of his opponents in Galatia, he declares: "Henceforth let no man trouble me; for I bear on my body the wounds [*stigmata*] of Jesus" (Galatians 6:17). He saw his own beatings, lashings, and stoning as equivalent to the wounds Jesus suffered, and as ample testimony to his special apostolic role (2 Corinthians 11:23–25).

When Paul first began to work in the provinces of Asia Minor and Greece in the early 50s A.D., he fully expected to live to see the return of Christ and the end of the age. In his earlier letters he writes in the first person of how "we who are alive" at that time will be lifted up into the clouds to meet the Lord in the air (1 Thessalonians 4:17). By the 60s A.D., when he had been imprisoned in Rome, he began to anticipate that his own life, like that of Christ, "would be poured out as a libation upon the sacrificial offering of your faith" (Philippians 2:17). The language here is difficult to translate, but Paul seems to be saying that as a priest he will bring the "faith" of his Gentile followers as an offering to God with the pouring of his own blood over it. He goes on to say, in the same letter to the Philippians, that he anticipates dying and being resurrected just as Christ had done:

> For his sake I have suffered the loss of all things . . . that I may know him and the power of his resurrection, and may share his sufferings, *becoming like him in his death*, that if possible I

may attain *being raised up out from [among] the dead.* (Philippians 3:8b, 10)

Even though this imitative language has generally been taken as
generic, that is, as applicable to the suffering of any follower of
Christ, in this context Paul has been contemplating his own immediate death, which he describes as "departing to be with Christ"
(Philippians 1:23). He also uses a rare compound verb, meaning
"to be raised up out of," found nowhere else in Jewish or Christian
writings. In the same way he had written to the Corinthians that as
an apostle he was "always carrying in the body the death of Jesus"
and "being given up to death for Jesus' sake," so that *life* would
come to them (2 Corinthians 4:10–12). He is comparing his own
state of suffering, for the sake of his followers, with that of Jesus.
It is in this context that he speaks of being "absent from the body"
but "present with the Lord," again speaking of his suffering and
death (2 Corinthians 5:6–9). The two passages are closely parallel
and they seem to refer to Paul alone.

Paul refers to those who die "in Christ" before the return of
Jesus as the "dead in Christ," or those who have "fallen asleep."
This is in keeping with the Hebrew view that the dead "sleep in
the dust" (1 Thessalonians 4:13; 1 Corinthians 15:20; Daniel 12:2).
They do not "depart" to be with Christ when they die but they rise
up to meet him, literally, "in the air," at his coming, raised *from* the
dead in their newly glorified bodies: "And the dead in Christ will
rise first; then we who are alive, who are left, shall be caught up
together with them in the clouds to meet the Lord in the air" (1
Thessalonians 4:16b–17).[10]

I am convinced, as Albert Schweitzer suggested, that Paul had
come to believe in the latter years of his life that he would likely not
live to see the return of Christ but that he was to receive a special
reward immediately upon his death.[11] Unlike others who "sleep in
Christ," awaiting the resurrection at Christ's coming, Paul seems

to believe that he will be raised up immediately out of Hades and taken to join Christ in heaven—being glorified together with him, as he has suffered and died with him. It is possible that he based this assurance of "departing to be with Christ" upon the special revelation he had when he was taken up into the third heaven and entered paradise. He indicates that he saw and heard things in that experience that he was not permitted to reveal (2 Corinthians 12:4).

We have no record of Paul's last years, assuming he was executed during the reign of Nero, perhaps in A.D. 64 during the great persecution at Rome. Our last authentic letters are Philippians and Philemon, written most likely when he was being held under guard in Rome, perhaps between A.D. 60 and 62. He seems to contemplate his death, but also anticipates some possibility of his release.[12]

Given Paul's extraordinary understanding of his special calling as an apostle, destined for a mission to the Gentiles ordained by God even before his birth, let's examine the unique message that he preached. Paul offered a new and different message—a "revelation of Jesus Christ" that had now been revealed only to him as the Thirteenth Apostle—last but not least. Paul transformed the message of Jesus from earth to heaven. In the following chapters we will see to what extent he redefined the role of the Messiah, the kingdom of God, the people of Israel, and the revelation of Torah to launch his brand of Christianity on a collision course with Judaism and pave the way for a new and separate Christian faith.

FIVE

A COSMIC FAMILY AND A HEAVENLY KINGDOM

Paul's greatest revelation is largely unrecognized. It was his main inspiration and motivation but few have even heard of it. He describes it as "the revelation of the *mystery* that was kept secret for long ages." The Greek word *mysterion* means "secret" and Paul believed that he had been specially chosen to reveal it (Romans 16:25). God purposely hid the secret from the beginning of time and only now, through Paul, was it being revealed. Paul says that if any of the rulers of the world had understood it they would not have crucified Jesus:

> But we speak the wisdom of God in a *mystery* [*mysterion*] that
> has been hidden that God decreed before the ages, *for our glo-*
> *rification*. None of the rulers of this age understood this; for
> if they had they would not have crucified the *Lord of glory*. (1
> Corinthians 2:7–8)

So what was this hidden cosmic secret? It has something to do with what Paul describes here as *glorification*—but what does that mean? And why does he call Jesus the "Lord of glory" in this context?

If you took a poll among Christians who are reasonably informed about their faith, asking them the one great teaching for which Paul is most remembered, most would probably say "justification by faith." Paul emphatically declared, "all have sinned and fallen short of the glory of God," and that humans can be "saved" only by grace through faith in Christ, not by their good deeds (Romans 3:21–24). For the most part the theologians would agree. From the great Catholic thinker Augustine to the Protestant Martin Luther, Paul's doctrine of "justification by grace through faith" has been considered the heart and center of his gospel message.

As central a teaching as "justification by faith" was to Paul, it could not be the secret revelation hidden through the ages to which he refers. To be justified means to be forgiven of one's sins. It is a legal term, equivalent to an undeserved pardon granted a convicted criminal. Grace, as Paul uses the term, means unmerited favor. But grace was nothing new and it was definitely not hidden. Paul argues in his letter to the Romans that God has always dealt with humans in this way, including Abraham, the father of the nation, and David, its first great king (Romans 4:1–8). Without the grace and forgiveness of God, no human being could stand before the Creator at the Day of Judgment.

Justification, or being forgiven of one's sins, is connected to another major concept of Paul—the notion of *salvation*. As with many of Paul's terms, the English word has been used so often in theological contexts that its common meaning is easily missed. The Greek word *soteria* refers to being rescued. It is not a special religious word. Paul writes in Koine, the commonly spoken Greek of his day. Years ago I remember reading a letter from a sailor in the Roman navy. It was written in Greek on a scrap of papyrus and had been dated to the second century A.D. The sailor was writing home to his father, giving the family greetings, and he thanked the god Serapis that, although he was shipwrecked, he had been *saved* from drowning in the sea—using the same Greek word Paul used.[1]

To understand what Paul means when he writes about salvation we need to ask—rescued *from* what and rescued *for* what? Paul teaches that humans can be saved or rescued from the "wrath" of God's judgment by having their sins forgiven (1 Thessalonians 5:9; Romans 5:9). But he sees this as merely a means to an end. To be saved, or forgiven of sins, is an essential first step, but it is only a means to a much greater end. It cannot be the center of Paul's message; in fact it is subsidiary to a larger revelation—the mystery held secret since before the Creation.

In Paul's letter to the Romans he spends the first seven chapters covering all the ins and outs of justification. It is no wonder people can get the impression that this is his main idea. Finally, when he comes to chapter 8 he tells them the secret—the hidden mystery involving the very purpose for creating human beings in the first place. He covers that in one chapter.

Paul mentions "the mystery" in passing only six times in his authentic letters, but without explaining much about what he means.[2] We are most fortunate to have Romans 8, since it is the only place he offers a full and systematic exposition of the revelation he had received. Without this chapter we would be hard-pressed to make much sense of the other passing references, where he assumes a familiarity on the part of his readers. For example, he writes the Corinthians that he did not come to them "proclaiming *the mystery* of God in lofty words of human wisdom," but he assumes, and does not say, what that mystery is (1 Corinthians 2:1). We have to remember that Paul's letters are occasional documents, written at various times and places to address specific issues. Much of the time he is handling emergencies, addressing practical problems and misunderstandings, responding to threats, and defending himself against enemies. He often assumes, but does not explain, the details of his teachings. His letter to the Romans is a fortunate exception to this general rule. It comes close to a formal treatise, expounding Paul's view of his gospel message.

The word "gospel" in Greek, *euangelion*, like the word "salvation," is another one of those words that have come to have an exclusively theological sound to our modern ears. It is commonly said to mean "good news" or "glad tidings," which is correct, but a more fresh translation might be an *announcement*, in the sense of a welcome proclamation. There are several Greek inscriptions and papyri dated before the Christian era where an announcement of the birthday of the emperor Augustus is proclaimed, using the word "gospel." These texts show that the word was commonly used in Koine and that it had no special religious meaning.[3]

I already pointed out in the introduction to this book that Paul uses the word "gospel" in a most proprietary way. He refers to "my Gospel," and it is clear he has something very specific in mind (Romans 2:16; 16:25; Galatians 1:11-12). As I mentioned, of the seventy-two occurrences of the term *gospel* in the entire New Testament, sixty are in Paul's letters![4] A better modern translation would be, again, "the Announcement," referring most specifically to Paul's revelation of the hidden mystery. As we will see, this is not the same as the gospel preached by the Jerusalem apostles but a revelation Paul insists was given to him alone, completely independent of them, not from the earthly Jesus they had known, but from the heavenly Christ who had chosen him even before his birth (Galatians 1:11–15). Notice Paul's very specific language about the timing of this revelation. He is speaking of what he calls "my Gospel" and says it is "the revelation of the mystery that was kept secret for long ages *but is now being disclosed*" through his preaching to the nations (Romans 16:25).

All the various aspects of "the Announcement" had further been confirmed to him by a series of subsequent "visions and revelations of the Lord," including being taken into heaven to see and hear "things unutterable" (2 Corinthians 12:1-4). When he uses the formula "I received from the Lord," he refers to a rich body of "revelations" that he has received, including direct sayings from

Jesus, teachings about the Lord's Supper, and details about how the end of the age will unfold.

THE HIDDEN MYSTERY REVEALED

At the core of the mystery announcement that Paul reveals is God's secret plan to bring to birth a new heavenly family of his own off-spring. In other words, God is *reproducing himself*. These children of God will represent a new genus of Spirit-beings in the cosmos, exalted in glory, power, and position far above even the highest angels.

That is part of the reason the plan was kept secret. Reflecting a common Greco-Roman view of the cosmos, Paul believed in a universe thickly populated by a vast hierarchy of angelic beings, demonic spirits, and spiritual forces both good and malevolent.[5] As a Jew he also believed in forces of darkness led by Satan and his angelic minions, whose entire concerted efforts were concentrated on opposing the ways of God in his dealings with humankind. For Paul, Satan was a very real entity with whom he has had personal dealings, not a metaphor for evil. Paul calls Satan "the god of this age" and refers to human history, under Satan's control, as "this present evil age" (2 Corinthians 4:4; Galatians 1:4). Various human kings, emperors, and potentates rule the visible world, but the invisible power behind the scenes is Satan. When Paul says the mystery was hidden from the "rulers of this age," or else they would not have crucified Jesus, he refers to Satan and his forces as much as the human rulers, Jewish or Roman, that they inspired (1 Corinthians 2:8). The death of Jesus was all part of God's secret plan, in order for Jesus to become the "firstborn" Son of this new heavenly family. Jesus' crucifixion looked like a defeat but it was actually God's surprise strategy to defeat the Satanic forces.

For Paul this cosmic birthing process is not a metaphor: it is as literal as the birth of a human child. In his letter to the Romans he offers a tightly worded sequential outline of what he calls God's purpose or *plan* of salvation:

> For those whom God *foreknew* he also *predetermined* to share the likeness of the image of his Son, in order that he might be the first-born among many brothers. And those whom he predestined he also *called*; and those whom he called he also *justified*; and those whom he justified he also *glorified*. (Romans 8:29–30)

The plan is laid out clearly here and its implementation involves five sequential steps: to foreknow, to predestine, to call, to justify, and finally to glorify. It is the final stage, that of *glorification*, that is the heart of the mystery: "But we speak the wisdom of God in a *mystery* (*musterion*) that has been hidden that God decreed before the ages, *for our glorification*" (1 Corinthians 2:7). This glorification involves, as Paul says, "sharing the likeness of the image of his Son," referring to Jesus' exalted glorified state, and thus becoming part of the new heavenly family.

Paul says the first step is the selection of a special group of chosen ones whose call to participate in the plan was determined before their birth. In other words, God both knew them and chose them in ages past. They are the ones "called" by God at the present time to participate in the plan. Paul refers constantly to his followers being "called to belong to Jesus Christ" (Romans 1:6). He trusts that the selection process is in God's hands and his role is only to proclaim the Announcement:

> We preach Christ crucified, a stumbling block to Jews and folly to Gentiles, but *to those who are called*, both Jews and Greeks, Christ, the power of God and the wisdom of God. (1 Corinthians 1:23–24)

> For consider your *calling*, brothers: not many of you were wise
> according to worldly standards, not many were powerful, not
> many were of noble birth. But God *chose* what is foolish in the
> world to shame the wise; God chose what is weak in the world
> to shame the strong. (1 Corinthians 1:26–27)

This is a common motif throughout Paul's letters. God does what
is least expected; it is all part of the mystery. While those in society
are impressed with the powerful, the wise, and the mighty, hidden
from their view is this tiny chosen group that is destined by God
to be exalted to the highest place in the universe. Just as Christ was
despised, rejected, and crucified, those who follow him will experience similar suffering that in turn will lead to their glorification:

> If we are children, then we are heirs—heirs of God and *fellow
> heirs* with Christ, provided we *suffer* with him in order that
> we may also be *co-glorified* with him. For I consider that the
> sufferings of this present time are not worth comparing with
> the *glory that is to be revealed* to us. (Romans 8:17–18)

The next step in Paul's sequence is justification. Those that God has
known, chosen, and called, who respond to the Announcement,
are justified by grace. They are forgiven their sins and they receive
this unmerited pardon through their faith that Jesus has died for
their sins and has been raised from the dead for their justification.
Paul expresses it like this: "Righteousness will be reckoned to us
who believe in him that raised from the dead Jesus our Lord, who
was put to death for our trespasses and raised *for our justification*"
(Romans 4:24–25). Here we see clearly that Paul specifies that justification depends not only on the death of Jesus for sins, but also
his resurrection from the dead.

As we have seen, for Paul, Jesus' resurrection from the dead is
not the resuscitation of his physical body, buried in a tomb, but his

transformation to a life-giving Spirit-being, with a glorious spiritual body. It is this glorified heavenly Christ that Paul claims to have "seen," and it is Jesus' transformation, from a "man of dust" to a "man of heaven," that guarantees the final step of salvation, the *glorification* of an entire new family of heavenly beings. Those who are known, chosen, called, and justified will finally be glorified.

When and how the final step of glorification takes place is fortunately a subject that Paul addresses in some detail in several places in his letters. Paul believes that he is living at the end of the age, very near the time when Christ will return from heaven. He expects to live to see Jesus appear visibly in the clouds, in the lower atmosphere, at which point he expects that he and the other chosen ones, including those who have died, will be instantly reclothed in their glorious new spiritual bodies. They will literally rise up into the air to meet him. He describes the scene in detail to the Thessalonians:

> For this we declare to you by the word of the Lord, that we who are alive, who are left until the coming of the Lord, shall not go ahead of those who have fallen asleep [i.e., died]. For the Lord himself will descend from heaven with a cry of command, with the archangel's call, and with the sound of the trumpet of God. And the dead in Christ will rise first; then we who are alive, who are left, shall be caught up together with them in the clouds to meet the Lord in the air; and so we shall always be with the Lord. (1 Thessalonians 4:15–17)[6]

Paul says he received this scenario "by the word of the Lord," which means it was part of the revelation he claims to have received directly from Jesus. What he doesn't explain in this text, but elaborates fully elsewhere, is that the living and the dead will experience, simultaneously, a transforming immortalization with a glorious new spiritual body. He writes the Philippians:

> But our citizenship is in heaven, and from it we await a Savior,
> the Lord Jesus Christ, who will change our body of humilia-
> tion *to be like his glorious body*, by the power that enables him
> even to subject all things to himself. (Philippians 3:20–21)

This change is what Paul means when he says the chosen group is
destined to "share the image of the likeness" of God's Son (Romans
8:29). It can only be done by Christ, who has been given this unique
creative power in his new role as vice-regent over the entire universe. Paul specifically tells the Corinthians that this transformation process *is the mystery*. He is again describing what will happen
when Jesus appears in the clouds of heaven:

> Behold! I tell you a *mystery*! We shall not all sleep [i.e., die be-
> fore Jesus appears], but we shall all be changed, in a moment,
> in the blink of an eye, at the last trumpet. For the trumpet will
> sound, and the dead will be raised imperishable, and we [the
> living] will be changed. For this perishable nature must put
> on the imperishable, and this mortal nature must put on im-
> mortality. (1 Corinthians 15:51–53)

Paul's designation of Jesus as the "firstborn of many brothers"
should not be taken as a reference to male gender (Romans 8:29). In
Hebrew thinking the male phrase "sons of Israel," like our English
word "mankind," often means the "children of Israel," which is generic and includes men and women. In the same way Paul refers
at one point to the cosmic revealing of the "sons of God," referring
to the glorification of this new God-family, but a few lines later
he refers to them as the "children of God," using generic language
(Romans 8:19, 21). A more proper translation might be "offspring."
The author of the gospel of Luke has apparently picked up a bit of
this from Paul when he explains Jesus' teaching about the resurrection as involving neither male or female, but nonetheless "Sons of

God, being sons of the resurrection" (Luke 20:34–36).[7]

Paul understands the birthing of these heavenly children of God as an ongoing process. They have received the "Spirit of his Son," which has joined with their spirits, making them "sons of God" (Galatians 4:6; 1 Corinthians 6:17). Paul calls this the "spirit of Son-ship," which signifies and guarantees the intimate relationship between father and child, as well as the full rights of inheritance:

> But you have received the spirit of Son-ship. When we cry, "Abba Father," it is the Spirit itself bearing witness with our spirit that we are children of God, and if children then heirs, heirs of God and co-heirs with Christ, provided we suffer with him in order that we may also be glorified with him. (Romans 8:15–17)

This infusion of the Christ-Spirit into the elect group makes them also "Christs," in that they participate fully in all that Jesus Christ has been given. Paul tells the group at Corinth: "It is God who establishes us with you in Christ, and he has *anointed* [*chrisas*] us; he has put his seal upon us and given us his Spirit in our hearts as a guarantee" (2 Corinthians 1:21–22). The Greek verb *chrio*, which Paul uses here, is the same one used for the Messiah or Christ—whom God has *anointed*. The idea of being "anointed by the Spirit" far supersedes a ceremonial anointing with oil, routinely used for kings and priests in ancient Israel. In Jewish expectation of this period, the Messiah to come in the Last Days has just such an anointing of the Spirit.[8] Paul and his followers, as anointed ones of the Spirit, are then "heirs of God and *co-heirs* with Christ" (Romans 8:17). The inheritance is theirs by *birthright*—in that like Christ, the same Spirit begets them.

Paul calls this Spirit the "Spirit of Son-ship" and it is the receiving of this divine Spirit that allows the children to cry out "Abba" to God as Father. "Abba" is the intimate term still used in Hebrew today when a child calls a father.[9]

Paul says that this Son-ship process is an ongoing one, much like the growth of an embryo or fetus in the womb of a mother. The "outer man is wasting away, while the inner self is being renewed day after day" (2 Corinthians 4:16). This is not Plato's dualism of mortal body and immortal soul. It is the life-giving Spirit of Christ, dwelling in the mortal, decaying body, and which brings life. Paul says that the process of inner transformation has already begun: "And we all, with unveiled face, beholding the glory of the Lord, are being transformed *into the same image* from one degree of glory to another. For this comes from the Lord who is the Spirit" (2 Corinthians 3:18). In that sense, Paul says that these chosen ones are not "in the flesh" but instead "in the Spirit," since the Spirit of Christ dwells in them, making their spirits alive, though their bodies are "dead" (Romans 8:9–11). The final step in the "Son-ship" is what he calls the "redemption" of the body, when it is set free from its bondage to decay (Romans 8:23).

THE LAST ADAM

Paul's core understanding of the mystery is based upon his teaching about two Adams, a first and a second, or last. Theologians use the term *Christology* to refer to the various views of Jesus that were developed and debated in the early church. In what ways was Jesus understood to be more than an ordinary human being? Within the New Testament one already finds a complex and diverse mix of views.[10] In Paul's letter to the Philippians he provides us with what is generally considered to be our earliest expression of Christology. His words are carefully chosen and formally set forth. Many scholars have argued that Paul inherited this confession of faith, because it has the making of a formal creed, but I regard Paul as its author and originator since it reflects his unique view of Christ so completely. It is very nicely written in Greek, in stanzas, much like a hymn. Here is a very literal translation:

> Though he [Christ] existed in the *form of God*, he did not consider being equal to God a thing to be grasped, but he emptied himself, taking the form of a slave, being *born in the likeness of a man*. And being so born, he humbled himself, becoming obedient to the point of death, even death on a cross.
>
> Therefore God has highly exalted him and favored on him the name that is above every name, so that at the name of Jesus every knee should bow, in heaven and on earth and under the earth, and every tongue confess that Jesus Christ is Lord, to the glory of God the Father. (Philippians 2:6–11)

The allusions to Adam in the Genesis story are unmistakable. Adam is the one who tried to "grasp" equality with God, and thus he lost his potential to eat of the Tree of Life and live forever (Genesis 3:5, 22–23). As a "man of dust," he and all his descendants were doomed to return to the dust, with no hope of escaping death (Genesis 3:19).

In contrast to Adam, Paul believed that Christ, before he was born as the human Jesus, existed from the beginning in the form of God, and had equality with God.[11] Whether Paul understood Jesus as a created being or one eternally existing with God, he never says. Paul does, however, believe that Christ was an agent in the creation in the world, and that he gave up the riches of his heavenly status, taking on the form of a mortal man:

> Yet for us there is one God, the Father, from whom are all things and for whom we exist, and one Lord, Jesus Christ *through whom* are all things and through whom we exist. (1 Corinthians 8:6)

> For you know the grace of our Lord Jesus Christ, that, *though*
> *he was rich*, yet for your sakes he became poor, that you
> through his poverty might become rich. (2 Corinthians 8:9)

The writer of the letter of Colossians, likely writing a decade or
more after Paul's death, possibly made use of some earlier material
from Paul, particularly on this topic. Here is how he fills out the
description of Christ before his human birth, something Paul himself does not elaborate in the letters we have from him:

> He [Christ] is the image of the unseen God, the first-born of
> all creation; for in him all things were created, in heaven and
> on earth, visible and invisible, whether thrones or dominions
> or principalities or authorities—all were created through him
> and for him. He is before all things, and in him all things hold
> together. (Colossians 1:15–17)

It seems reasonable to assume Paul had something like this in
mind.[12] Christ would have been the very first of God's creation, put
over everything else, whether the invisible angelic hosts, or the visible things on the earth. The letter of Hebrews, which was also written
after Paul, but probably influenced by his thinking, says that Christ
was the one "through whom God created the world" (Hebrews 1:2).
But all this was before the human being Jesus existed.

According to Paul, by emptying himself and being born of a
woman as a flesh-and-blood mortal we know as Jesus, and then
showing his willingness to be obedient to God by suffering to the
point of death on a cross, Jesus was raised from the dead by God.
His resurrection was a victory over sin and its resulting process—
death. As we have seen, according to Paul, Jesus was not merely
a "man of dust" restored to mortal life, but one transformed into
a "man of heaven," whom God exalted above every other created
being in the universe. He becomes the first "man of dust," ever

transformed into heavenly immortality and glory, inaugurating the process of salvation for others who would follow his example of obedience and suffering.

By becoming like the first Adam, Jesus has paved the way for a group of second or last Adams, that is, a new genus of heavenly beings, transformed from dust to Spirit as he had been. Paul explains this to the Corinthians:

> The first man was from the earth, a man of dust; the second man is from heaven. As was the man of dust, so are those who are of the dust; and as is the man of heaven, so are those who are of heaven. Just as we have borne the image of the man of dust, *we shall also bear the image of the man of heaven.* (1 Corinthians 15:47–49)

Paul explains that the first Adam, of the dust, was an earthly parallel to the last Adam, who becomes a life-giving Spirit. "It is not the spiritual that is first, but the physical, and then the spiritual." Adam and Eve were made in the image and likeness of God in the very beginning: "So God created man in his own image, in the image of God he created him; male and female he created them" (Genesis 1:27). However, they were perishable physical models or prototypes, reflecting the image and likeness of God, but made of dust and thus subject to death. Since they greedily grasped at their potential to be "equal to God," they were banished from his presence. When Christ was born in human likeness, taking on the form of a man, he represented a potential reversal of the process, in which one who bears the image of the man of dust could undergo the glory and transformation to immortality.

Even though Paul's language here can sound symbolic, analogical, and even mythological to our modern ears, for him the process of bringing about the birth of this new family of heavenly beings was as real as the air he breathed and the ground he walked upon.

After all, he believed that he was the chief agent God had chosen to reveal the Announcement of the mystery to all nations. He also believed the time he had to complete his mission was quite short. He was driven night and day by the visions and revelations that he believed he had received from Christ. At any moment he expected to look up to the sky and see Christ there, come to initiate with unimaginable power and glory the final stages of human history.

A HEAVENLY KINGDOM

Paul does not tell us much about what he thinks will happen after the arrival of Christ in the clouds of heaven when "those who belong to Christ," whether living or dead, will be glorified and lifted up into the heavens. He refers several times to "inheriting the kingdom of God," referring to the heavenly glorification that his followers were expecting to receive: "Now this I say brothers, that flesh and blood cannot inherit the kingdom of God; neither does the perishable inherit the imperishable" (1 Corinthians 15:50). He warns his followers any number of times that if they persist in immoral behavior they will "not inherit the kingdom of God" (1 Corinthians 6:9–10; Galatians 5:21).

In the teachings of John the Baptizer and Jesus, where the proclamation of the kingdom of God is central, the emphasis is on an era of justice, righteousness, and peace among all nations when the "will of God is done on earth as it is in heaven."[13] Sometimes this view of the kingdom has been labeled as "earthly" or "physical," as opposed to a "heavenly" or "spiritual" kingdom, but this is a misunderstanding of the Hebrew notion of the messianic age. Although it is "on earth," it is surely seen as an era of spiritual advancement, and Jesus regularly spoke about receiving "eternal life" in the age to come:

Jesus said, "Truly, I say to you, there is no one who has left house or brothers or sisters or mother or father or children or

lands, for my sake and for the gospel, who will not receive a
hundredfold now in this time, houses and brothers and sisters
and mothers and children and lands, with persecutions, and
in the age to come eternal life." (Mark 10:29–30)

According to Jesus, in the "age to come" the Messiah will sit on
his throne of glory and judge all the nations (Matthew 25:31).
Abraham, Isaac, Jacob, and all the righteous of all ages will be
raised from the dead and "sit at table in the kingdom of God" (Luke
13:29). It is spoken of as a "new world," but there is no idea of leaving the earth and going to heaven: "Truly, I say to you, in the new
world [literally, "re-created"] when the Son of Man will sit on his
glorious throne, you who have followed me will also sit on twelve
thrones, judging the twelve tribes of Israel" (Matthew 19:28).

Paul, in contrast, is radically oriented toward a heavenly kingdom; one that flesh and blood cannot inherit. Rather than a reordered earth, however transformed, he envisions a reordered cosmos.
He tells his followers at Corinth: "Do you not know that the chosen
ones will judge the cosmos? And if the cosmos is to be judged by you,
are you incompetent to try trivial cases? Do you not know that we are
to judge angels? How much more matters pertaining to this life!" (1
Corinthians 6:2–3). He rebukes the Corinthians for taking their disputes to the Roman legal authorities when in fact their heavenly destiny is to rule with Christ over the entire universe—angels included.
Earlier in the same letter he sarcastically chides them for putting
their expectations of future glory ahead of the suffering that must
come first: "Already you are filled! Already you have become rich!
Without us you have become kings! And would that you did already
reign, so that we might share the rule with you!" (1 Corinthians 4:8).

Paul is so convinced the end of the age has drawn near that he
tells people not to marry and he encourages them to minimize all
their dealings within society. Everything is about to be turned upside down. Here are his words:

I mean this brothers, the appointed time has grown very short; and from now on, let those who have wives live as though they had none . . . and those who buy as though they had no goods, and those who deal with the world as though they had no dealings with it. For the *outward form of this cosmos is passing away.* (1 Corinthians 7:29–31)

For Paul the rule of Christ is a cosmic one and involves the subjugation of "things in heaven, things on earth, and things under the earth" (Philippians 2:10). In the heavenly realms this involves, first and foremost, the defeat of the "principalities" and "powers," including Satan himself and all his angels, who are in rebellion against God—"the God of peace will crush Satan under your feet shortly," he tells the Romans (Romans 16:20; 8:38). On earth all human rule, authority, and power will be deposed and replaced by the rule of God through Christ and the glorified God-family. "Things under the earth" refers to the world of the dead, Sheol or Hades, where the departed spirits await resurrection and judgment.

Paul's most comprehensive statement on the future heavenly kingdom of God is as cryptic as it is tantalizing. It has been the subject of endless debate among Paul's interpreters. In just a dozen or so lines he pulls back the veil a tiny bit and allows us to peek into the future. Here is the full quotation:

For as by a man came death, by a man has come also the resurrection of the dead. For as in Adam all die, so also in Christ shall all be made alive. But each in his own order: Christ the first fruits, then at his coming those who belong to Christ. Then comes the end, when he delivers the kingdom to God the Father after destroying every rule and every authority and power. For he must reign until he has put all his enemies under his feet. The last enemy to be destroyed is death. For [scripture says] "God has put all things in subjection under his feet." But when it says, "all things are put in subjection," it is plain that he is excepted who put all things in subjection under him. When all things are subjected to him, then the Son himself will also be subjected to him who put all things in subjection under him, that God may be all in all. (1 Corinthians 15:21–28)

Paul believes that God has a universal plan for all the descendants of Adam: "For as in Adam all die, so also *in Christ* shall all be made alive" (1 Corinthians 15:22), but he believes this process unfolds only in stages. As he says, "God was *in Christ* reconciling the cosmos to himself," but in the present age, before the return of Christ, there is only a select number called to be part of the chosen ones (2 Corinthians 5:19). Accordingly, it is only the "dead in Christ" who are lifted up and glorified when Christ appears, not all the dead of all ages (1 Thessalonians 4:16). Though Paul believes in the general resurrection of all the dead, as did Jesus and the Pharisees, he never mentions it directly and only hints at it here— *all shall be made alive.* His entire concentration is upon the tiny initial group that he calls "the elect," who he believes is being collected together just before the end of the age.

When Paul says "by a man came the resurrection of the dead" he refers, of course, to Christ, as the second or last Adam, who inaugurated the process of *glorification* for all of Adam's descendants who are "of the dust" and thus subject to death. Based on the notion of the universality of the death that came through Adam, Paul says that the remedy of death, which is heavenly glorification, will be as universal as the fate of death. In other words *all* human beings will eventually be born into the God-family. Paul never mentions any idea of hell or eternal punishment in any of his letters, but he did believe that those who are chosen first can escape the wrath of God that will come with God's judgment at the end of the age.

Paul goes on to say there is an ordered process involved that unfolds in two distinct stages. Stage one takes place at the coming of Christ, when only those "in Christ," whether living or dead, experience their glorification, putting off the mortal and being reclothed in immortality. Elsewhere he refers to this event as the "revealing of the sons of God" (Romans 8:19). This group, the select ones God has chosen and called, whom Paul is gathering through his preaching, are compared to the "first fruits" of a harvest. This analogy is well-known in the Hebrew Bible. It involves a select portion of produce to be dedicated first to God, before the full harvest is carried out.[14] This select group does appear before the judgment seat of Christ to receive commendation and rewards, and if necessary punishments, to enable it to carry out its exalted destiny:

> Therefore do not pronounce judgment before the time, before the Lord comes, who will bring to light the things now hidden in darkness and will disclose the purposes of the heart. Then every one will receive his *commendation* from God. (1 Corinthians 4:5)

Paul warns his followers frequently of this judgment, which he calls the "judgment seat of Christ," admonishing them to "judge themselves" now so they will not have to be judged and thus condemned along with the world: "For we must all appear before the judgment seat of Christ, so that each one may receive good or evil, according to what he has done in the body" (2 Corinthians 5:10).

Stage two, which Paul calls the "end" (Greek *telos*), follows, but only after an indeterminate period of time. That is when Christ, who has been given all rule, authority, and power, is able to successfully put "all his enemies under his feet." Presumably, during this interim period, he will be assisted by his newly glorified heavenly family—thus Paul's statement that they will be future judges of the world and the angels (1 Corinthians 6:2–3). Paul never writes explicitly of "hell" as a final state of those judged as wicked.

He does believe in the "wrath" of God against sinners who do not repent when Jesus appears as judge in the clouds of heaven: "The day of the Lord will come as a thief in the night. When people say, 'There is peace and security,' then sudden destruction will come upon them as travail comes upon a woman with child and there will be no escape" (1 Thessalonians 5:2–3). In contrast, those "in Christ" are saved from this wrath (1 Thessalonians 1:10; 5:9–10). Presumably, as victorious glorified Spirit-beings, these members of the God-family assist their older brother Jesus Christ in adjudicating the fate of all humanity—whether living or dead. Paul apparently conceives of this as a process involving dispensing of rewards and punishments impartially to all human beings: "There will be tribulation and distress for every human being who does evil, the Jew first, but also the Greek [i.e., Gentile], but glory, honor and peace for every one who does good, the Jew first and also the Greek" (Romans 2:9–10).

The last enemy to be destroyed is death, which seems to imply a full resurrection of *all* the dead in Hades, but since "everything" becomes subject to Christ, and all those who died "will be made alive," the implication, at least, is of universal salvation.

Paul ends the long passage from 1 Corinthians 15 with his final, most cryptic statement: "When all things are subjected to him [Christ], then the Son himself will also be subjected to him who put all things under him, *that God may be everything to everyone*" (verse 28). Here we see that in Paul's view the rule of Christ, as well as those who assist him in this cosmic transformation, is an intermediate and functional rule. It is for a specified period of time, to accomplish a designated end. Once that goal is achieved and the universe reaches a complete harmony, "God will be everything to everyone." The phrase in Greek, *panta en pasin*, is difficult to translate but literally says, "That God may be all things in everything."

The author of the letter of Ephesians, an obvious devotee of

Paul writing in Paul's name several decades after his death, seems to offer a fair summary of what we can otherwise deduce directly from Paul's letters about the mystery: "For God has made known to us in all wisdom and insight the *mystery* of his will, according to his *predetermined purpose* that he set forth in Christ, as *a plan* for the fullness of time, to *unite all things in him*, things in heaven and things on earth" (Ephesians 1:9–10).

Salvation then, for Paul, is, in the end, *rescuing the entire human race* from the disharmony and death that pervade the entire cosmos as a result of the rebellion of the angelic hosts. Christ, along with his newly empowered family of chosen ones, must reign until they have destroyed "every rule, authority, and power," so that God can be all things to all. Ultimately, Paul says, the "creation itself will be released [i.e., "saved"] from its bondage to decay" (Romans 8:21).

Paul believed that his own experience as well as that of his followers verified the Announcement he proclaimed, this gospel of the mystery of God, uniquely revealed to him. He is adamant that he received his extraordinary personal revelations directly from Christ, swearing to his followers, "In what I am writing you, before God, I do not lie!" (Galatians 1:20). He even went so far as to place a curse on himself, or anyone else, who would dare to change his message, or depart from it. Paul also regularly appealed to the specific ecstatic spiritual experiences of his followers, who he believed had been "joined to the Lord, having become one Spirit with him."

In the following chapter we will see the radical implications of these shared spiritual experiences. For Paul, being "united with Christ" was not merely a metaphor expressing solidarity and unity of faith but an experiential reality that he and his followers relied upon as evidence of their salvation. As we will see, baptism was not merely a symbolic water purification ritual but a means to achieve direct possession of the Spirit of Christ. Those so united with Christ, through being possessed of his Spirit, became one spiritual "body" with him and were spiritually sustained by eating the flesh and drinking the blood of Christ through the Eucharistic meal of bread and wine. This transformation of the Jewish rituals of water purification and the blessing of God for bread and wine took Paul and his followers far afield from the practices of Jesus and his first followers and would have been viewed as shockingly pagan by James and the leaders of the Jerusalem church.

SIX

A MYSTICAL UNION
WITH CHRIST

What does it mean to be "in Christ"? I don't mean believing in Jesus in the sense of having *faith* in Christ, but literally *being in Christ*. The phrase might be familiar to readers of the New Testament or to churchgoers, but what does it mean and where did it come from? The Hebrew Bible speaks often about believing and trusting in God, but never about *being in* God, and Jews don't talk about *being in* Abraham, Moses, or any of the Prophets.[1]

The phrase "in Christ" belongs exclusively to the thought world of Paul and he uses it more than fifty times in his genuine letters.[2] It is *never* used in the New Testament Gospels, either by Jesus or anyone talking about Jesus. That alone should give us pause. No matter how familiar the phrase might be, or what we think we might understand about it, we need to first hear the words of Paul in the context in which he uses them. As we will see, Paul's concept of *being in Christ* is a key to understanding his view of what it meant to be a Christian.[3] It is the underpinning of his teaching about God creating a new heavenly family of glorified Spirit-beings and it forms the basis of the experiences he and his followers were convinced showed that they were dealing directly with Christ as a living Spirit-being.

I have often thought of my task as a historian as trying to make the familiar strange and the strange familiar. It is all too easy to think that we understand some aspect of the past when in reality we are more likely looking through the tint of our modern assumptions. If we can distance ourselves in order to see the ways in which the past is strange to us, then we have a chance to understand it in a new and more authentic way.

One of my professors in graduate school at the University of Chicago once said to us, "If you had a time machine and traveled back to Greece in the first century A.D., dropping in to observe a gathering of a cell group of Paul's followers meeting in Corinth, don't assume you would have even the slightest idea of what was going on." At that time I thought he was exaggerating for effect but my decades of research in the history of ancient religions has convinced me that his was an understatement.

He was referring not so much to obvious language and cultural barriers as to his contention that we have largely missed Paul's strangeness. It is easy to assume, based on our familiarity with modern forms of Christianity, that earliest Christianity would have some basic resemblance to what we know today; maybe not pews, pulpits, and stained glass windows, but surely the essential content of the worship services. This might be the case for Christianity in the fourth or fifth century, when the liturgy, creeds, and certain patterns of language were taking a more definitive shape—at least in the pockets of Christianity that Rome controlled. But it would be decidedly untrue for Paul's time. Paul's Christianity can be understood only against the worlds of mysticism, magic, miracles, prophecy, and the supernatural manifestations of the spiritual world—both angelic and demonic—so alien to our modern scientific worldview. At the very core of these religious experiences of Paul and his followers were his two great innovations, baptism and the Lord's Supper, which he introduced in wholly new form to his wing of the Jesus movement.

BEING IN CHRIST

For Paul the heavenly cosmic Christ is no longer the historical figure Jesus. He speaks of having "faith in Jesus" a few times but he never speaks of being *in Jesus*, only of being *in Christ*.[4] The distinction is neither accidental nor academic, but indeed essential to his understanding of how the process of cosmic salvation works.

The man Jesus, born of a woman, as a flesh-and-blood mortal human being, Paul calls "Christ according to the flesh":

> From now on, therefore, we regard no one [of our group] according to the flesh, even though we once regarded Christ according to the flesh, we regard him such no longer. Therefore, if anyone is in Christ, he is a new creation. The old has passed away; behold, the new has come. (2 Corinthians 5:16–17)

This old way of remembering Jesus has now passed. That is why, in all of Paul's letters, he tells his converts nothing about the *life* of Jesus on earth. This is quite remarkable. Paul relates nothing of Jesus' birth, that he was from Galilee, that he was baptized by John the Baptizer, that he preached that the kingdom of God was near, healed the sick, and worked miracles. Paul never quotes directly a *single* teaching of Jesus. It is possible, but not certain, that he alludes to two or three sayings of Jesus, but even these are uncertain.[5] Paul could summarize Jesus' entire life and teachings in a single sentence: God sent forth his Son, born of a woman, who died for sins and was raised from the dead. That is it.

As Paul tells the Corinthians, "I decided to know nothing among you except Jesus Christ and him crucified" (1 Corinthians 2:2). As we have seen, the "Gospel" for Paul was not the message that Jesus preached, or anything Jesus taught, but rather the message of what the man Jesus had *become*—the firstborn of the new cosmic family. This was Paul's "Gospel"—his secret Announcement.

Paul believed that Christ had transcended his mortal human identity to become the firstborn Son of the new creation, a second or last Adam, and so the man Jesus is no more. Paul prefers the term "Christ," using it over a hundred and fifty times, almost as if it is a new proper name replacing Jesus. The phrase "the Lord," referring to Christ, he uses over a hundred times. Another hundred times in his letters he uses combinations such as "Jesus Christ" or "the Lord Jesus Christ." The single name Jesus occurs only eleven times.

This reflects and reinforces his view that the revelations he has received from the heavenly Christ are far superior to anything anyone received from the earthly Jesus. Also, since the process of salvation involves the human Jesus becoming a glorified Adam of the new creation, it made no sense to Paul to dwell on a past that is fading away when a much more glorious present has already been inaugurated. This perspective, as we will see, has applications to everything he teaches, including social relations, ethical norms, and his understanding of the place of the Torah, or Law of Moses, in the Plan of God. But most important, it shaped the contours of this new form of Christianity for the next nineteen hundred years, a Christianity wholly oriented to salvation in the heavenly world, in sharp contrast to the movement Jesus the Jewish Messiah had inspired with its emphasis on a kingdom of peace and justice on earth.

As we saw in the previous chapter, Paul says that it was Christ, and not the human Jesus, who existed from the beginning of creation in the "form of God" but then subsequently emptied himself, being born in the likeness of a mortal human being (Philippians 2:6–7). Paul makes the rather startling assertion that this cosmic Christ, ages before he was born as a human being, had manifested himself as Yahweh, the God of Israel! He does not dwell on this point, but he is quite clear about it. He refers particularly to the time of Moses, when the Israelites "saw" Yahweh as a mysterious cloud-fire pillar: "And Yahweh went before them by day in a pillar of cloud, to lead them the way, and by night in a pillar of fire, to give them light, that they might go by day and by night" (Exodus 13:21).

Paul says that the God who led the Israelites through the Red Sea and in their desert wanderings for forty years, the one they called the Rock, *was* Christ (1 Corinthians 10:4; Deuteronomy 32:4, 18). He does not explain the particulars of his view, but the idea that there was an "upper" Yahweh, who remains unseen, sometimes called "God Most High," as well as a "lower" manifestation of that same God, called the "messenger Yahweh," who appears from time to time in human history in a visible manner on earth, was common in various forms of Judaism of Paul's time.[6] This lower Yahweh is not flesh and blood, even though in some of the stories he seems to "materialize," but when he appears he is then "taken up" or in one case he just disappears in a flame of fire.[7]

This is very much akin to the Greek notion of the ineffable God manifest in the lower world as the "Word" or *Logos*, which was an integral part of Platonic and Stoic cosmology. The Logos idea was appropriated by the Jewish philosopher Philo, a contemporary of Paul, to deal with passages in the Hebrew Bible that seem to refer to these two Yahwehs, an upper and a lower. In the New Testament the gospel of John adopts the Logos idea wholesale, but makes the shocking assertion that "the *Logos* became flesh," referring to the birth of Jesus (John 1:1, 14).[8] This is akin to Paul's view of the preexistent Christ, in the form of God, who emptied himself and was born of a woman.

Paul says little more about the preexistent Christ as a manifestation of Yahweh other than that he was present in the days of Moses. Paul is focused entirely on the other end of history, the termination of what he calls "this present evil age" (Galatians 1:14). What Jesus represents to Paul is one thing and one thing only— the cosmic, preexistent Christ being "born of a woman," as a flesh-and-blood mortal human being now transformed to a life-giving Spirit. This is what drove Paul and excited him most. For him it explained the Genesis creation itself and accounted for all the subsequent "blood, sweat, and tears" of the human story. Humans were created to become Gods! "This slight, momentary affliction" was preparing them for an "eternal weight of glory beyond all comparison" (2 Corinthians 4:17).

In the Hebrew Bible, Yahweh, the One God of Israel, had declared: "Turn to me and be saved, all the ends of the earth! For I am God and there is no other . . . To me every knee shall bow, every tongue shall swear (Isaiah 45:22–23). Paul quotes this precise phrase from Isaiah but now significantly adds: "At the name of Jesus every knee should bow, in heaven and on earth and under the earth, and every tongue confess that Jesus Christ is Lord, to the glory of God the Father" (Philippians 2:10–11). Christ as the newly exalted Lord of the cosmos is the functional equivalent of Yahweh.[9]

As lofty and esoteric as these concepts might be, Paul and his followers believed that their experiences of Christ were real and direct. The mystical rites of baptism and eating the Lord's Supper were their means of uniting with Christ and being possessed by his Spirit.

IMAGINING PAULINE BAPTISM

Paul invented Christian baptism. Along with the Lord's Supper, or the Eucharist, it has proven to be his most enduring contribution to Christianity. For Paul these were not merely symbolic acts, but mystical rites that were efficacious in bringing about union with Christ's Spirit.

I say Paul invented baptism because, so far as we know, none of the apostles was ever baptized in the name of Christ. They did indeed practice a form of baptism for their followers, but it was not the "baptism into Christ" that Paul taught, as we will see, but a continuation of the baptism taught by John the Baptizer.

When we first read of baptism in the New Testament it is from

John the Baptizer, who told the crowds that flocked to the banks of the Jordan River to repent of their sins since the kingdom of God had drawn very near. The arrival of God's kingdom meant God's wrathful judgment, so John's was a "baptism of repentance for the remission of sins" to prepare one for the impending apocalypse (Mark 1:4). John the Baptizer was considered an important enough threat that he came to the attention of Herod Antipas, ruler of Galilee, who had him killed. Josephus, the first-century Jewish historian, mentions John, explaining that he was so popular with the people that Herod feared his preaching might lead to an uprising. Josephus comments on John's practice of baptism, explaining that it was a "consecration of the body implying that the soul was already cleansed by right behavior."[10]

Various rites of ritual purification requiring immersion in water were common in Judaism but John's baptism was something different since it was connected to repentance and forgiveness of sins.[11] To be baptized by John was to respond to his apocalyptic call to be part of a special group who had dedicated themselves to live righteously at the end of days. The apocalyptic community that wrote the Dead Sea Scrolls, usually identified as the Essenes, had a similar practice of initiating members into their exclusive community through a ceremony involving water immersion.[12]

Jesus was baptized by John, and Christians would have difficulty explaining why he would be baptized for the "remission of sins."[13] Apparently, Peter and John, at least, had been disciples of John even before Jesus joined the baptizing movement (Acts 1:22; John 1:35–42). Jesus teamed up with John the Baptizer and began to preach the same message: that the kingdom was at hand and people should repent of their sins and be baptized (John 3:22). When John was arrested and killed by Herod Antipas, Jesus took over the leadership of this apocalyptic baptizing movement. The last week of Jesus' life he brought up the subject of John's baptism, indicating that it had been the litmus test of his generation.

According to Jesus those who rejected John's baptism had rejected God, because John was one of his greatest prophets (Mark 11:29–33; Luke 7:26–30).

The new idea of baptism "in the name of Christ" as practiced by Paul and by Christians today is dramatically different from John's baptism. The book of Acts reports that Peter and the rest of the apostles began to preach this new kind of Christian baptism within weeks of Jesus' crucifixion, telling people to repent and be baptized in the name of Jesus Christ for the remission of their sins in order to receive the gift of the Holy Spirit (Acts 2:38). Ironically, the author never reports that any of the Twelve were ever rebaptized in this new way, but he insists that they began to require it of others.

It is hard not to hear Paul whispering in the background here. The author of Acts is imposing Paul's view of Christian baptism on his narrative so as to give it apostolic legitimacy decades after the deaths of James, Peter, John, and the first-generation leaders of the movement. He is not writing history but theology—and Pauline theology at that.

At one point in his narrative he unwittingly reveals this. He relates that a married couple named Priscilla and Aquila, disciples of Paul, ran into a Jewish-Christian preacher named Apollos at Ephesus. Although Apollos was a disciple of Jesus and a powerful preacher of the Christian message, he had never even heard about being baptized into Christ—and the author of Acts admits it! The year is A.D. 54—nearly twenty-five years after Jesus' death. The way Acts describes Apollos is quite striking:

> Now a Jew named Apollos, a native of Alexandria, came to Ephesus. He was an eloquent man, competent in the Scriptures. He had been instructed in the way of the Lord. And being fervent in spirit, he spoke and taught accurately the things concerning Jesus, though he knew only the baptism of John. (Acts 18:24–25)

This is rather telling evidence regarding an original form of baptism associated with John the Baptizer and Jesus that had nothing in common with Paul's baptism.

Shortly thereafter Paul arrived in Ephesus, where he encountered a group of Christians of similar views to those of Apollos. Paul asks them, "Into what were you baptized?" and they reply, "Into John's baptism." They say they have never even heard of "receiving the Holy Spirit" (Acts 19:1–7). According to the author of Acts they were glad to be updated and Paul baptized them immediately "into Christ" and put his hands on them, at which point they received the Holy Spirit and began to speak ecstatically and utter prophecies. What the author of Acts does not say, perhaps because he did not dare make such a claim, is whether Apollos, the eloquent leader of the group, had submitted to such a rebaptism.

This becomes doubly interesting in that by the time Paul got to Ephesus, Apollos had left and gone to Corinth, where Paul had just spent the previous eighteen months, setting up a cell group of his followers. In Paul's letter 1 Corinthians the group is hopelessly divided, with some saying "I belong to Paul" but others saying "I belong to Apollos." It is surely no accident that the mysterious Apollos is suddenly mentioned in Paul's letter. But even more to the point, Paul indicates that the divisions among the Corinthians were demarcated by what kind of baptism they had received (1 Corinthians 1:10–17). Paul rebukes the Corinthians from a long distance, through his letter, trying to shame them by saying he could not teach them the full mystery of his gospel because they were not yet ready, with some claiming to follow him, but others claiming to follow Apollos (1 Corinthians 3:1–4). Unfortunately we have no way of knowing Apollos's side of the story. All we are left with is the implication in the book of Acts that he and his disciples, who knew only John's baptism, quickly came over to Paul's side. But apparently things were not nearly so harmonious.

For the author of Acts to admit that a form of Christianity was actively and openly operating in Asia Minor and Greece, even into the mid-50s A.D., holding loyally to the baptism of John the Baptizer, the very baptism that Jesus himself endorsed and practiced, is a valuable witness to this form of lost Christianity before Paul. He wants his readers to view this odd group as an anomaly, a kind of backwater phenomenon that quickly shifted to the new baptism "into Christ" that Paul preached. From his second-century vantage point such might have been the case, but in forty or so years following the death of Jesus the proper baptism was that practiced by John and Jesus. Paul's innovation had barely begun to take hold.

If the picture of harmony that Acts presents between Paul and the original apostles is a fiction, this tiny glimpse we get of Apollos and his understanding of baptism is quite telling. It shows that even decades after the death of Paul, when the book of Acts was composed, the author still felt the need to counter contrary views by retroactively projecting Paul's views of baptism as the norm to be accepted in the entire Christian movement.

Paul gives us a thorough exposition of his understanding of baptism in his letters. There are three main texts:

> For in Christ Jesus you are all sons of God, through faith. For as many of you as were baptized into Christ have been Christ-clothed. There is neither Jew nor Greek [i.e., Gentile], there is neither slave nor free, there is neither male nor female; for you are all one in Christ Jesus. (Galatians 3:26–27)

> For by one Spirit we were all baptized *into one body*—Jews or Greeks, slaves or free—and all were made to drink of one Spirit. (1 Corinthians 12:13)

> All of us who have been baptized into Christ Jesus were baptized *into his death*. We were buried therefore with him by

baptism into death, so that as Christ was raised from the dead by the glory of the Father, so we too walk in a new life. (Romans 6:3-4)

Through Paul's baptism one becomes a "Son of God," stripped of the old but reclothed in Christ. Baptism was a means of uniting oneself with the cosmic Christ, and thus becoming *one* spiritual body with all those who are likewise so joined. The former person is dead and buried—literally, in a kind of watery grave of baptism, but then resurrected to a new life in the Spirit. All former personal identities are obsolete—whether ethnic, social, or gender based. This kind of mystical union can come about only by the agency of the one Spirit that animates the collective divine body of Christ as a whole.

This can sound complex, abstract, and theological to us today but for Paul and his followers it was as real as the physical creation, even though the internal transformation was not externally visible. As we saw in the previous chapter, Paul believed that while the outer body of flesh was in the process of dying, the inner person, now united with Christ as one Spirit, was being renewed each day (2 Corinthians 4:16; Romans 8:10). Being "united in a death like his" opens the way for "the Spirit of the one who raised Jesus from the dead to give life to your mortal bodies through his Spirit that dwells in you" (Romans 8:11). Jesus, raised from the dead as the last Adam, had become this life-giving Spirit.

It should be noted that Paul does not distinguish between "the Spirit," "the Spirit of God," "the Spirit of Christ," or the "Spirit of the One who raised Jesus from the dead" (Romans 8:9-11). That is why he can say, "The Lord is the Spirit," and that the transformation "from one degree of glory to another" comes from "the Lord, who is the Spirit" (2 Corinthians 3:17-18). This sounds a bit confusing unless one realizes that in Paul's understanding the One God manifests himself in the world through the agency of the

Spirit. The generic word "spirit" in Greek is *pneuma*. It refers to an unseen force and is the normal word for "wind." In these contexts it refers to the unseen agency of the One God in the visible world—and that agent is the cosmic Christ—who *is* the Spirit. That is why it makes sense in Paul's thinking to speak of his followers as "being in Christ" but also of "Christ being in them." Through their baptism they have become united with Christ, in the one spiritual body of Christ, but that union comes from Christ, who is the Spirit, dwelling in each of them.

For Paul baptism is not a symbolic ritual but a powerful spiritual activity that effected real change in the cosmos. Paul, for example, refers to some who "baptized in behalf of the dead," evidently referring to a practice of proxy baptism for loved ones who had died before experiencing their own baptism (1 Corinthians 15:29).[14] Whether Paul endorsed the practice or not we cannot be sure, but it would be unlike Paul to refrain from condemning a practice he did not at least tolerate. After all, there is a sense in which *all* baptism is "for the dead" since it represents a "burial" of the dying mortal flesh in preparation for receiving the life-giving Spirit. Whatever the case, this practice of "baptism for the dead" shows just how efficacious the activity was understood to be as a means of invoking the Christ-Spirit—even for those who had died!

Given this conceptual framework, we can try to imagine what the baptism experience might have been like in Paul's churches. I base the following on what we know of ancient Jewish practice, our earliest surviving Christian liturgies, reports on the early Christians made by the Romans, and the few hints that Paul gives us.

Baptism was conducted in a river or stream since Paul's cell groups were illegal and meeting in private homes. There were, of course, no church buildings or formal places of worship.[15] It is possible in some cases that a wealthier patron or host of the group might have had an inside pool or bath.

We can imagine that the candidate would have entered the

water naked, leaving behind the old clothing, trampling it under-foot.[16] Standing waist high in the water, accompanied by the one administering the baptism, he or she was likely asked: "Do you confess that Jesus is Lord and believe in your heart that God has raised him from the dead, calling upon his name to save you from your sins?" Paul refers to this specific moment when this "confession of the lips" brings salvation (Romans 10:9–11). The candidate would have confessed out loud, perhaps bending the knees slightly as a gesture of submission: "I believe that Jesus is Lord!" followed by the cry in Aramaic: *Maranatha!*—meaning "May our Lord come!" Those observing the baptism would then likely all cry out "Amen!," which means in Aramaic, "Let it be so!" This ritual gesture of the bowing of the knees, practiced in ancient Jewish daily prayers at the mention of God's name, is alluded to by Paul in his letter to the Philippians: "that at the name of Jesus every knee should bow, in heaven and on earth and under the earth, and every tongue confess that Jesus Christ is Lord, to the glory of the Father" (Philippians 2:10–11).

Paul invokes the Aramaic cry *"Maranatha!"* at the end of his first letter to the Corinthians (16:22). It was used as a formulaic way of summoning the Christ-Spirit, either as a curse or a blessing. According to the *Didache* it was also pronounced in a similar way at the end of the Eucharist meal, to separate those worthy from those unworthy (*Didache* 10:6). The idea was to call upon the Jesus as Lord and bid him to unite at that moment with the person being baptized. The corporate response using the Aramaic word *Amen*, familiar to Christians today, would have been strange and new to a Greek-speaking group. Paul had introduced it as a formal response at group gatherings (1 Corinthians 14:16).

Next, based on the Jewish practice of the *mikveh* or ritual bath, the candidate buckled the knees completely, submerging the body underwater until the head was covered, basically kneeling underwater. Standing up one would cry out ecstatically, "Abba, Abba!"

using the Aramaic word for "father." This was a cry of intimate rec-
ognition by the new spiritual child, signifying that the Spirit had
indeed entered the candidate and possessed him or her. Paul refers
to this precise moment twice in his letters and it is obvious that he
is thinking of a formal cry that he connects to the moment one receives the Spirit at baptism:

> And because you are sons, God has sent the Spirit of his Son
> into our hearts, crying out, "Abba! Father!" (Galatians 4:6)

> You have received the spirit of Son-ship. When we cry out,
> "Abba! Father!" it is the Spirit himself bearing witness with
> our spirit that we are children of God. (Romans 8:15–16)

This ecstatic cry at baptism, signifying the coming of the Spirit of
Christ into the candidate, was viewed as a guarantee of the legitimacy of the "Son-ship." Twice Paul tells the Corinthians:

> But it is God who establishes us with you in Christ, and has
> *anointed* us; he has put his seal upon us and given us his Spirit
> in our hearts *as a guarantee.* (2 Corinthians 1:21–22)

> He who has prepared us for this very thing [i.e., the trans-
> formation to Spirit] is God, who has given us the Spirit as a
> guarantee. (2 Corinthians 5:5)

Paul uses a particular Aramaic word here (*arrabon*) translated as
"guarantee." Literally, it refers to a first installment—much like
"earnest money" put down on a purchase.

Still standing in the water, the person administering the baptism would put his hands on the head of the candidate and ask
God to confirm the presence of the Spirit openly as a witness to all
present by giving the person his or her spiritual "gift."[17] These were

specific manifestations of the Spirit given to those "baptized by one Spirit into one body" according to God's choosing (1 Corinthians 12:4–13). Some would begin to speak ecstatically in languages (*glossolalia*) they had never learned, whether human or angelic; others would utter prophecies, demonstrating supernatural wisdom, knowledge, or insight; while others were given the power to work miracles or to perform healings.

As the candidate came up out of the water he or she would be clothed in a new white garment, picturing the new spiritual body they would receive at the resurrection. Each member of the group would then greet the newest member with a familial kiss on the mouth, referred to in several of Paul's letters. He calls it "the kiss of holiness," presumably to avoid any connotation of sexual impropriety or indecency.[18]

This imaginary attempt to sketch a scene of baptism in Paul's churches is based on evidence that comes directly from Paul. These powerful and evocative Aramaic words—*Maranatha*, *Abba*, and *Amen*—are each attested as formulaic utterances in Paul's letters. To Paul's Greek-speaking converts these would have a foreign, magical sound. It is likely that baptisms were done in secret and at night, as we will see below, so the atmosphere of mystery and intrigue would have been all the more heightened. As vital as baptism was, it was initiatory and done only once for each new Christian, whereas the ongoing power of Christ's Spirit was sustained by a mystical meal that Paul introduced to his churches as the "Lord's Supper."

EATING THE LORD'S SUPPER

Reading the New Testament backward could hardly be more critical than when it comes to examining the sacred meal that Paul calls the "Lord's Supper." This most central of all Christian rites, the Eucharist or Holy Communion, involving eating the flesh and drinking the blood of Christ, however understood, is at once as familiar as it is strange. Here is what Paul writes to the Corinthians around A.D. 54:

> For I received from the Lord what I also handed on to you, that the Lord Jesus on the night when he was betrayed took bread, and when he had given thanks, he broke it, and said, "This is my body which is [broken] for you. Do this in re-membrance of me." In the same way also he took the cup, af-ter supper, saying, "This cup is the new covenant in my blood. Do this, as often as you drink it, in remembrance of me." (1 Corinthians 11:23-25)

Mark, our earliest gospel, written between A.D. 75 and 80, has the following scene of Jesus' Last Supper:

> And as they were eating, he took bread, and after blessing it broke it and gave it to them, and said, "Take; this is my body." And he took a cup, and when he had given thanks he gave it to them, and they all drank of it. And he said to them, "This is my blood of the covenant, which is poured out for many." (Mark 14:22-24)

The precise verbal similarities between these two accounts are quite remarkable, considering that Paul's version was written at least twenty years earlier than Mark's. Where would Paul have got-ten such a detailed description of what Jesus had said on the night he was betrayed? The common assumption has been that this core tradition, so central to the original Jesus movement, had circu-lated orally for decades in the various Christian communities. Paul could have received it directly from Peter or James, on his first visit to Jerusalem around A.D. 40, or learned it from the Christian con-gregation in Antioch, where, according to the book of Acts, he first established himself (Acts 11:26).

What Paul plainly says is easy to overlook: "*For I received from the Lord what I handed on to you.*" His language is clear and unequivocal. He is not saying, "I received it from one of the apostles, and thus indirectly it came from the Lord," or "I learned it in Antioch, but they had gotten it by tradition from the Lord." Paul uses precisely the same language to defend the revelation of his gospel and how it came to him. He says he did *not* receive it from any man, nor was he taught it, but swears with an oath, "I received it through a revelation of Jesus Christ" (Galatians 1:11–12). This means that what Paul passes on here regarding the Lord's Supper, including the words of Jesus over the bread and the wine, comes to us from Paul and Paul alone!

We have every reason to take him at his word. Though it might sound strange to us that anyone would claim to have received by revelation a narrative of Jesus' last meal with his disciples years after the event, Paul considered that sort of thing a normal manifestation of his prophetic connection with the Spirit of Christ. One of the gifts of the spirit was a "word of knowledge," and such a revelation could apply to the past, the present, or the future. In the same way Paul claims to have received a detailed scenario of precisely what will happen in the future when Jesus returns. He prefaces his revelation with the claim "For this I declare to you *by the word of the Lord*" (1 Thessalonians 4:15). Paul says that he hears from Jesus. To speculate as to where Paul derived the ideas he claims were given to him by revelation is to enter into his personal psychology to a degree to which we have no access. To try to do this would be outside the realm of historical inquiry.

Since Paul's account is the earliest we have of the Last Supper, we have to be very careful in reading the gospels of Mark, Matthew, and Luke, all of which record a similar account but were written decades later. In other words we can't begin with Mark, our earliest gospel, and assume that Jesus actually said these words at the Last Supper, and then go to Paul, who comes after Jesus, as if he were just echoing the primary account. Things are precisely the other way around. We have every reason to believe that Mark got his tradition of the words of Jesus at the Last Supper from Paul. Matthew and Luke, who then use Mark as a source, also repeat what Paul had said decades earlier.[19]

One way of sharpening this inquiry is to ask two questions that take us beyond Paul and back to Jesus. Is it historically probable that Jesus held a Last Supper with his disciples on the night before his death? Is it historically probable that Jesus uttered words about the bread being his body and the cup of wine his blood?

For the first question we have two independent ancient sources: Mark (who is echoed by Matthew and Luke) and the gospel of John. Both report that Jesus ate such a meal and it is reasonable to assume such is the case. For the second question Paul is our only source reporting that Jesus spoke of the bread as his body and the wine as his blood—assuming that Mark, Matthew, and Luke derive their accounts from him. John reports an intimate meal Jesus had with his disciples but never says anything about words such as these spoken over bread and wine. It is difficult to imagine John, who was aware of the other gospels, leaving such an important tradition out of his gospel except by intention. His silence is essentially his "no" vote on the historical reliability of our single source—Paul.

But there is another reason for doubting the historical validity of Paul's account. Other than Paul, our earliest record of the words spoken at a Christian Eucharist celebration over the bread and the wine come from the *Didache*, mentioned previously, and they have no correspondence whatsoever to the words of Jesus that Paul reports:

You shall give thanks as follows: First, with respect to the cup: "We give you thanks, our Father, for the holy vine of *David, your child*, which you made known to us through Jesus your child. To you be the glory forever." And with respect to the fragments of bread: "We give you thanks our Father, for the life and knowledge that you made known to us through *Jesus your child*. To you be the glory forever." (Didache 9:2–3)[20]

This precious text provides us with clear evidence that early Christian communities were gathering together for a common thanksgiving meal called the Eucharist, blessing bread and wine, but with no connection whatsoever to the Pauline words associated with the Lord's Supper that became the norm within Christianity. It is also noteworthy that both Jesus and David are equated in this prayer as "your child," showing the fully human understanding of Jesus as a bloodline descendant of David and thus heir of his royal dynasty. As we have seen, the *Didache* as a whole shows no influence of Paul's teachings or traditions. It fits well with the broader picture we have seen based on the Q source, the letter of James, and the scattered texts that we can identify from later Jewish-Christian sources.

What Jesus said at his Last Supper with his disciples we have no way of knowing but there is evidence he thought of that meal as a "Messianic banquet" to be eaten in anticipation of their table fellowship in the future kingdom of God. He tells the Twelve: "You are those who have continued with me in my trials: and I assign to you, as my Father assigned to me, a kingdom, that you may eat and drink at my table in my kingdom and sit on thrones judging the twelve tribes of Israel" (Luke 22:28–30). This saying of Jesus is from the Q source, not from Paul, but Luke connects it to the Last Supper. Luke relies on his source Mark for his Lord's Supper account, including the Pauline tradition of the words about eating the body and drinking the blood of Jesus. But surprisingly, Luke knows another source with no such language! He places both into his narrative, juxtaposed one after the other:

[*Tradition A: Alternative Source*] And he said to them, "I have earnestly desired to eat this Passover with you before I suffer.

For I tell you I will not eat it until it is fulfilled in the kingdom of God." And he took a cup, and when he had given thanks he said, "Take this, and divide it among yourselves. For I tell you that from now on I will not drink of the fruit of the vine until the kingdom of God comes." (Luke 22:15–18)

[*Tradition B: Mark Source*] And he took bread, and when he had given thanks, he broke it and gave it to them, saying, "This is my body, which is given for you. Do this in remembrance of me." And likewise the cup after they had eaten, saying, "This cup that is poured out for you is the new covenant in my blood. (Luke 22:19–21)

When one reads both traditions as a unit it makes little sense, because Jesus ends up taking the cup twice but saying entirely different things. When the two traditions are separated, each forms a discrete unit.

This becomes all the more significant since Luke's Tradition A fits with what we might expect Jesus to have said in a Jewish messianic context. Oddly, Mark appears to preserve just a bit of this more primitive Jewish tradition, since Jesus concludes the meal by saying: "Truly, I say to you, I shall not drink again of the fruit of the vine until that day when I drink it new in the kingdom of God" (Mark 14:25). Matthew includes this verse as well, copying it from Mark (Matthew 26:29). The reason it is odd is that it does not fit well with the Pauline "this is my body" and "this is my blood" tradition that Mark makes the center of his Last Supper scene. Jesus is obviously not anticipating one day drinking his own blood with the disciples in the kingdom. Evidently Mark knew something of the two traditions but mutes the one while playing up the other. He was perhaps bothered by the idea of two different scenes of Jesus blessing the cup, but with different words of interpretation, so he drops the first one. Luke leaves them both, juxtaposed, even though they might be seen as contradictory. This convolution of Luke was sufficiently bothersome to some scribes that the Western text tradition (based on the fifth-century A.D. Codex Bezae) *drops* the second cup scene (verses 19b–20) entirely; leaving a contradictory combination of Tradition A and B that makes little sense.[21]

Luke's Tradition A, supported by Mark's words of Jesus at the end of the meal, is probably as close as we can get to what Jesus might have said on the last evening of his life. What he expects is a celebratory meal of reunion in the kingdom of God. This idea, often referred to as the "Messianic Banquet," is described clearly in the Dead Sea Scrolls. When the Messiah comes, all his chosen ones sit down at a common table with him, in the kingdom, with blessings over bread and wine:

> When God brings forth the Messiah, he shall come with them at the head of the whole congregation of Israel with all his brethren, the sons of Aaron the Priest . . . and the chiefs of the clans of Israel shall sit before him . . . And when they shall gather for the common table, to eat and to drink new wine . . . let no man extend his hand over the firstfruits of bread and wine before the Priest; for he shall bless the firstfruits of bread and wine . . . Thereafter, the Messiah of Israel shall extend his hand over the bread and all the congregation of the Community shall utter a blessing . . .[22]

One thing seems clear. The idea of eating the body and blood of one's god, even in a symbolic manner, fits nothing we know of Jesus or the Jewish culture from which he comes. The technical term *theophagy* refers to "eating the body of one's god," either literally or symbolically, and various researchers have noted examples of the idea in Greek religious traditions in which the deity was symbolically consumed.[23] Although some scholars have tried to locate Paul's version of the Eucharist within the wider tradition of "sacred banquets" common in Greco-Roman society, his specific language about participating in the spiritual efficacy of Jesus' sacrificed body and blood by eating the bread and drinking the wine seems to take us into another arena entirely.[24] The closest parallels we have to this kind of idea are found in Greek magical materials from this period. For example, in one of the magical papyri we read of a spell in which one drinks a cup of wine that has been ritually consecrated to represent the blood of the god Osiris, in order to participate in the spiritual power of love he had for his consort, Isis.[25]

Jesus lived as an observant Jew, keeping the Torah or Law of Moses and teaching others to do the same. Jews were strictly forbidden to consume blood or even to eat meat from which the blood had not been properly drained and removed (Leviticus 7:26–27). The Jewish followers of Jesus, led by Jesus' brother James, were quite stringent on this point, insisting that it applied equally to non-Jews as well as Jews, based on the prohibition to Noah and all his descendants after the Flood. They forbade non-Jewish followers of Jesus to eat meat that had been killed by strangling, or to consume any blood (Acts 15:19–20). Paul was admittedly lax on these restrictions and tells his followers they can eat any kind of meat sold in the marketplace, presumably even animals killed by strangulation, so long as no one present happens to notice and object on the basis of biblical teachings (1 Corinthians 10:25–29).

Given this background I think we can conclude that it is inconceivable that Jesus would have had his followers drink a cup of wine as a representation of his blood, even symbolically, or break bread to represent his flesh, sacrificed for their sins.[26]

WHEN YOU ALL COME TOGETHER

Participation in the memorial meal of the Lord's Supper was a corporate event in Paul's churches. The followers were all to gather in one place, waiting until everyone is present, and separating any common meals they might eat together from this sacred moment (1 Corinthians 11:33). Ideally, this gathering of the body of Christ was a time when the Christ-Spirit would be manifested in extraordinary ways, with gifts of the Spirit abundantly demonstrated. This could include speaking ecstatically in exotic languages, uttering prophecies, healing the sick, and pronouncing blessings and curses. Paul devotes four chapters in his first letter to the Corinthians in an attempt to bring some order to the chaos that had begun to characterize these meetings (1 Corinthians 11–14). He had received reports that the group was engaging in gluttony and drunkenness and had divided up into various factions. Their gatherings had become loud and disorderly, with the Spirit given free rein to guide each individual as he or she was moved. People were interrupting one another, all speaking at once, with ecstatic outbursts of every description. Some of the women in the group, who were allowed a limited amount of participation if they had the gift of prophecy but otherwise were to be silent in the gatherings, were speaking out, asking questions, and expressing their views.

Paul was fearful, from the reports that he had received, that demonic spirits might have invaded their Christian space and were the source of some of the chaos—impersonating the Spirit of Christ. One of the gifts of the Spirit was the ability to supernaturally "discern" whether a spirit speaking was that of Christ or an imposter (1 Corinthians 12:10). Paul even refers to a case where someone was yelling out "Jesus be cursed!" while claiming to be speaking through the Spirit of Christ (1 Corinthians 12:1–3). Apparently this was a way of cursing the human Jesus, who was seen now as separate from the divine Spirit of Christ. Though Paul strictly forbade such conduct, it is clear that the roots of such practices represent extensions of his own teachings taken to extremes, as he was the one who had emphasized that those "in Christ" were freed from the Torah, that "all things were lawful," and that Jesus as an observant Jew "according to the flesh" was no longer the focus of the followers of Christ (2 Corinthians 5:16–17). In the place of the historical Jesus, Paul had now put his own example, urging his followers: "Be imitators of me, as I am of Christ" (1 Corinthians 11:1).

It is hard for us to imagine such a scene. It must have been something akin to the behavior reported at the Salem witch trials in the seventeenth century, or perhaps at some of the early-nineteenth-century revivals in frontier America, with people shouting, running wildly, falling to the ground, and even barking or laughing uncontrollably.[27]

Central to the early Pauline gathering was participation in eating the Lord's Supper together. The point that Paul emphasizes most was that this was no ordinary meal and should be completely separate from common meals of social fellowship. What he teaches about the meal gives us an insight into why he insists that Jesus referred to the bread as his body and the cup of wine as his blood. Paul reminds the Corinthians: "The cup of blessing that we bless, is it not a *participation* in the blood of Christ? The bread that we break, is it not a *participation* in the body of Christ?" (1 Corinthians 10:16).

The cup of wine and the bread were not merely symbolic, reminding one of Jesus' death: they were understood to be *instrumental*—allowing one who is *united with Christ* in the One Body to *participate* in Jesus' death. Protestants and Roman Catholics have debated this point for centuries, with the Catholics insisting that the bread and wine, once consecrated, become, in a deeply mystical sense, the "real" body and blood of Christ. This idea reflects the teachings of Paul. Some Protestant scholars have resisted such a sacramental understanding of Paul's mysticism, considering it magical and superstitious and thus incompatible with Paul's deep spirituality.[28] There is a real peril here in trying to "modernize" Paul, who is hardly a post-Enlightenment rationalist. Paul's world is thick with angels and demons and he believes he is locked in battle with cosmic forces. The fantastic and the miraculous are to be expected at every turn. His cosmos is that of Hellenistic Judaism, with levels of heavens, astral spirits, and a Hadean underworld.[29]

We can assume that some special words of "consecration" were spoken over the bread and wine, perhaps using the Aramaic or Hebrew phrases *ze hu guphi* and *ze hu dami* ("this is my body," "this is my blood"), with the Aramaic cry *"Maranatha!"* to summon the Spirit of Christ to be present at the meal. The meal was called a "memorial," but the Greek word implies not just recalling a past event, but participating in something presently being reenacted by invoking the deity. By taking this bread and this wine into one's own body, one is uniting with the body and blood of Christ. Paul explains that eating the Lord's Supper is a terribly awesome act before which one must undergo deep self-examination so as to participate in a "worthy manner." To do otherwise, without discerning the body of Christ, is to bring judgment upon oneself (1 Corinthians 11:27–32).

The early Christians influenced by Paul took up this view of the Lord's Supper with enthusiasm. Ignatius, the early-second-century bishop of Antioch, calls the Eucharist the "medicine [*pharmakon*] of immortality, the antidote that we should not die but live through all eternity in Jesus Christ" (Ephesians 20). He roundly condemns other Christian groups who "do not confess that the Eucharist is the flesh of our Savior Jesus Christ" (Smyrneans 7). He says to avoid such people and not even speak about them—indicating there was disagreement in the early second century between groups of Christians who follow Paul and those who maintain a tradition like that found in the *Didache*. A few decades later, the Christian apologist Justin, who lived in Rome, stated Paul's perspective unequivocally:

> For *not as common bread and common drink* do we receive these; but in like manner as Jesus Christ our Savior, having

been made flesh by the Word of God, had both flesh and blood for our salvation, so likewise have we been taught that the food which is blessed by the prayer of His Word, *and from which our blood and flesh by transmutation are nourished, is the flesh and blood of that Jesus* who was made flesh. (*Apology* 1.66)

Irenaeus, a highly influential late-second-century bishop of Lyons, insisted that eating the body and blood of Christ ensured the future resurrection of the corruptible flesh: "Having received the Word of God, the Eucharist, which is the body and blood of Christ; so also our bodies, being nourished by it, and deposited in the earth, and suffering decomposition there, shall rise at their appointed time" (Against Heresies 5.2.3).

This kind of personal identification between consuming the transformed elements of the Eucharist and one's hope of giving life to the mortal body is not as far removed from Paul as it might first sound. When he instructs the Corinthians about the way in which they must approach this sacred meal with awe and proper preparation, Paul observes that some of them, who have disregarded the "body of Christ," have become "weak and ill, and some have died" (1 Corinthians 11:30). He means this quite literally. He links the physical health and well-being of their bodies to the way in which they are participating in the Lord's Supper. The implication is that if one properly participates in this sacred meal one will be preserved "body, soul, and spirit" in sound health until the arrival of Christ in the clouds of heaven (1 Thessalonians 5:23).

When the Christians of Asia, where Paul had worked for many years, first came to the attention of the Romans in the early second century A.D., they were viewed with suspicion as an illegal cult, given to "superstition" and suspected of practicing "abominations." The Romans suspected them of eating human flesh, drinking blood, practicing magical curses and spells, and holding nocturnal meetings involving men and women of all classes at which they would remove their clothing and engage in vile sexual acts of every description.[30] Pliny the Younger, appointed by the emperor Trajan as a provincial governor in Bithynia-Pontus, in northern Asia Minor, around A.D. 110, had Christians arrested and interrogated on suspicion of such crimes. The Christians, of course, maintained their innocence, and one of the things they emphasized was that when they gathered together to eat their sacred meals they consumed only "ordinary harmless food," and that they took oaths to never lie, steal, kill, or commit adultery. In contrast, Jews were accepted in Roman culture as a legal religion with a high standard of ethics. It is not hard to imagine how an outside observer might have so characterized Paul's "mystery religion," when he himself had trouble keeping things in check.

By the end of the second century Paul's triumph was complete. His views of baptism and the Lord's Supper had been accepted as orthodox Christian teaching and his emphasis on the cosmic Christ over the human Jesus predominated. The editing of the New Testament, with the gospels, the book of Acts, and Paul's thirteen letters following, more or less sealed the orthodox interpretation. The Christianity of James and the original apostles began to fade in influence.

Despite Paul's efforts at propagating the validity of these spiritual experiences and practices among his followers, his message faced major difficulties. As we will see in the following chapter, both his experiences and his message were grounded in his conviction that the end of the age was near and that his followers very shortly would experience the full transformation from flesh to spirit, which had been only partially realized in their initial union with Christ. Time was not on Paul's side, and as a result his followers increasingly had to face the hard reality of continued life in a world that remained very much as it had always been. They were truly trapped between two worlds.

SEVEN

ALREADY BUT NOT YET

Paul and his followers faced an insurmountable problem, and unwittingly their failure to overcome it resulted in incalculable human suffering and misery. They had pushed themselves hard up against the cruel reality of time. It is one thing to believe that one is living at the end of history, right on the cusp of its transformation, but quite another to continue to deal with the hard, relentless reality of ordinary day-to-day life, unchanged year after year. The passing of time is something that every apocalyptic group has had to face, in whatever period they have lived.

However, for Paul and his followers it was even worse. It was not just a matter of time, of waiting. Not only did they believe that the transformation of the world was near: they were convinced it *had already begun*—but it had not yet arrived! They believed they were "in Christ," and thus *already* participating in God's grand reshaping of the cosmos. At the same time, "outside" in the natural world, human life and history continued as always. They were not simply living between two worlds, waiting for one to end and the other to begin. They were living within two worlds. Plato had taught that one could leave this world and go to a higher heavenly existence. Jesus and other apocalyptic Jews expected the imminent end of this world and the arrival of the new age. Paul's gospel said that the chosen ones were already in the kingdom of God, by being in Christ even while waiting for its arrival.

The term "kingdom of God" refers to the reign of God, usually understood in Jewish apocalyptic texts in this period as the time when God decisively intervenes in human affairs to bring about a new age of God's righteous rule. God's anointed one, or Messiah, was expected to usher in this dramatic halt and turnabout of human history. The Messiah would be exalted above every other authority so that through his reign the will of God would be done on earth, as it is done in heaven. Paul taught that Jesus, who was a royal descendant of David, had fulfilled the role of the expected Messiah. But more important to Paul, he had been "declared Son of God in power by his resurrection." Paul believed that Jesus had been raised from the dead and glorified to sit "at the right hand of God" (Romans 1:3–4). Since his reign was a heavenly one, *the kingdom of God had already arrived* and would shortly be manifested to the surprise of the entire world.

As we have seen, Christ's rule from heaven, not just over the earth, but the entire cosmos, will continue until he destroys all rule, authority, and power, putting "all things" under his feet (Romans 8:34; 1 Corinthians 15:25). Paul's cosmos is a disrupted one, a cosmos in rebellion, currently controlled by Satan, "the god of this age." But Satan's time is short-lived. Paul triumphantly declares to the Christians at Rome: "The God of peace will *shortly* crush Satan under your feet" (Romans 16:20). This was in the late 50s A.D., during the reign of Nero.

The final result of Christ's heavenly exaltation and reign is that *every knee will bow, every tongue confess,* that Jesus is *Lord.* The word "Lord" (Greek *kurios*) means master, ruler, or potentate. It is the same word that the Roman emperors put on their coins and demanded in oaths of allegiance. That Jesus *is* already "Lord" means that his reign has been inaugurated. *It is already here, but not yet consummated.*

Stage one in the plan for extending the reign of God to the entire cosmos was the selection and preparation of a special group of human beings who would receive the same exaltation as the Messiah, in order to share in his reign. Those "in Christ" were already "in the kingdom." There was indeed a battle raging, not with "weapons of worldly warfare" but divine power to destroy strongholds, particularly the grip of Satan and his demons upon those whom God had chosen (2 Corinthians 10:3–6). Paul says that once those "in Christ" learn to complete their own obedience, they will then be ready to punish every disobedience—empowered as co-rulers with Christ.

During this interim period, as the reign of Christ is being extended, there will be persecution and outside opposition. This the group could handle, even if it might seem to contradict their faith that Christ was the new cosmic ruler. They had been taught that in order to be glorified they must first suffer, as Christ had suffered. Paul tells them they should even "rejoice" in sufferings, since it will result in great reward (Romans 5:3). They expected the natural world to continue, temporarily, on its tired and worn path of birth and death, disease and decay, and sin and injustice. Paul had told them that Satan was the *god* of "the present evil age" and that he had "blinded the eyes of the unbelievers" (Galatians 1:4; 2 Corinthians 4:4). Satan had been attacked by Christ's victory over death, but not yet defeated. Those in Christ still had to live in the old world, but without being contaminated by it. The tensions, stresses, persecutions, and even temptations were considered necessary tests that would only make them stronger (Romans 8:18; 2 Corinthians 12:9). Paul had taught his followers that "all things work together for good for those called [literally, "invited"] according to his purpose" (Romans 8:28). This is not a general promise of divine providence for humankind in general, but a specific promise made only to the elect group. No matter what came their way, even if it had been sent by Satan, God would use it to perfect them: "For the sake of Christ, then, I am content with weaknesses, insults, hardships, persecutions, and calamities. For when I am weak, then I am strong" (2 Corinthians 12:10).

The challenge, and the insurmountable problem, was to work out the conflict between the intersection of the old world and the new in the present. Paul tried his best to provide guidance and instruction. He stressed and sometimes even demanded what he believed was the *ideal*, but the cost of denying one reality at the expense of another often proved too great.

Albert Schweitzer once characterized the teachings of Jesus as "interim ethics." He was thinking of the ways in which an apocalyptic view of history could radicalize one's ethics to a degree that would be foolishly impractical if the "end" did not arrive as expected. In other words, an individual who believed that the end of history was very near might well choose to "turn the other cheek," forgive enemies, refrain from resisting evil, or sell what he has and give to the poor. This is what Schweitzer meant by "interim ethics," meaning they made sense only *if* God's intervention to bring about justice in the world did in fact come. In a world that continued on, generation after generation, one might even consider such ethical standards to be unjust since they would enable oppression and wickedness to thrive.

Paul's ethics were decidedly apocalyptic, but he took things a step further, giving a new definition to the idea of radical. He asked that people behave "as if" the heavenly transformation had already taken place, even if by every visible indication it had not. This perspective profoundly affected his views on human sexuality, economic and social inequities, and religious and ethnic divisions.

NEITHER MALE NOR FEMALE

Let's begin with Paul's view of men and women. He describes to his followers in Galatia the ultimate ideal of God's kingdom: "For as many of you as were baptized *into Christ* have put on Christ. There is *neither Jew nor Greek, there is neither slave or free, there is neither male nor female,* for you are all one in Christ" (Galatians 3:27–28). Clearly Paul did not imagine that these ethnic, economic, and gender categories had somehow magically disappeared through the act of baptism into Christ—or did he? His letters are filled with instructions about how to handle various problems related to ethnicity, economics, and gender, as well as similar problems, but on another level he expects the new reality "in Christ" to have raised his followers far above the fray of *all human* failings and disruptions. What does Paul mean by his claim that sexual distinctions between male and female no longer exist in the one body of Christ?

As a Jew Paul believed that God had created humans as male and female in the beginning: "So God created man in his own image, in the image of God he created him, male and female he created them" (Genesis 1:27). The very first command God gives Adam and Eve in the Genesis account is "Be fruitful and multiply, and fill the earth and subdue it," which certainly puts God's positive blessing upon reproductive sex (Genesis 1:28). Throughout the creation story everything that God has made is pronounced as good, and at the end the whole is declared "very good." This notion that a good God created and blessed the good earth is fundamental to most forms of Judaism in this period. In certain Hellenistic and gnostic systems of thought the physical creation was viewed negatively, the unfortunate creation of an inferior deity, so that the "fall" of humans into the lower world, and their fracture into male and female, was seen as a problem from which one needed to be "saved." Recall the Greek understanding of the physical body as a repository for the soul, something to be discarded so the soul could be free.

Paul is no gnostic. He accepts that human sexuality is part of the intended order of God's good creation. He also accepts the notion in Genesis that the woman is to be *subject to* the man, and is, in that sense, *inferior to* the man. He writes the Corinthians: "For a man ought not to cover his head since he is the image and glory of God; but woman is the glory of man. For man was not made from woman, but woman from man. Neither was man created for woman, but *woman for man*" (1 Corinthians 11:7–8). Paul has been blessed as well as damned for these clear and definitive words.[1] What he says here has put him at the center of heated discussions about the role of women in the church and society that are as active today as they were anciently. The difference is that the Church largely went the way of Paul, especially from the second century A.D. on, so that the emphasis in the Hebrew Bible regarding the essential goodness of the physical creation and blessings upon male and female sexual union were muted in contrast to Paul's otherworldly perspectives.

The context of Paul's declaration was a controversy over whether women in the Corinthian church should pray or prophesy in the group gatherings with their heads covered or uncovered. The covering referred to is not a cloth or veil, even though some English translations give that impression—it is the woman's hair. Paul addresses the issues of both hair length and style.[2] He explains: "If a woman has *long hair*, it is her pride. For her hair is given to her for a covering [i.e., veil]" (1 Corinthians 11:15). Paul insists that if a woman has shorter hair, or puts her hair up in common Greco-Roman style, exposing her neck and ears, she is getting out of her place in God's created order, as well as being immodest.[3] In contrast, a man with long hair shames his head. Men submit themselves directly to God, while women are to bow their heads to their husbands, with their long hair as a sign of that submission: "For a man ought not to cover his head, since he is the image and glory of God; but woman is the glory of man" (1 Corinthians 11:7).

Paul bases his position on his assertion that there is a rigid hierarchy of the created order, moving from God, to Christ, to the man, and last of all, at the bottom of the chain of authority—the woman: "But I want you to understand that the head of every man is Christ, the head of a woman is the man, and the head of Christ is God" (1 Corinthians 11:3). For a woman to wear her hair immodestly dishonors her "head"—referring to her husband as her head, as well as her head itself, a kind of play on the word. Paul then says something commentators have puzzled over for the past eighteen hundred years. A literal translation reads: "Neither was man created for woman, but woman for man. On *account of this* a woman ought to have *power* [Greek *exousia*] on her head, because of the angels" (1 Corinthians 11:9–10). Some have taken this to mean a "symbol of authority," that is her covered head, but grammatically the noun is active, not passive. The reference is to something the woman controls, not something that controls her. The idea is that the woman who covers her head exercises power or authority over her head, and thus does not expose it to immodesty—namely to the lustful gaze of the angels! Here Paul likely alludes to the story in Genesis where the angels or "sons of God" lusted after women, left their proper place in heaven, and came down to earth and impregnated them (1 Corinthians 11:10; Genesis 6:1–2).[4] The woman was made *for* the man, not for these rebellious angels, so in the dynamic, charismatic manifestation of prayer and prophecy, when the heavens are open and the spiritual energy is flowing from heaven to earth and back again—a woman must guard herself.

Paul believed that angels, and possibly uninvited demonic spirits as well, were present in the charismatic gatherings of his followers as they invoked the Spirit of Christ, who shows his presence and power through manifesting various gifts of the Spirit.[5] Eating at the "table of the Lord," as Paul refers to their sacred meal, is an occasion of segregated holiness for the group, when the spiritual presence of Christ is quite literally imbibed through the bread and the wine (1 Corinthians 10:21). Paul entertains the possibility that demons might be brought along by those who might have also eaten recently at an idol's temple and been unwittingly bonded with them (1 Corinthians 10:14–21). These spiritual realities and dangers make the proper conduct and modesty of women of vital importance to the well-being of the group as a whole. Paul had just warned the group that those who were punished in the days of Moses had eaten and drunk in holiness but then "rose up to dance" in sexually immodest ways (1 Corinthians 10:6–7).

Paul is adamant about his stance. His tone is strident and uncompromising. He sarcastically says that if women insist on cutting their hair they should just shave their heads like common prostitutes—and if they find that shameful, then they should cover their heads! (1 Corinthians 11:5–6).

Paul obviously anticipates that some women will object to his views, some perhaps because of Greco-Roman fashion, in which women routinely put their hair up above their neck and ears. However, it is possible that others object on the grounds of what Paul has taught them, that there was "no longer male or female" in Christ. If such was ever the case, would it not be so in the assembly, when all were gathered as one, eating the flesh and drinking the blood of Christ's body? Also, since these women were praying and giving prophecies ecstatically in the Spirit, were they not acting directly under the authority of Christ? Would they need any man as their "head" or mediator?

Surprisingly, Paul considers none of this and abruptly closes the door on further discussion with his final declaration: "If anyone is disposed to be contentious, we recognize no other practice, nor do the churches of God" (1 Corinthians 11:16). But even while laying down the law Paul cannot resist giving at least a nod to the ideal. Even though these male and female roles are still operative in the "old" creation, he observes, almost parenthetically: "Nevertheless, *in the Lord* woman is not without man, nor man without woman; for as woman was made from man, so *the man* is now born of woman. And all things are from God" (1 Corinthians 11:11–12). Since Paul is speaking of an alternative to the order of creation in which woman was made *from* man and *for* man, he must here have the "new creation" in mind, or as he says—*in the Lord*. The reference to "the man" seems to refer then to Christ, the new Adam/Man, even if by extension all the select group, whether male or female, who are "born of women" are included as part of the new Adamic race. The idea is that in the old creation woman needed man to exist (Eve from Adam), but in the new creation the male needs the woman to exist (Jesus from Mary)—not referring primarily to human birth in general, but the birth of *the* Man— Jesus Christ, through the woman Mary. As Paul says in Galatians, "When the fullness of time arrived, God sent forth his Son, *born of a woman*" (Galatians 4:4). I am convinced this is the best interpretation of these difficult verses. Paul's affirmation that the first creation, while important to honor, is balanced by the new creation, with the ultimate "Man" (i.e., Christ as "last Adam") coming from a woman, fits precisely the tension Paul faces in both affirming the old reality and denying its priority over the new.

Although Paul apparently allowed women a limited role in the group gatherings, so long as they were exercising prophetic gifts of the Spirit, he lays down a general rule a bit further on in the same letter to the Corinthians:

> As in all the churches of the saints [the chosen ones], the women *should keep silent* in the churches. For they are not permitted to speak, but *should be in submission*, as the Law also says. If there is anything they desire to learn, let them ask their husbands at home. For it is shameful for a woman to speak in church. (1 Corinthians 14:34–35)

By referring to the Law or Torah, Paul is going back again to the created order in Genesis. When Adam and Eve were expelled from the Garden of Eden, Eve was told that, as part of her punishment, "your desire shall be toward your husband and *he shall rule over you*" (Genesis 3:16). As with Paul's previous discussion about women covering themselves with their hair, Paul will brook no compromise on this point, ending his discussion with an appeal to his own authority as one in contact directly with Christ: "If anyone thinks that he is a prophet, or spiritual, he should acknowledge that the things I am writing to you are a *command of the Lord. If* anyone does not recognize this, *he is not recognized*" (1 Corinthians 14:37–38). Here we see that in Paul's churches the single test, in the end, was whether one submitted to what Paul said or not—regardless of any kind of claim to one's own spirituality or prophetic gifts.

Paul's rigid instructions demanding that women be modest, silent, and submissive, with no direct access to Christ other than through their husbands, seems to stand in blatant contradiction to Paul's teaching about baptism into the one body and *being in Christ*. Some interpreters of Paul have gone so far as to suggest that Paul's insistence on the silence of women in 1 Corinthians 14:33b–36 is an interpolation added by a later pious scribe who wanted to take the opportunity to bring Paul into conformity with the writer of 1 Timothy, writing as late as A.D. 100, who had claimed his letter was from Paul:

> Let a woman learn quietly with all submissiveness. I do not permit a woman to teach or to exercise authority over a man; rather, she is to remain quiet. For Adam was formed first, then Eve; and Adam was not deceived, but the woman was deceived and became a transgressor. (1 Timothy 2:11–14)[6]

As appealing as such a suggestion might be as a way to ethically "sanitize" Paul for our modern sensitivities, I think we should resist this kind of editing of his letters. There are no manuscripts of 1 Corinthians that omit this passage, and Paul's demand that women be silent and submissive fits precisely with what he says earlier in his discussion of women's hair. He grounds his dogmatic rulings on the public behavior of women in his understanding of Genesis, which describes how God set the parameters of the present physical creation.

What is much more likely is that the author of 1 Timothy, based on his reading of 1 Corinthians 11, is repeating and expanding Paul's advice. He specifically mentions that women should not braid their hair or wear provocative attire, and that their learning in silence also prohibits them from *teaching* or having any kind of authority over men! The writer, however, in reinforcing Paul's point about the woman being created *after* the man, expands this view of subordination with a new argument, also taken from Genesis: "For Adam was formed first, then Eve; and Adam was not deceived, but the woman was deceived and became a transgressor. Yet the woman will be saved through *the birth of the child*" (1 Timothy 2:14–15).

This passage, like Paul's statement in 1 Corinthians that "in the Lord" *the* man comes from *a* woman, might be taken as a general affirmation of "childbirth," but in both passages the definite article is used with a rare noun that refers to the birth of a child.[7] I am convinced this makes it more likely that the reference is to the birth of Jesus as the second Adam. The author of 1 Timothy is not discussing a woman's general well-being, but how she can be *saved*, having become a transgressor, and having led all of humankind in that fallen direction.[8] Christians came to believe that the reference in Genesis 3:15 to the "seed" of the woman crushing the head of the Serpent, or Satan, was a reference not to offspring in general but to Jesus Christ (Romans 16:20).

How, then, does Paul's view that there is no longer "male nor female" for those baptized into Christ fit with his insistence that the old order of the physical creation, with its male and female roles, be respected and maintained? To answer that question we need to look at his earlier discussion, also in 1 Corinthians, about marriage and celibacy. If there is no longer male or female in Christ, then how are people to live with one another when sexual differences and desires, not to mention married and unmarried states of life, are an ever-present reality that *has not passed away*—outside of Christ?

Paul's advice to the Corinthians on sex and marriage is about as complex and as convoluted as anything he ever wrote, but packed into the single chapter of 1 Corinthians 7, it is the key to understanding the dilemma he and his followers faced. The topic comes up because the Corinthians have written him a letter, apparently quoting back to him a teaching he had given them: "It is good for a man not to touch a woman" (verse 1).

Paul sticks by that general principle while at the same time allowing variation. He clearly would prefer that his followers live a nonsexual life, and cites his own choice of celibacy as an example—"as one who, by the Lord's mercy, is faithful" (verses 7–8, 25). He advises those who are single or widowed, unless they are "aflame with passion," to remain single and celibate (verses 8–9). Marriage is not the ideal, or even the best choice, but is preferable over sexual immorality for those who lack the "gift" to live the nonsexual life (verse 9).

If a couple is engaged, it is better not to marry if they have their sexual desires under control (verses 36–37). If a man and woman are already married, they are not to divorce, except in the case where an "unbeliever" refuses to stay with a Christian partner (verses 12–16). If both are Christians the marriage cannot be broken, though a temporary separation is allowed, either when there are problems or in the case of one or the other wanting to withdraw temporarily to experience the nonsexual life for spiritual reasons (verses 5, 10–12). Several times Paul emphasizes that he is not commanding or requiring celibacy, and just as many times he goes on to say it is nonetheless the better choice.

To support his contention that the nonsexual life is preferable,

Paul stresses that people are living in an acute apocalyptic situation. He refers to *the impending distress* (verse 26) and tells the Corinthians that *the appointed time has grown very short* (verse 29). Paul and his followers expected to live to see Christ return in the clouds of heaven. He believed there was little time left to pursue a normal life: marrying, having children, or going into business. Paul expected society to begin to come unraveled, with social and economic uncertainties, persecutions, and natural disasters:

> *From now on* let those who have wives live as though they had none, and those who mourn as though they were not mourning, and those who rejoice as though they were not rejoicing, and those who buy as though they had no goods, and those who deal with the world as though they had no dealings with it. For the *present form* [*schema*] *of this world is passing away* (29–31).

And that is just the problem. The present world order *is passing away* but it is also still here. Men are men, and women are women, and sexual desires are real and powerful. Marriages have their normal stresses, and people are being born as well as getting sick and dying. In Paul's ideal world of *being in Christ*, none of these things should be happening. Men and women should already have transcended their physical, sexual lives. No one should be getting sick or dying. Sexual immorality should be no temptation whatsoever. If Christ is in them, and they are in Christ, why should any realities of the old creation have any sway? Why should there be any struggle "against the flesh." After all, the "outer nature" is fading while the "inner nature" is being renewed day by day (2 Corinthians 4:16). Paul is profoundly disappointed in his followers, whom he chastises for still living "according to the flesh." He suggests that the reason some are dying is that they have not properly participated in the Lord's Supper (1 Corinthians 11:30). He knows he cannot command sexual abstinence but he had somehow hoped they would have already made their own decisions to take this higher path of spirituality.

For Paul, as a Jew, sexual immorality (*porneia* in Greek) refers to any sexual activity outside a marriage between a man and a woman. This means that he condemns a wide range of sexual practices within Greco-Roman society that were commonly accepted, including homosexuality and sexual intercourse with prostitutes (Romans 1:26–27; 1 Corinthians 6:9–19). He is clear and uncompromising—those who practice such things will *not* inherit the kingdom of God. He avows that the instructions he has given are "through the Lord Jesus," that "the Lord is an avenger of all these things" as he had solemnly warned them, and that anyone who disregards these teachings is disregarding God (1 Thessalonians 4:6). Marriage is an available "remedy" but even better is a pure devotion to Christ.

Paul is giving the Corinthians practical advice. Though baptized into Christ, they are nonetheless part of the "old world" that is passing away. He tells them it is better not to marry "to spare them worldly troubles," or so they can be "free from anxieties," since the apocalyptic crisis is upon them (1 Corinthians 7:28, 32). Those women who have chosen to marry must be submissive to their husbands, as God decreed to Adam and Eve from the beginning. They have chosen the old world, so they must continue to live within it. He is particularly concerned that they behave in ways that promote what he calls "good order" (1 Corinthians 7:35; 14:40). The word he uses in Greek, *euschemonos*, means "a good arrangement." It refers to a proper standard of ordered decency. But the problem, of course, is that he also says the present *schema*, or "order" of things, is passing away. In the end he can't resist pointing out that those who like him cast aside their sexuality through the gift of the Spirit experience purer devotion to Christ. They are holy *in body* as well as in spirit. But even after saying that, he repeats once again that he wants to lay no necessity upon them (1 Corinthians 7:34–35). He is having difficulty balancing his instruction between the old order and the new one.

NEITHER SLAVE NOR FREE

Paul compounds his claim that there is neither male nor female "in Christ" with the equally startling claim that slavery and freedom no longer exist, either (Galatians 3:28). If the one is gender nonsense the other is surely socioeconomic naïveté, to say the least. After all, Paul admits that his gospel was "foolishness" (literally "moronic") to those who are perishing, but contained a secret wisdom and power only those chosen could understand through the Spirit (1 Corinthians 1:18–24; 2:12–13).

During Paul's lifetime, under the emperors Augustus, Tiberius, Caligula, Claudius, and Nero, the practice of slavery was widespread and even those of modest means routinely owned a few slaves.[9] It is estimated that out of a population of 45 million in the empire under Augustus (31 B.C. to A.D. 14), at least 20–30 percent were slaves. The majority of them had become slaves as a result of Roman military conquest. Slaves worked in private homes, on farms and estates, in factories and mines, on public projects. They were absolutely essential to the vast imperial governmental network spread throughout every Roman province, not to mention the bureaucratic central administration in Rome. In Italy the percentage of slaves was much higher, estimated as high as 40 percent of the population. Some were poor and destitute, others were quite privileged and educated, but even household slaves were provided food, clothing, and shelter of significantly less quality than family members enjoyed. Slaves were considered property and owners exercised absolute *dominium* or "lordship" over them. Legally, slaves had no rights, even to family or property. Children born to slaves belonged to the owner. Even though there were some laws against the extreme abuse of slaves, they could be beaten, punished, and used sexually as their owners pleased.[10]

There were also large numbers of ex-slaves or freedmen, called *libertini*, who enjoyed limited rights of voting and ownership of property after their legal manumission. Many visitors to Pompeii have marveled at the luxurious House of the Vettii, owned by the Vettius brothers, who evidently were freedmen. Cicero, the first-century B.C. Roman philosopher and statesman, had a slave named Tiro who served ably as his secretary and confidant. Cicero and his children loved him. In A.D. 53 Cicero freed Tiro when the latter was fifty years old. Tiro edited some of Cicero's letters after he died and even composed a biography of his former master. He is credited with perfecting a form of shorthand and is thus responsible for the recording of so many of Cicero's speeches.[11]

Obviously, for a slave to obtain freedom was a highly prized opportunity. Paul has been roundly criticized for condoning slavery by not demanding that Christian slave owners free their slaves. But his position on slavery, as with all issues of social and ethnic identity, is consistent. Three times in this context Paul repeats what he calls his "rule in all the churches," namely that everyone should lead the life that "the Lord has distributed to him" at the time he or she was "invited" through the gospel (1 Corinthians 7:17). He explains:

> Everyone should remain in the calling in which he was called. Were you a slave when called? Never mind. Even if you can gain your freedom, make use of [the slavery].[12] For he who was called *in the Lord* as a slave is a freedman of the Lord. Likewise he who was free when called is a *slave of Christ*. (1 Corinthians 7:20–22)

In Paul's view, even if one is a slave he or she is actually free—*in the Lord*. And those who are free are "slaves" of Christ—so all such differences are of no consequence. They exist but they don't exist, depending on which "world" is one's reference point.

Paul repeats for a third time his general rule: "So, brethren, in whatever calling each was called there let him remain *with God*" (1 Corinthians 7:24). His rule here is precisely parallel to what he says about marriage: "Are you bound to a wife? Do not seek to be free. Are you free from a wife? Do not seek marriage" (1 Corinthians 7:27). And though he does not forbid marriage, he also would not forbid that a slave accept manumission—he just prefers that everyone remain as they are since God was the one who put them in such circumstances in the first place. Paul believed that *all things* work together for good for those who are called according to his purposes (Romans 8:28). That means to be a slave could potentially be a good thing, since God is the one who has ordered everything.

Paul's rule, thrice repeated here, is laid down in the context of his expectation of the impending apocalypse, so that if the "appointed time has grown very short," no current state of life in which one finds oneself is a lasting condition. But what is more important, any "calling" one finds oneself in is just that—one that he says the Lord assigned, for his own purposes.

As with marriage and sexuality, however, the short time left before Christ returns is not as important a factor as the spiritual reality one already has *in Christ*. With God there is neither male nor female, neither slave nor free. On the level of what he calls "the flesh," such matters might seem important, but from the viewpoint of those *in Christ*, all such states of life are transcended by the new creation, which is already here—but has not yet arrived!

Paul applied this principle of living lawfully within the society and accepting things as ordered by God even to the Roman governing authorities: "Let every person be subject to the governing authorities. For there is no authority except from God and those that exist have been instituted by God. Therefore he who resists the authorities resists what God has appointed and those who resist incur judgment" (Romans 13:1–2). Christians are to pay their taxes, showing respect and honor to those in authority (Romans 13:7). Considering that Paul's life spans the reigns of Roman emperors of the likes of Caligula and Nero, notorious for their cruelty and ruthlessness, this instruction is really quite remarkable. One might think that Paul's apocalyptic stance regarding the imminent overthrow of the present evil world, not to mention the Roman military occupation of his homeland, would preclude his referring to the Roman authorities as God's servants. In Paul's view the present economic and social configuration of society was a matter of indifference. God orders present circumstances but all is in the process of passing away.

Toward the end of his life, when Paul was imprisoned in Rome in the early 60s A.D., contemplating that he might not live to see the return of Christ, he took a much more practical approach to slavery. It just so happens that the last letter we have from him, only a page or two in length, deals with this very subject. Paul writes from prison in Rome to Philemon, one of his more well-to-do converts, who lived in Asia Minor. Paul had chanced upon a runaway slave, named Onesimus, belonging to Philemon and whom he had converted to Christianity. Roman law required that runaway slaves be sent back to their owners and anyone aiding such a fugitive could be liable for damages. Paul writes from prison that he is sending Onesimus back, and subtly hints, but does not demand, that Philemon free him to serve Paul. He even offers to pay any damages Onesimus might owe. Paul suggests that perhaps Onesimus's running away was for some greater purpose, so that Philemon could "have him back forever, no longer as a slave but more than a slave, as a beloved brother . . . *both in the flesh and in the Lord*" (verse 16). Paul still maintains that one's state of life "in the flesh" is nothing to compare to one's "freedom" in the Lord—but nonetheless, he sees that being free in the flesh, as well as in the Lord, could have a decided practical advantage.

One might see some inconsistency here in that Paul expects the life of the flesh to go on with respect to slavery, paying taxes, and living in submission to Roman civil rule, while he seems to expect his followers somehow to transcend the flesh with respect to matters of sexuality, marriage, ethnic identity, and vocation. It is obvious that he himself is caught up in the very tensions implied by his "already but not yet" stance regarding the imminent termination of history with the arrival of Christ in the clouds of heaven, and its "delay" as the decade of the 50s passed. What he most wants to see is harmony and good order in his communities, so that within and without, peace can prevail. He is forging new ground in that he is willing to take his followers outside the parameters of Jewish culture, in which matters of life in this world and the world to come were generally balanced in favor of the former. The danger was that his form of "Christianity," freed from the practicalities of the Torah while attempting to live "as if" this world were already passing away, led to constant confusion and conflict among his followers.

Not the least of these conflicts created by Paul's teaching about the new world, already here, but not yet fully realized, had to do with the thorny question of ethics. How were those who were united with Christ to live in the present world? Judaism pointed to the revelation of the Torah given by Moses, but Paul had decidedly declared that his followers were no longer subject to that system of law and ethics, being instead "free in Christ." In the following chapter we will see how Paul's creation of a new "Torah of Christ" paved the way for a decisive break between him and the Jewish apostles and followers of Jesus who remained firmly rooted in their Jewish heritage.

EIGHT

THE TORAH OF CHRIST

Was Jesus a Jew or a Christian? I often pose this question to my students as we begin my college course called Christian Origins. The course takes a broad overview of the development of earliest Christianity just past the end of the first century. The question is intentionally provocative, posed to get at the heart of the matter. How was it that Jesus the Jew founded a movement that eventually made a clean break with Judaism, casting it aside as obsolete, and went on its way as a separate new religion called Christianity?

Did Jesus plant the seeds of that definitive split? Did James the brother of Jesus, along with Peter and the other twelve apostles, remain Jews, observing the Torah and maintaining the traditions of their Jewish heritage? What about Paul? Did he remain a Jew, observant of Torah, as the book of Acts maintains, insisting only that his non-Jewish converts not be forced to become Jewish? Or did his understanding of his newly revealed Gospel so completely supersede his former Jewish faith as to transform it into what could only be called a new religion?

Scholars have devoted an inordinate amount of attention to this "parting of the ways," that is, the eventual break between Judaism and Christianity and how and when it came about.[1] What we can be quite sure of is that by the second century and beyond, Jews did not want to be confused with the Christians and the Christians wanted nothing to do with the Jews, considering them a rejected people without Christ.[2] Ignatius, bishop of Antioch, writing around A.D. 110, could hardly be any clearer:

> Do not be deceived by strange doctrines or antiquated myths, since they are worthless. For *if we continue to live in accordance with Judaism*, we admit that we have not received grace. (*Magnesians* 8:1)

> It is utterly absurd to profess Jesus Christ and to practice Judaism. For Christianity did not believe in Judaism, but Judaism in Christianity, in which "every tongue" believed and "was brought together" to God. (*Magnesians* 10:3)

> But if anyone expounds Judaism to you, do not listen to him. For it is better to hear about Christianity from a man who is circumcised than Judaism from one who is not. But if either of them fail to speak about Jesus Christ, I look on them as tombstones and graves of the dead, upon which only the names of men are inscribed. (*Philadelphians* 6:1)

The term "Christianity" (*Christianismos*) appears here for the first time in any ancient source, showing how early this separate religion was emerging, in distinction from Judaism, its ancient mother faith. The verb Ignatius uses here, translated as "practice Judaism" ('*ioudaizo*), means to "live like a Jew," referring particularly to the identifying marks of inclusion in the Mosaic covenant, such as the dietary laws, the observance of the Sabbath and Jewish festivals, and the circumcision of male children. The concern that Ignatius and other early Christian leaders had over the next two centuries was that Gentile Christians would continue to be attracted to Jewish observances.[3] Apparently this concern was justified because statements repudiating the Jews as an obstinate race from whom God's favor had been removed, as well as strong prohibitions against any sort of Jewish observances, are common throughout the writings of the early Christian fathers.

Paul insisted that none of his Gentile converts was bound to keep the Jewish commandments but the issue of what Paul himself practiced as a Jew, and what he told other Jews, either openly or secretly, about their obligations in the Jesus movement brought him into the sharpest conflict he had with the Jewish Christianity espoused by the Jerusalem church, led by James and the apostles. For any Jew to disregard these commandments and related observances as obsolete and superseded by the coming of Christ amounted to nothing less than the abolition of Judaism. If Jews ceased to practice circumcision or any of the distinctive observances that separated them from the "nations," it would be only a matter of a generation or two that their "Jewishness," even by the most general definition, would disappear. If they, in addition, took on the practices and faith of a new religion, particularly one that espouses tenets that are alien to Judaism, the rupture and loss of identity would become complete.

I believe that Paul is indeed a "second" founder of Christianity and that he departed from his former Jewish faith in such a radical way that his gospel cannot by any stretch of definition be called "Judaism." Paul never uses the word "Christian," nor does Jesus for that matter, but I am convinced that Paul promulgated his version of messianic "Christ faith," which he calls his gospel and which laid the foundation for a new religion, entirely separate from Judaism. All labels are inadequate, and pigeonholing is difficult, since the definitions one ends up using for either the term "Christian" or "Jew" can vary so much, but the positions Paul takes on the fundamental tenets of Judaism are quite clear. I use the term "second founder" because I want to reserve the use of the term "Christian" to describe a form of the faith associated with Jesus, his brother

James, Peter, and the rest of the twelve apostles, who I argue stood in solidarity together.

NEITHER JEW NOR GREEK

The Romans divided the world into "Greeks" and "barbarians," that is, those who were civilized through exposure to the language and culture of Greco-Roman society, and those on the frontiers of the empire who "babbled" in a foreign tongue. The Jews had their own sharp, twofold division of humankind—themselves and all who were non-Jews. If one was not Jewish, either by birth or conversion, one was classified as among the "nations"—which meant the rest of the world. The word "nation" in Greek (*ethnos*) meant "Gentile" for the Jews.

For the Jews such a division of humankind was not merely a matter of ethnic or cultural solidarity. Jews were scattered throughout the Roman Empire and beyond, speaking various languages, and many Jews living under Roman rule were thoroughly "Greek" in both language and culture. What separated Jews from all the other "nations" was a double claim. First, that they served the only true and living God, so that the so-called gods of the nations were mere idols—which meant "no gods," or even false gods. Second, that God had chosen Abraham and his descendants, had made a special covenant with them, and had revealed to them the Law, or Torah, of Moses, the observance of which set them apart from all the other nations. Not all Jews believed or accepted these claims in the same way, or agreed on what it meant to live as a Jew according to the Torah. Jews, and the forms of "Judaism" they practiced, or chose to ignore, were as varied in Roman times as they are today.[4]

Non-Jews were not left out of this Jewish vision of humanity, since God was the Creator of all humankind and on the Day of Judgment would hold Jews and non-Jews alike accountable for their behavior.[5] Righteous Gentiles were to shun the worship of idols, turn to the one true God, and live by the universal ethical precepts revealed in the Torah as applicable to all humankind. This did not make one a Jew, and conversion to Judaism was neither required nor expected. Such Gentiles were known as "God-fearers" who, alongside the people of Israel, stood as witness to the one God and his ethical standards of righteousness. At Jewish synagogues, spread through all the cities of the ancient Roman world, one would find non-Jews gathered alongside the Jewish worshippers to hear the reading of the Torah and the Prophets and to listen to the preaching of Moses.[6] In the gospels, Jesus once commended a Roman centurion at Capernaum in Galilee as having more faith than he had found in all of Israel—warning the people that the kingdom of God would include those from all nations, gathered alongside Abraham, Isaac, and Jacob, with Jews who were unrighteous cast out (Luke 7:1–10; Matthew 8:5–13). Paul shared this perspective, contrasting one who is "uncircumcised" but lives a moral life with one who is "circumcised" but lives immorally (Romans 2:25–29). It was his view that the non-Jew would have favor with God while the Jew would be condemned at the Judgment.

If Paul had left it at that, his position would have been acceptable to other Jews, including James, Peter, and the Jerusalem church. But he said things that they found unacceptable. To say that a "righteous" Gentile is more acceptable to God than an "unrighteous" Jew is one thing, but then to go on to affirm that such a Jew, without Christ, is not a "real Jew" while the righteous Gentile is actually the *true* Jew is quite another. That would imply that the Gentile has thus "replaced" the Jew, an idea that would have been repudiated by most Jews.

What Paul's Jewish teachers would have said is that Jews remain Jews no matter what their level of adherence to God's covenant with Israel, while Gentiles remain Gentiles, whether righteous or unrighteous—but that both will be judged by the moral standards applicable to each. In other words faith in God and living a moral life are *not* the determiner of Jewishness, but rather participation in the special covenant made with Abraham is. One became part of that Abrahamic covenant by birth, since God had made the covenant with Abraham and *his descendants*. One could also become a Jew through conversion to Judaism. If a Gentile underwent such a formal conversion he or she was considered thereafter a Jew, or member of the house of Israel, and no longer a Gentile. Even a Jewish figure as illustrious as the great second-century A.D. rabbi Akiva ben Joseph was from a family of converts to Judaism. Indeed the rabbis say it is forbidden, once one has converted to Judaism, even to refer to the person's past.[7] From a Jewish perspective Jews remain Jews, Gentiles remain Gentiles, and God will judge both accordingly.

As a Jew Paul had accepted the basic pillars of Judaism—one Creator God, Israel as the chosen people, and the Torah divinely revealed to Moses—as well as the place of Gentile God-fearers in God's plan. He says, "I advanced in Judaism beyond many of my own age among my people, so extremely zealous was I for the traditions of my fathers" (Galatians 1:14). He lived strictly as a Pharisee and he says that when it came to the Torah and its observance he was "blameless" (Philippians 3:5–6). Paul would have valued the various markers of Israelite distinction and identity, setting the Jews apart from the nations, whether by circumcision, dietary laws, observance of Sabbaths and festivals, or laws of ritual purity.

Once Paul received his revelation from Christ, accepting Jesus as cosmic Lord, exalted to the right hand of God, everything changed. Paul refers to his former life as a Jew as "rubbish" compared to the new status of being in Christ (Philippians 3:8). His core beliefs were not merely modified, updated, or amplified: they were wholly recast in the light of what he calls the "mystery" of the gospel he had received.

In Paul's new vision of things, a non-Jew, in order to be "saved" from God's judgment, must turn from idols to the one God and also bow the knee in worship to Jesus as Lord—something Jews would be forbidden to do. In the *Amida*, the central Jewish prayer that dates back to pre-Christian times, one bows the knee three times at the mention of God's holiness.[8] The prophet Isaiah had said that in the time to come "every knee would bow, and every tongue confess" that Yahweh is God and there is no other (Isaiah 45:23). Paul amends that very text to say that every knee would bow and every tongue would confess *Jesus as Lord*—to the glory of God the Father (Philippians 2:10–11). This single move, in which a human being is considered equal to God and thus worthy of worship, separates Paul's version of Christianity from Judaism and effectively creates a new "religion" separate from most mainstream Judaism.[9] But Paul goes much further.

Paul denigrates the Jewish people as "Israel according to the flesh," broken off the tree of Israel, cut off from God, and dying like cast off branches on the ground, because of their unbelief in Jesus as Lord and Christ. They are now replaced by a new and true Israel—according to the Spirit. Finally, Paul says that the Torah of Moses was never intended to be permanent; it was given through the mediation of angels, not directly by God, and having served its temporary purpose in leading both Jews and Gentiles to Christ, it has been superseded. Here are a few samples of his clear declarations on these points:

The One God

> We know that an idol has no real existence, and that there is *no God but one*. For although there may be so-called gods in heaven or on earth—as indeed there are many "gods" and many "lords," yet for us there is one God, the Father . . . *and one Lord, Jesus Christ*. (1 Corinthians 8:4–6)

> You turned to God from idols, to serve a living and true God, and to wait for his Son from heaven, whom he raised from the

dead, Jesus who delivers us from the wrath to come. (1 Thessalonians 1:9b–10)

The Chosen Nation Israel

For we are the true circumcision, who worship by the Spirit of God and put no confidence in the flesh. (Philippians 3:3)

For neither circumcision counts for anything, nor uncircumcision, but a new creation. (Galatians 6:15)

The Torah of Moses

For Christ is the end of the Torah, that everyone who has faith may be justified. (Romans 10:4)

Now before faith came, we were confined under the Torah, kept under restraint until faith should be revealed. So the Torah was our custodian until Christ came, that we might be justified by faith. But now that faith has come, we are no longer under a custodian. (Galatians 3:23–25)

Paul's statements in these three areas not only separate him from the various forms of Judaism of his day; they also serve to exclude Jews, who do not bow the knee to Jesus as Lord, from the "new Israel" that Paul believes God is creating through one's union with the Christ-Spirit. Simply put, the implication of what Paul teaches is no less than the demise of Judaism.

Circumcision means "being a Jew," either by birth or conversion, but that genealogical connection to Abraham counts for nothing now that the new creation has come. However, as was the case with male and female, or slave and free, the problem that Paul and his adherents faced was that Jews and Judaism did not disappear with the coming of Christ. Far from it. The Temple in Jerusalem continued as Judaism's center, the Torah was honored and observed, Jewish learning flourished, and there were synagogues in every major city and town throughout the Roman Empire. Even those Jews who accepted Jesus as Messiah never imagined that this implied they should cease to practice their Jewish faith or that the coming of Jesus redefined the Jewish people. Jesus himself had lived as an observant Jew. His brother James was known for his piety and devotion to the Torah.

James and the Jerusalem apostles would have agreed with Paul on many points but the Jewish people were still Israel, the Torah remained valid "until heaven and earth passed away," and God alone was to be worshipped, with none beside him. Jesus had not come to destroy the Torah. He had upheld even the "least" of its commandments.

FOLLOWING THE TORAH OF CHRIST

Paul finds himself caught between two worlds and cannot resist operating, even as a Jew, as if the old world has already passed away and been replaced by the new creation. He adopts a situational stance that was difficult to characterize, since he believed that whether one lived as a Jew or as a Gentile was a matter of indifference to one *in Christ*. He offers this surprisingly candid assessment of his own approach to Jews as well as Gentiles:

> To the Jews I became as a Jew, in order to win over Jews; to those under the Torah I became as one under the Torah—though not myself under the Torah—that I might win those under the Torah. To those outside the Torah [i.e., Gentiles], I became as one outside the Torah—not being without "To-

rah" to God, but under the Torah of Christ—that I might win
those outside the Torah. (1 Corinthians 9:20–21)[10]

Paul says here that all of those in Christ, whether Jew or Gentile,
are under a new Law or Torah—the Law of Christ. He clearly has
no written code in mind, so what is this *Law of Christ*—what are
its precepts and contents and what does it mean to be under its jurisdiction? The answer is quite surprising.

Paul believed that Gentiles, who he says are "outside the Torah,"
were not part of the special covenant God made with the nation of
Israel and thus had no formally written Law. He also agreed with
the rabbis who taught that the nations of the world were still morally responsible for a minimum set of universal human ethics that
had been revealed to Noah as the father of the entire human race
after the Flood. These "Noahide" laws were variously enumerated
in Jewish sources, both before and after the time of Jesus, but they
included prohibitions against idolatry, sexual immorality, murder,
stealing, cruelty to animals, and eating blood, as well as positive
injunctions to honor parents and practice social justice, including
loving one's neighbor.[11] Like other Jews of his time, Paul considered all humankind morally responsible to God as Creator through
the gift of reason and the natural law revealed by one's conscience.
Paul believed that Gentiles had no excuse for turning from worship of the Creator to worshipping the forces of nature. He writes
the Romans:

> For the invisible things of him since the creation of the world
> are clearly seen, being perceived through the things that are
> made, even his everlasting power and divinity; that they may
> be without excuse: because that, knowing God, they glorified
> him not as God, neither gave thanks; but became vain in their
> reasoning, and their senseless heart was darkened . . . they
> changed the glory of the incorruptible God for the likeness

of an image of corruptible man, and of birds, and four-footed beasts, and creeping things. (Romans 1:20–23)

This is a common Jewish polemic against the Gentile world and what was viewed as their willful foolishness in turning to idols. Paul follows here, almost word for word, the thoughts of the author of the *Wisdom of Solomon*, a first-century B.C. Jewish text now included in the Apocrypha:[12]

> For all people who were ignorant of God were foolish by nature; and they were unable from the good things that are seen to know the one who exists, nor did they recognize the artisan while paying heed to his works . . . Yet again, not even they are to be excused; for if they had the power to know so much [about science] they could find sooner the one who made these things. (*Wisdom* 13:1, 9)

The author of the *Wisdom of Solomon* goes on to argue that "the idea of making idols was the beginning of sexual immorality," which then led to all other sins, and Paul follows his chain of thought precisely, offering a long litany of Gentile vices:

> For this cause God gave them up unto vile passions: for their women changed the natural use into that which is against nature: and likewise also the men, leaving the natural use of the woman, burned in their lust one toward another . . . being filled with all unrighteousness, wickedness, covetousness, maliciousness; full of envy, murder, strife, deceit, malignity; whisperers, backbiters, hateful to God, insolent, haughty, boastful, inventors of evil things, disobedient to parents, without understanding, covenant-breakers, without natural affection, unmerciful: who, knowing the ordinance of God, that they that practice such things are worthy of death. (Romans 1:26–32)

According to Paul, God's general principle of judgment will be to hold Jews, who are "under the Law," responsible for what the Law demands, while holding Gentiles, who are "without the Law," responsible for the law "written in their hearts," with their conscience either accusing or excusing them accordingly (Romans 2:12-16).

There is nothing in Paul's position as expressed here in the opening chapters of Romans that is antithetical to Judaism. The rabbis of Paul's day would have agreed with his essential points regarding the sinfulness of both Jews and Gentiles and God's righteous judgment of all humanity.

In his letters Paul frequently offers a basic moral catalogue of prohibited activities, insisting quite adamantly that his followers live up to such minimal standards of moral behavior:

> Do you not know that the unrighteous will not inherit the kingdom of God? Do not be deceived; neither the immoral, nor idolaters, nor adulterers, nor those receiving sodomy, nor those committing sodomy, nor thieves, nor the greedy, nor drunkards, nor revilers, nor robbers will inherit the kingdom of God. And such were some of you. But you were washed, you were sanctified, you were justified in the name of the Lord Jesus Christ and in the Spirit of our God. (1 Corinthians 6:9-11)

That is why Paul is so outraged when he receives the report that one of the brothers at Corinth is living with his father's wife, apparently his stepmother—a kind of sexual immorality, he says, that is "not even found among the Gentiles" (1 Corinthians 5:1-5). Paul demands that the man be expelled immediately from the congregation in a formal ceremony that would deliver him back to Satan—a kind of reverse baptism, so that he is no longer considered in Christ.

Sexual immorality (Greek *porneia*), along with idolatry, and eating blood, seemed to be the three points of the Noahide laws that presented the most difficulties for Gentile God-fearers—whether Christian or not. Prohibitions against murder, stealing, and injustice, as well as honor of parents, would be upheld in Greco-Roman culture as much as among the Jews, so they were not matters of dispute. But what did it mean to "turn from idols"? It was understood that one would no longer worship at a temple of one of the dozens of Greco-Roman gods, but what about ancillary activities such as eating meat sold in the marketplace that had been sacrificed to a pagan god, or attending a festival connected to one of the gods as part of a civic celebration? Sexual immorality was defined much more broadly within Judaism as well. Prostitution, homosexuality, and sex of any kind before or outside marriage were considered sinful and broadly categorized as *porneia*. Eating blood was almost inevitable, since the techniques of butchering animals used in Greco-Roman society did not include the elaborate Jewish measures to remove all blood from the flesh. In fact, animals were often strangled and hung up in the meat market with all the blood and organs intact. Those living a strict Jewish life would consider all such behavior as unrighteous and they would expect God-fearers to do so as well.

Paul deals with all of these topics in some detail, particularly in his first letter to the Corinthians. The stance he takes is complex and a bit confusing because his instincts are to allow "freedom in Christ" and not put his followers "under law" in a formal and legalistic way. On sexual matters he is quite strict and uncompromising, whereas on food and diet he tends to be openly liberal. With regard to "meat offered to idols" he had emphasized that "an idol is nothing" so that these sacrifices to "nothing" should be inconsequential to one who has the proper knowledge. He says one can eat whatever meat is sold in the marketplace without raising questions about where it came from—that is, had it been slaughtered on an altar in the temple of one of the Greco-Roman deities? Whether this would include meat from animals killed without draining their blood ("things strangled") Paul never specifies, but one has the impression he was not stringent on that point. He tells the Corinthians that if they are invited to dinner at the house of a nonbeliever in Christ, to just go ahead and eat whatever is served, and presumably this could include meat from animals that had been strangled, or slaughtered at an idol's temple (1 Corinthians 10:25–26).

He had taught his followers the general principle that "all things are lawful," and the Corinthians quote this back to him, but he did not intend that to be applied to justify sexual immorality. He had to clarify and back off considerably on that point. Some of the Corinthians were apparently frequenting the brothels and Paul was quite outraged (1 Corinthians 6:15–16). Others, as we have seen, were attending festivals at temples and participating in the meals, in effect, as Paul puts it, "eating at the idol's table" and thus essentially worshipping demons! (1 Corinthians 10:14–22).

In all of these areas Paul tries to walk a thin line between allowing freedom, considering the scruples of Jews and other God-fearers who might be stricter in their interpretations, while maintaining a strict standard against any kind of sexual immorality or involvement at local temples that might involve spiritual bonding with demonic forces. Paul expects that these principles, along with his basic moral catalogue of prohibited activities, which he derived from his Jewish background, would be an obvious minimum standard of behavior for "those in Christ," but they did not even touch the new Law of Christ.

For this reason Paul was profoundly disappointed with all his churches. They never seemed to grasp what he believed was their heavenly calling—to be part of the glorified God-family—so that such petty minimal standards, either of the Jewish Torah, or the Noahide laws, would pale in significance before the spiritual Law of Christ. Paul mentions the term "Law of Christ" only two times in his letters—in 1 Corinthians and Galatians. These communities

were his most fractured and troubled, and his frustrations and disappointment with both are evident. He told the Corinthians that
living as a Jew under the Torah, or as a non-Jew "outside" the Torah,
were of no consequence or interest to him—since he considered
himself "under the Law of Christ." He puts it to the Galatians as an
exhortation: "Bear one another's burdens, and so fulfill the Law of
Christ!" (Galatians 6:2). He had just explained that only those "led
by the Spirit" were no longer "under the Law," and that if one practiced what he calls the "works of the flesh," including such things
as sexual immorality, idolatry, envy, murder, and selfishness, one
would be excluded from inheriting the kingdom of God—in other
words one's newly engendered life as a potential glorified child of
God would be aborted (Galatians 5:18–21).

The Law of Christ is not a list of precepts or prohibitions, but
rather involved what Paul calls "walking by the Spirit." Paul believed that only those who were *united with Christ*, who had the
Spirit of Christ, could "put to death" the desires of the flesh and be
led by the Spirit. He saw this as a deeply internal moral battle, not
a set of external behavioral measures—but it is a relentless struggle that continues daily. It never ceases and it is never won: "For
the desires of the flesh are against the Spirit, and the desires of the
Spirit are against the flesh; for these are opposed to each other, to
prevent you from doing what you would" (Galatians 5:17).

In his letter to the Romans he explains more fully, and here one
sees clearly Paul's "already but not yet" dilemma working to its full-
est. Those who have the Spirit of Christ are "not in the flesh" but
"in the Spirit," yet their life in the body continues, and the body remains "dead" because of sin. Paul sees this as an existential condition, a dichotomy of being—never to be solved by moral victory but
only to be resisted and struggled against. He goes so far as to say
that when one sins, it is not really that person who sins—but their
sinful "flesh" that does so. He explains this on a very personal level,
speaking of his own unending struggle with sexual temptation:

I do not understand my own actions. For I do not do what I want, but I do the very thing I hate. Now if I do what I do not want, I agree that the law [against "lust"] is good. So then it is no longer "I" that do it, but sin that dwells within me. For I know that nothing good dwells within me, that is, in my flesh. I can will what is right, but I cannot do it. For I do not do the good I want, but the evil I do not want is what I do. Nor if I do what I do not want, it is no longer "I" that do it, but sin which dwells within me (Romans 7:15–20).

Paul had introduced the description of this struggle by quoting one of the Ten Commandments: "You shall not desire [Greek *epithumeo*] your neighbor's wife" (Deuteronomy 5:21; Exodus 20:17). He says that as a child one would not be aware of this "Law" against coveting, but once one was able to realize the implications of the commandment, most likely as an adolescent, the prohibition itself, finding opportunity "through sin," caused "all sorts of lust in me" (Romans 7:8–9). He does not fault the "Law" itself, which he calls "good, holy, and just," but rather the "sin" that dwelt in his fleshly nature.

According to Paul there is no solution to this struggle, no victory to be won over the "flesh" until the body is shed at the resurrection and one becomes wholly transformed. Yet in the meantime, one has no choice but to resist—and that is the most that can be expected and required. He writes, "if you live according to the flesh you will die, but if by the Spirit you put to death the deeds of the body you will live. For all who are led by the Spirit of God are sons of God" (Romans 8:14). Paul's point here is that "to put to death the deeds of the body" is not to win the battle against sin—in this case sexual lust—but to denounce the flesh itself. That is the operational base of the problem. That way when one does "sin" it is not the person who is sinning, but their "flesh," which they have denounced.

Such a view of sin and human responsibility runs directly counter to what finds in the Torah, or in most forms of Judaism. Though there is within Jewish tradition what is called a *yetzer ra*, an "inclination to do evil," there is also, equally at work, the *yetzer tov*, the "inclination to do good." They are not mismatched, but represent two choices, and one can overcome the other. God warns Cain when he is incensed with jealousy against his brother Abel: "If you do well, will you not be accepted? And if you do not well, sin is couching at the door; its desire is for you, but you must master it" (Genesis 4:7). Moses, in rehearsing all the commandments of the Torah before the assembly of ancient Israelites, states:

> For this commandment that I command you this day is not too hard for you ... But the word is very near you; it is in your mouth and in your heart, so that you can do it. See, I have set before you this day life and good, death and evil. ... therefore choose life, that you and your descendants may live ... (Deuteronomy 30:11–19)

In Paul's experience such is not the case. God's standard of judgment—to reward those who do good, whether Jew or Gentile, and punish those who do evil, whether Jew or Gentile—becomes moot because ultimately there are none who can do the good (Romans 2:9–12; 3:9–10). The giving of the Torah to Israel at Sinai ironically only served to "increase sin," since it set forth standards that were even more demanding than those of the Noahide laws (Romans 5:20). Everything was calculated in God's plan to bring humankind, both Jew and Gentile, to Christ, since it was only in Christ that the "flesh," along with sin and death, could eventually be destroyed.

I don't mean to suggest here that Paul was indifferent to sin and moral failure in his claim that all one could do was struggle. It all has to do with whether one is in Christ or outside. The Law of Christ, which operates by the Spirit of Christ dwelling within a person, is a strategy of resistance, activated by "yielding" to the Spirit and not to the flesh. Those who live "according to the flesh," without actively engaging in the struggle, he says, will be excluded from the kingdom.

IMITATE ME

Even though Paul believes his followers have been baptized into Christ and thus have received the Spirit of Christ, he likens their utter failure to grasp the implications of the freedom in Christ, under the Torah of Christ, to stunted spiritual growth. He writes the Corinthians:

> But I, brethren, could not address you as spiritual men, but as men of the flesh, as babes in Christ. I fed you with milk, not solid food; for you were not ready for it; and even yet you are not ready, for you are still *of the flesh*. For while there is jealousy and strife among you are you not of the flesh, and behaving like *ordinary men*. (1 Corinthians 3:1–3)

Paul's language is most interesting here. To be "of the flesh" is to behave in ordinary, normal, human ways, whether one is a Jew or a Gentile, whereas to be "of the Spirit" is to leave behind petty human regard for self-promotion. As we have seen, the list of problems in the Corinthian group that have been reported to Paul include bitter divisions into factious groups, taking one another to court in lawsuits, going to brothels, a case of incest, drunkenness, eating at idol temples, and abusing the sacredness of the Lord's Supper.

Paul's disappointment stems from his perspective of the exalted "heavenly" status of these Spirit-engendered followers. He finds it hard to comprehend how such a cluster of weaknesses would even arise in the first place. He says, for example, "To have lawsuits at all with one another is a defeat for you," implying that they have not

even taken the first tiny step toward any kind of spiritual maturity
(1 Corinthians 6:7).

Paul's approach is a complex mixture of sharp rebuke, sham-
ing, admonition, and encouragement, but in the end, since the
freedom under the Law of Christ seems so elusive to the group, he
demands that they look to him as a kind of "second" Christ:

> I am not writing you to shame you, but to admonish you as
> beloved children. For if you have numerous guides in Christ,
> you do not have many fathers, since *I begot you in Christ Jesus
> through the Gospel.* I urge you, *imitate me!* This is why I sent
> Timothy to you . . . to remind you of *my ways in Christ* as I
> teach them in all the churches. Some are arrogant as though I
> were not coming to you, but I will arrive soon, if the Lord wills,
> and I will ascertain the power of these puffed up ones, not their
> talk. For the Kingdom of God does not exist on talk but on
> power! What do you prefer? Shall I come to you with a rod,
> or with love in a spirit of gentleness? (1 Corinthians 4:14–21)

This language implies far more than the idea of "follow my example." What Paul suggests here is that he has effectively become an
extension of the Christ-Spirit in the world—at least for those he has
"fathered" through his Gospel. He tells the group that when he arrives to visit them he will come with the power of Christ behind
him, and like a parent will either treat them with gentleness or punish them with a thrashing. This sense in which Paul sees himself
as an extension of Christ is very clear in his instructions of how to
deal with a man who is having sexual relations with his stepmother:

> For though absent in body *I am present in Spirit,* and I have
> already pronounced judgment *as present,* in the name of the
> Lord Jesus on the man who has done such a thing. When you
> are assembled, and *my Spirit is present,* with the power of our

> Lord Jesus, you are to deliver this man to Satan for the de-
> struction of the flesh, that his spirit may be saved in the day of
> the Lord Jesus. (1 Corinthians 5:3–5)

Here we see that Jesus is present in power *through* Paul's "Spirit,"
which I put in upper case to indicate that he has become the operational locus for the Spirit of Christ. This rather bizarre ceremony, a kind of "reverse exorcism," will effectively put the guilty
man "outside" of Christ, back in the realm of Satan, who is the "god
of the world." Like baptism and the Lord's Supper, such a Spirit-
empowered activity is far from symbolic. In such a state the man
can be buffeted and attacked freely by Satan, whose powers he had
once escaped, with the hope that he might realize his error and
perhaps return to the fold. Socially such a one was to be shunned.
Paul sternly demands that they are "not even to eat with such a
one" (1 Corinthians 5:11). Here Paul not only speaks "in" or "for"
Christ, but in a representative sense he *is* the Christ-Spirit, manifest in the world. To disregard him is to disregard God, who has
given him this position. Faithfulness to God is indeed faithfulness
to God's message, with all its implications. But in a practical sense
this faithfulness is demonstrated by submission to Paul:

> Be imitators of me, as I am of Christ. (1 Corinthians 11:1)

> If anyone would like to argue, we recognize no other practice,
> nor do the churches of God. (1 Corinthians 11:16)

> If anyone considers himself to be a prophet or a spiritual one,
> let him acknowledge that what I write you is a command of
> the Lord. If anyone disregards this then he is disregarded. (1
> Corinthians 14:37–38)

Paul's precise mode of exercising his apostolic authority varies according to the degree of resistance he anticipates encountering. In 1 Corinthians and Galatians, where he is addressing serious problems among his followers, and some in the group are openly challenging his authority, he is dogmatic, unbending, and even threatening. In his letter to the group at Thessalonica he has confidence that his instructions will be well received, so he tends to be more gentle:

> But we were gentle among you, like a nurse caring for her children, so being affectionately desirous of you, we were ready to share not only the gospel of God with you, but our very selves, since you had become so dear to us. (1 Thessalonians 2:7–8)

> For you know how, like a father with his children, we exhorted each one of you and encouraged you and charged you to lead a life worthy of God who calls you into his own kingdom and glory. (1 Thessalonians 2:11–12)

Similarly, when he writes to his followers at Philippi he clearly expects them to receive his instructions positively, so his tone is encouraging, but nonetheless, obedience to Christ is to be gauged by obedience to the apostle and the degree to which they follow him:

> Thus my beloved ones, as *you have always obeyed*, so do so now, not only when I am present, but even more when I am absent—work out your own salvation with fear and trembling. (Philippians 2:12)

> Brothers, join in *imitating me*, and keep your eyes on those who walk according to the example you have in us. (Philippians 3:17)

> What you have learned and received and heard and seen in

me—do! And the God of peace will be with you. (Philippians 4:9)

At the same time he makes it clear that his instructions are not based on human authority, but backed by the power of Christ. He goes on to remind the Thessalonians that they are to avoid any form of sexual immorality, ending his instructions with the stern warning: "Therefore whoever disregards this, disregards not man but God, who gives his Holy Spirit to you" (1 Thessalonians 4:8).

But even with the Corinthians and the Galatians, where there are those that are openly opposing him and his apostleship, he mixes his firm instructions with emotional pleas based on their personal bond established by his "fathering" them. To the Galatians he says he is like a parent watching over the birth of a child: "My little children, with whom I am again in the anguish of childbirth until Christ be formed in you! I could wish to be present with you now and to change my tone, for I am perplexed about you" (Galatians 4:19–20). To the Corinthians he pleads:

> Even if I am not an apostle to others at least I am to you; for you are the seal of my apostleship in the Lord. (1 Corinthians 9:2)

> Our mouth is open to you Corinthians, our heart is wide . . . open your hearts to us; we have wronged no one, we have corrupted no one, we have not taken advantage of anyone. I do not say this to condemn you, for I said before that you are in our hearts . . . (2 Corinthians 6:11; 7:2–3)

But then in the same letter, though perhaps in a section written a bit later, when he has received reports of their possible resistance, he once again stresses his authority, his impending visit, and warns them of the consequences they will face if they resist him:

I beg you that when I am present I may not have to be over-bearing with the kind of persuasion I plan on employing against those who accuse us of walking according to the flesh. (2 Corinthians 10:2)

For even if I boast a bit of our authority (which the Lord gave for building up, not for destroying you) I will not be put to shame. (2 Corinthians 10:8)

I warned those who sinned before and all the others, and I warn them now while absent, as I did then when I was there on my second visit, that if I come again I will not spare them— since you want proof that Christ is speaking through me. (2 Corinthians 13:2–3)

I write this while I am away from you, in order that when I come I may not have to be severe in my use of the authority that the Lord has given me for building up and not for tearing down. (2 Corinthians 13:10)

Notice that it is Christ who has given Paul his authority and al-though, ideally, this authority is for "building up," it can be equally powerful for "tearing down" and thus destroying. In the end Paul expects obedience and he wants his followers to soberly consider what is at stake in their losing their salvation, and thus coming under the wrath of God. One must always keep in mind the apoca-lyptic context of everything Paul writes. For him, as well as for his communities, the "day of the Lord," when Christ appears in the clouds of heaven to judge the world, could come at any time:

We overthrow argument [i.e., with the weapons of divine power—verse 4] and every proud obstacle to the knowledge of God, and take every thought captive to obey Christ, having prepared to punish every disobedience, *when your obedience is complete.* (2 Corinthians 10:5–6)

The destructive use of his authority is intended for the outsider or the opponent, not for the obedient child who imitates the father. The situation at Corinth and with the Galatians is so desperate that the "children" themselves are in danger of moving into the category of the "outsider," and thus suffering the destruction of divine power mediated by the apostle. This is very serious business, with cosmic consequences. In Galatians he uses hyperbolic language with a full repertoire of cursing, sarcasm, dire threats, and warnings:

I am amazed that you are so quickly deserting him who called you . . . (1:6)

If anyone is preaching to you a gospel contrary to the one you received, let him be damned! (1:9)

O foolish Galatians! Who has bewitched you? (3:1)

I have confidence in the Lord that you will *take no other view than mine* and that the one troubling you will bear his condemnation, whoever he is! (5:10)

The threat Paul sees among the Galatians is apparently a specific person, unnamed, who has challenged Paul's apostolic authority and his message that the Torah of Moses has been superseded by the coming of Christ. Conversion to Judaism, signified by the rite of circumcision in the case of males, was always an open option for Gentiles in the Jesus movement. It was not required or even expected, but those who felt so drawn to become part of Israel were welcome. Paul is adamant, to the point of vulgarity, in resisting this option. There were apparently some among his group of followers who were encouraging those who wanted to take this step. He declares: "I wish the ones who are troubling you would cut themselves off!" referring to a slip of the circumcision knife, and he warns that anyone who does become circumcised has severed himself from Christ! (Galatians 5:4, 12).

DOES GOD CARE FOR OXEN?

Perhaps the most telling indication of Paul's approach to the Torah comes in his defense of his right as an apostle to be supported financially by his followers. Some of Paul's opponents had apparently denied his apostleship and influenced some of his followers at Corinth to question his status compared to Peter, James, and the other Jerusalem apostles. He adamantly defends himself:

> Am I not an apostle? Have I not seen Jesus our Lord? Are not you my workmanship in the Lord? If to others I am not an apostle, at least I am to you; for you are the seal of my apostleship in the Lord. (1 Corinthians 9:1–2)

He then compares himself to the Jerusalem apostles directly:

> This is my defense to those who would examine me. Do we not have the right to our food and drink? Do we not have the right to be accompanied by a wife as the other apostles and the brothers of the Lord and Cephas? (1 Corinthians 9:3–5)

Although Paul insisted that out of dedicated service to his followers he worked as a manual laborer and did not ask them to support him financially, he is quite insistent that like the apostles at Jerusalem he had every right to do so (1 Corinthians 9:12, 18). Paul appealed to the example of the priests who serve at the temple in Jerusalem, noting that the Torah commands that they share in the offering brought by the people. He even refers to a teaching of Jesus: "In the same way the Lord commanded that those who proclaim the gospel should get their living by the gospel," perhaps alluding to Jesus' teaching that "the laborer deserves his wages" (1 Corinthians 9:14; Luke 10:7). However, his main support for his position comes from his citation of the Torah itself:

> Do I say this on human authority? Does not the Torah say the same? For it is written in the Torah of Moses, "You shall not muzzle an ox when it is treading out the grain." Does God care for oxen? Does he not speak *entirely for our sake*? . . . if we have sown spiritual good among you is it too much if we reap your material benefits? (1 Corinthians 9:8–11)

What Paul argues here is not just a multilayered interpretive meaning for a command of Torah, with a literal as well as an allegorical meaning. That was common among the rabbis, who might agree that although this command of the Torah was given to ensure the proper care of animals, how much more so, in principle, would it imply the proper care of humans. But Paul takes an opposite approach. He insists that this Torah command has nothing at all to do with the welfare of the animal—asking "Does God care for oxen?"—and asserting that this Torah command was entirely intended to support his position that he as a spiritual laborer had the right to be supported financially.

This allegory encapsulates the implications of Paul's way of thinking, which are monumental. What he does here he does on a grander scale with the entire Torah, and with the central tenets of Judaism as a whole—moving everything from literal to allegorical, from earth to heaven. Israel is no longer the physical nation; rather, the "true Israelites" are those who are "in Christ," having been "circumcised" in heart (Galatians 6:16; Philippians 3:3). The honored

messianic Davidic bloodline means nothing, as God creates many
brothers of the Messiah who will reign as "kings" with him spiritually (Romans 8:17; 1 Corinthians 4:8; 6:2–3). The kingdom of God
is no longer on earth but God's real "commonwealth" is in heaven
(Philippians 3:20). Jerusalem is no longer the city blessed and chosen by God. God has cursed Jerusalem and its Jewish inhabitants;
now the "true" Jerusalem is in heaven (Galatians 4:25–26). Those
who were once blessed by keeping all the commandments of the
Torah are now under a curse, while those who follow the "Torah of
Christ" are blessed (Galatians 3:10; 6:2). All human relations, from
the sexual to the social and economic, are losing importance as the
"form of this world is passing away" (1 Corinthians 7:31). Paul's assertion that God does not care for animals, even the lowly laboring
ox, represents an entire world of Torah overthrown in the interest
of the world to come. In terms of its full implications it might be
the most telling sentence we have from Paul. It implies that Paul's
new "Torah of Christ" has cut itself off from any real stake in the
transformation of this world into the kingdom of God, where the
will of God is done *on earth* as in heaven. Given these perspectives on the Torah, along with their implications for Judaism more
generally, it should not surprise us that Paul ended up in a bitter
struggle with Peter, James, and the original apostles, who claimed
to faithfully carry on the message of Jesus. We have only Paul's side
of that conflict, and his decisive break with Jerusalem is glossed
over in Acts, but there is enough evidence still to piece together
the story.

CHAPTER NINE

THE "BATTLE OF THE APOSTLES"

There is good evidence that the two great apostles of Christianity, Peter and Paul, ended up bitter rivals. They seem so inseparably tied together in later Christian history and tradition that the idea of a severe quarrel between them seems inconceivable.

The first time I stood in St. Peter's Square in Rome and approached the steps leading up to St. Peter's Basilica, I was struck by the twin colossal statues of Peter on the left and Paul on the right. Both hold scrolls in their left hands but Peter holds a golden key in his right hand, symbolizing his authority as head of the Church, and Paul holds a sword, representing the "Word of God."

In the center of the square, certainly more imposing, is an ancient Egyptian solar obelisk, complete with sun dial and zodiac signs, towering a hundred feet. It was once inscribed to the "Divine Augustus" but now the inscription reads: "Christus Vincit, Christus Regnat, Christus Imperat"—Christ Conquers, Christ Reigns, Christ Rules. It is topped with a bronze cross, said to contain a fragment of Jesus' original wooden cross. The emperor Caligula brought the original obelisk to Rome in A.D. 37 from Heliopolis,

Egypt, to stand in the Circus Maximus. It was a silent witness to the martyrdom of Peter and Paul and other Christians during the reign of Nero. Pope Sixtus V moved it to St. Peter's in 1585 as testimony to the triumph of the Christian Church over the worldly power of Rome, and by extension over the entire ancient world. Surrounding the square are 140 statues of saints atop the massive oval colonnades. But Peter and Paul, standing together as the patron saints of Christianity, hold center place, leading into the basilica, the world center of Roman Catholic Christianity.[1]

All over Rome it is the same—Peter on the left, Paul on the right, standing watch over the entrance to the bridge San Angelo crossing the Tiber River, or leading up to the central altar of the Basilica San Paolo, where Paul's tomb is located. At the Basilica of St. John Lateran, there are relics from both Peter's and Paul's heads—skull bones—kept inside statues in the canopy high over the altar. In countless cathedrals and churches around the world, the pair invariably and inseparably appear, whether at the Cathedral Basilica of Sts. Peter and Paul in Philadelphia, or the famed Peter and Paul Cathedral in St. Petersburg, where the Russian emperors and empresses are buried.

This legendary heroic pairing hangs on a surprisingly slim historical thread. The earliest reference dates to the early second century A.D. in a letter traditionally ascribed to Clement, an early bishop of Rome:

> Let us set before our eyes the good apostles: Peter, who because of unrighteous jealousy suffered not one or two but many trials, and having thus given his testimony went to the glorious place that was his due. Through jealousy and strife Paul showed the way to the price of endurance . . . he gave his testimony before the rulers, and thus passed from the world and was taken up into the Holy Place, the greatest example of endurance. (1 *Clement* 5:3–7)

This is a remarkable text. What Clement fails to say is as telling as what he seems to know, which is precious little. He mentions nothing about the manner of the deaths of either apostle: that Paul was beheaded, or that Peter was crucified. He does not even pair their deaths together in Rome, under Nero. Since Clement, as bishop of the Roman church, is presumably writing just a few decades after their deaths, one would expect some details about their martyrdom or the veneration of their tombs in Rome. One is tempted to wonder whether Clement knows any more about the deaths of Peter and Paul than one finds implied in the New Testament.[2] The only basis upon which he pairs them at all is in a context in which he is encouraging his readers to bear up under persecution so as to receive a heavenly reward.

Irenaeus, the late-second-century bishop of Lyons, mentions the tradition of "the two most glorious apostles, Peter and Paul" as founders of the church at Rome, but he gives no details of their deaths under Nero.[3] Eusebius, the fourth-century church historian, knows of a late-second-century source, Gaius of Rome, whom he paraphrases: "It is related that in his [Nero's] time Paul was beheaded in Rome itself, and that Peter likewise was crucified, and the title of "Peter and Paul," which is still given to the cemeteries there, confirms the story, no less than does a writer of the church named Gaius" (*Church History* 2.25.5–6). If Eusebius had had something more, or even a source that was more substantial than Gaius, a "writer of the church," he would surely have made use of it.

Most scholars, including leading Roman Catholic ones, are agreed that given such sparse evidence, the tradition of Peter and Paul as founders of the Roman church, much less Peter as first bishop of Rome, is more likely a fourth-century tradition overlaid on a very flimsy factual foundation:

> As for Peter, we have no knowledge at all of when he came
> to Rome and what he did there before he was martyred.

Certainly he was not the original missionary who brought Christianity to Rome (and therefore not the founder of the church of Rome in that sense). There is no serious proof that he was the bishop (or local ecclesiastical officer) of the Roman church—a claim not made till the third century. Most likely he did not spend any major time at Rome before 58 when Paul wrote to the Romans, and so it may have been only in the 60s and relatively shortly before his martyrdom that Peter came to the capital.[4]

The only thing we can say with any reasonable measure of possibility is that both Peter and Paul ended up in Rome during the reign of Nero and were executed, most likely following the fire that broke out in Rome the summer of A.D. 64 when Nero blamed the Christians and had many of them killed.[5] If they were in Rome at the same time, the evidence might well indicate, as we will see, they were there as rivals, not as co-apostles and founders of the Roman church.

There were Christians at Rome long before Paul or Peter ever set foot in the capital. When Paul writes his letter to the Romans, around the year A.D. 56, it is intended to serve as his "calling card," as he sets forth an exposition of what he calls "my Gospel" to introduce himself formally to them. He is neither their founder nor their spiritual "father," and the tone of the letter is more formal and much less personal than when he is writing to one of his own groups. He gives greetings at the end of the letter to various individuals by name, indicating that he has connections with a few dozen of their community (Romans 16:1–16). He does not mention Cephas or Peter. He refers to groups meeting in various homes, so we should imagine a network of cell meetings, perhaps loosely organized, likely diverse in beliefs and practices (Romans 16:4–5). One of Paul's main purposes in writing the letter was to make a plea for tolerance of different religious observances, including observing holy days and abstaining from certain foods—both clearly touchstone issues between Jewish and non-Jewish Christians (Romans 14:5–9). He also devotes a long section of his letter to his claim that the Jewish people, though temporarily cut off from God if they do not accept Jesus as Messiah and Lord, will soon come around to such a faith once they see the myriads of Gentiles who are turning to the God of Israel through their faith in Christ as a result of his work (Romans 9–11).

There was a sizable Jewish population in Rome with many synagogues. Suetonius, a Roman historian of the period, indicates there were heated disputes among the Jews of the city over "Chrestus," which led to the emperor Claudius banning them from the city precincts in A.D. 49.[6] This is likely a reference to disputes within the various Jewish communities over the newly imported messianic faith in Jesus (i.e., Chrestus = Christus), which had reached Rome by this time. According to the book of Acts, when Paul finally did arrive in Rome, around A.D. 58, under house arrest for fomenting disturbances in the Temple at Jerusalem, he set up shop in a rented house and began presenting his gospel to the local Jewish population. These encounters resulted in heated disputes, leading Paul to denounce the Jews and vow that he would preach only to non-Jews in the future (Acts 28:23–28).

In order to understand the relationship between Peter and Paul we need to leave behind the legendary tales of their heroic co-martyrdom in Rome and examine the evidence in Paul's genuine letters, our only contemporary sources.

A MAN CALLED PETER

We know precious little about the *historical* Peter, since as we will see, he has been made over in the New Testament writings in the image of Paul—but we do have some reliable evidence to go on. His Hebrew name is Simon (*Shimon*), the most common Jewish male name in Palestine in that period—one of Jesus' four brothers was also named Simon, plus there was Simon the Zealot among the Twelve. Simon had a brother named Andrew; they were fishermen on the Sea of Galilee (Mark 1:16). He is called "Simon bar Jonah," which is Aramaic for Simon *son of* Jonah—their father. Simon had a house in the fishing village called Capernaum ("village of Naum") on the northwest edge of the Sea of Galilee, where he lived with his wife, who is unnamed, and possibly his brother Andrew and family as well (Mark 1:29). They, along with Philip, another of the Twelve, are originally from Bethsaida, a village further to the east, also on the Sea of Galilee (John 1:44). Jesus moved to Capernaum, along with his mother and brothers, as he began his public work, making Simon's house his home base and headquarters (Matthew 4:13; John 2:12). There is a site today in Capernaum called the house of Peter, which became a Byzantine church, built over a first-century dwelling. Jesus chose Simon along with his brother Andrew, and two other fishermen brothers, James and John, as the core of his twelve apostles (Mark 3:16–17). Jesus gave Simon the surname Cephas, an Aramaic nickname meaning "rock," which was translated into Greek as Peter—the name most familiar to us today (John 1:42).

Peter, James, and John become a triumvirate among the Twelve; Jesus deals with them separately as his core leaders on a number of occasions (Mark 5:37; 9:2; 14:33). Peter is always mentioned first and functions as the "lead" apostle. The half-dozen stories about him in the gospels emphasize his enthusiasm for Jesus along with his impetuousness, and of course he is known best for denying Jesus three times the night of Jesus' arrest in order to save his own life, then repenting bitterly. According to Paul, as well as some of our gospel sources, it was Peter who first "saw" Jesus after his death, when he returned to his fishing business in Galilee.

Perhaps our best clue to Peter's religious background is that according to the gospel of John, he, along with Andrew, as well as the apostle Philip, were disciples of John the Baptizer before they joined forces with Jesus (John 1:35–41). Everything we know about John indicates that he was a fiery apocalyptic preacher, zealous for Israel's messianic redemption, and a strict adherent to the Torah. Many scholars have associated his message and his Jewish piety with the kind of apocalyptic nationalism that we find in the Dead Sea Scrolls. That Peter would have been drawn to this movement, as was Jesus, gives us a reliable profile of his zealous orientation toward his ancestral faith.

One might expect that the letters in the New Testament bearing Peter's name might be the best indication of what he believed and taught and what kind of Christianity he espoused. Although scholars do not think either 1 Peter or 2 Peter was actually written by Peter, it is abundantly clear that the letter we call 1 Peter is in fact a production of an early-second-century Pauline group, the same ones who produced 1 and 2 Timothy and Titus. The ideas in the letter are so close to those we associate with Paul in the later pseudonymous letters attributed to him that the resemblance is unmistakable. 1 Peter is a Pauline-style letter written in Peter's name, an obvious attempt to associate Peter's theology with that of Paul.

Paul knows Peter as Cephas, using his Greek name Peter only twice (Galatians 2:7–8). What Paul reveals is sparse but quite telling. Cephas is second next to James the brother of Jesus, along with John the fisherman as a third, in a new leadership triumvirate that Paul refers to as the "pillars" of the Jerusalem-based Jesus movement (Galatians 2:9). In Judaism this is called a *bet din* or "house of judgment." That James is in charge, flanked by Peter as his chief confidant, is quite telling since James is known in all of our sources as extremely zealous for the Torah—much as John the Baptizer had been. According to Matthew, Jesus had given Peter the "keys" of judgment, with binding and loosing power, which in Judaism means he functions as a judge over matters of Jewish law and observance for the Christian community (Matthew 16:19 and especially 18:18).

When Paul first visits Jerusalem, three years after his sojourn in Arabia and his revelatory experiences, he goes first to Peter, who then arranges for him to meet James (Galatians 1:18–19). Peter functions as a viceroy for James, and is apparently sent throughout the regions of Judea, Galilee, Syria, Asia, and Greece to represent the Jerusalem leadership and make sure that things are operating smoothly among the various branches of the Jewish-Christian movement outside the Land of Israel. Paul mentions that Peter travels about with his wife, supported by the Jerusalem headquarters, and Peter has apparently even visited Paul's group at Corinth (1 Corinthians 9:5; 1:12).

When Paul appeared before the Jerusalem Council around A.D. 50 to defend his independent preaching among the Gentiles for the previous fourteen years, he and the Jerusalem apostles apparently reached a kind of "live and let live" agreement to not interfere with one another's work. They agreed that Paul was to preach among the Gentiles a form of the Jewish messianic faith in Jesus applicable to non-Jews as God-fearers. Peter would head the missionary work to Jews scattered throughout the world. Most important, the Jerusalem leadership would not support any insistence that Paul's converts become circumcised and convert to Judaism. This is what Paul says in Galatians, and it fits well with what is reported by the author of Luke about the meeting in Acts 15.

What never came up, and what the Jerusalem apostles would never have imagined, given Paul's devotion and training in the Jewish faith, was that Paul believed that with the coming of Christ, the Torah of Moses, which he called "the old covenant," had been superseded and was "fading away," as we have seen in his letters. That means that even Jews were no longer "under the Torah," or obligated to observe the laws of traditions of the ancestral faith— particularly circumcision, the Sabbath, the Jewish festivals, the dietary laws, and ritual purity. We know from Paul's letters that he went much further than this, even to the point of teaching that the Torah had been given by angels, not directly by God, and that those who were under its tutelage were slaves to these inferior cosmic powers, which was no better than serving idols (Galatians 4:8–10).

Some have maintained that Paul wrote the negative things he did about the Torah only in the context of insisting that his Gentile converts not be forced to live as Jews, but his language is quite clear in this regard. He constantly uses the first-person plural—"we," including himself as a Jew. The Torah lasted from Moses to Christ, so *we* are no longer confined "under the Torah" but are released from its bondage (Galatians 3:23–4:10). According to Paul, as we have seen in previous chapters, if one is in Christ, whether Jew or Gentile, one is responsible only for the Torah of Christ.

We can be sure that Peter, James, and the Jerusalem apostles knew nothing about the full implications of Paul's teaching, especially that Jews need no longer follow the Jewish Torah. The author of the book of Acts tries to present a picture of harmonious cooperation between Paul, Peter, and James—they were all preaching the same gospel message. At the very end of his book, when Paul visits Jerusalem for the last time, before his imprisonment in Rome, Acts reveals more—perhaps more than intended—and the truth seems to come out, at least by implication.

According to Acts, toward the end of his career Paul arrived in Jerusalem and appeared before James and all the elders of the Jerusalem church. At issue was a "rumor" that James wanted to dispel, namely that Paul was teaching Jews that they could disregard the Torah. Acts records James addressing Paul: "You see brother how many thousands there are among the Jews of those who have believed; they are all zealous for the Torah, and they have been told about you that you teach all the Jews who are among the Gentiles to forsake Moses, telling them not to circumcise their children or observe the customs" (Acts 21:20–21). James then proposes that, to let everyone know that this rumor is false and that Paul himself lives in observance of the Torah, he participate in a purification ceremony in the Jerusalem Temple, which would involve bringing an offering and entering the sacred areas within the Temple court-yard where only Jews were allowed to go.

What is striking about this scene in Acts is that Paul says abso-lutely nothing. He neither confirms nor denies the rumor, though he does go along with the purification ceremony. But we know from Paul's own letters that he has established an operational pol-icy that when he is among the Jews, he becomes as "one under the Torah," and when he is with Gentiles, he lives as a Gentile (1 Corinthians 9:20–21).

That any scene like this ever took place seems doubtful, at least not in the way Acts reports it. We know that James and the rest of the Jewish followers of Jesus, like Jesus himself, were zealous for the Torah and their ancestral faith. One might also expect that the author of Acts would have Paul *deny* the truth of the rumor, but it seems he dare not do that, perhaps because he knows the picture of harmony he is trying to pass off here had no basis in fact and Paul was indeed teaching Jews and Gentiles that they were now under what he called the new covenant—the Torah of Christ. The main point we learn from Acts here is that the author felt he had to address this issue—and somehow dispel it. It was not something that could be ignored.

Since we know from Paul's letters that he unquestionably taught the very thing that James, in this concocted scene, is satis-fied he does not teach, we have to ask whether Peter, James, and the other apostles did in fact ever learn of Paul's real modus operandi in dealing with both Gentiles and Jews, and the full implications of his Gospel, which we have examined in previous chapters.

FALSE APOSTLES, SERVANTS OF SATAN

We have seen previously that Paul refers to the Jerusalem lead-ership of James, Peter, and John in a rather sarcastic and dismissive manner when he recounts his initial appearance before the Jerusalem leaders around A.D. 50:

> And from those who were reputed to be something—
> what they were makes no difference to me! God shows no
> partiality—those, I say, who were of repute added nothing to
> me ... and when they perceived the grace that was given to
> me, James and Cephas, and John, who were reputed to be pil-
> lars, gave to me and Barnabas the right hand of fellowship,
> that we should go to the Gentiles and they to the circumcised.
> (Galatians 2:6–9)

We can see here Paul's approach that it does not really matter what these leaders said or might have said, since he was taking his orders and had gotten his gospel directly from Christ. Because they apparently agreed to let him be, he was content.

The first hint of a rift that we get comes at Antioch, where there was a church composed of both Jews and Gentiles that Paul had apparently used as a base of operations for his preaching in Asia Minor over the previous decade, and where he had teamed up with Barnabas, a leading Jewish member of the Antioch community. When the group gathered they apparently had separate tables, for practical reasons, at which Jews could eat with the assurance that the food served was in keeping with Jewish dietary laws, and one where Gentiles could have any sort of food, so long as it did not include meat without the blood properly drained. This arrange- ment was not viewed as discriminatory, but one that allowed the group to meet together harmoniously. Unfortunately we only have Paul's side of the story, but he claims that Peter was "eating with the Gentiles" until a delegation from James showed up, then he moved to the Jewish table, thus playing the hypocrite. He says that Barnabas, Paul's partner, stood with Peter in doing the same. Paul clearly acknowledges here that James and his representatives would have insisted on strict standards of Jewish observance, including in the matter of dietary laws.

Paul says that he stood up before the entire group and publicly denounced Peter, as well as his own co-worker Barnabas: "If you though a Jew, live like a Gentile and not like a Jew, how can you compel the Gentiles to live like Jews?" (Galatians 2:14). The charge as stated here by Paul really makes no sense, since even if Peter and Barnabas had eaten unfit food at the table of the Gentiles, they would not thereby be compelling the Gentiles to live like Jews. But the idea that Peter would have disregarded dietary laws in the first place goes against everything we know of his leadership status alongside James in an observant Jewish-Christian community following the Torah. It is possible Peter was simply sitting with the Gentiles, not actually eating with them, but that when those from James arrived, Peter joined them at their kosher table and Paul interpreted this as a kind of social shunning.

But it is likely something much more significant is going on here, something Paul would never want to let out. If Paul's charge that Peter was "compelling the Gentiles to live like Jews" has any force at all, it must reflect Peter's sympathy with the idea that it was a perfectly fine and good thing if Gentiles who had become followers of Jesus were subsequently drawn toward Judaism and decided to convert. The issue would not be compulsion but free choice. Since the main issue Paul is addressing in the letter of Galatians is that his Gentile converts should not, under any circumstances, convert to Judaism, but remain as they are, Paul's denunciation of Peter and Barnabas likely reflects his consternation at their welcoming Gentiles who wanted to convert. Judaism did welcome sincere converts and there is every reason to think that Peter, James, and the others would have done the same. Requiring conversion and welcoming those who might choose it, however, are two entirely separate issues. Paul's position with his Gentile converts was that they did not need to convert to Judaism or keep the Torah in order to have a right relationship with God. That is not the same as saying that those who might choose to convert, having joined the Christian community as Gentiles, should be forbidden to do so. And that is the position that Paul took with his own converts. He tells them that if they receive circumcision, they are "cut off from Christ" (Galatians 5:2–4).

That Barnabas sides with Peter is quite telling, since he had spent years loyally working with Paul as a missionary partner. According to Acts he was a Levite, a member of a group that required the strictest observance of Torah, and he had the trust of the Jerusalem apostles (Acts 4:36). Apparently at this confrontation Paul begins to reveal a side of his teachings about the Torah of which even Barnabas, who had worked by his side, was not aware; otherwise surely Barnabas would have supported Paul on this occasion. It is also noteworthy that Barnabas is the one, according to Acts, who first introduced Paul to the Jerusalem church and vouched for him at Antioch as well (Acts 9:27; 11:25–26). Barnabas was closely tied to James and the Jerusalem apostles. He had been sent by them to provide leadership to the newly formed group in Antioch some decades earlier (Acts 11:22). The relations between Antioch and Jerusalem were close, as evidenced by the delegation from James arriving shortly before Paul's outburst (Galatians 2:12).

As noted, we have only Paul's side of the story and one should not assume that Peter and Barnabas agreed with Paul or were somehow properly rebuked and put in their place by Paul's harsh denunciation. They might well have defended themselves quite ably against his charges and it is very possible that given the circumstances it was Paul who was rebuked at Antioch. If Peter had apologized or acknowledged that Paul was correct, we surely would have Paul including that fact as part of his account. The fierceness of this confrontation was likely the first crack in the façade of harmony between Paul and the Jerusalem leadership.

It is quite significant that Acts records that right after the

Jerusalem meeting of A.D. 50, when Paul and Barnabas had returned to Antioch, they had a "sharp contention" and permanently split, never to work together again (Acts 15:39). Acts says the reason was whether to take Mark with them as they planned their next missionary trip—Paul objected and Barnabas wanted him along. It seems more likely that the confrontation with Peter and Barnabas over eating with the Gentiles, which Paul reports and Acts ignores, may have been the real cause of their bitter split.

What this evidence appears to indicate is that up until around A.D. 50, during the first decade of Paul's missionary work in the cities of Asia Minor, when he was working with Barnabas, he was not expressing, at least publicly, the full implications of his views about the Torah of Moses being invalidated by the new covenant he was preaching. It is possible that Paul only gradually came to this view. In his earliest letter to his congregation at Thessalonica, probably around A.D. 51, he says nothing controversial about the Jewish Torah and seems to be expounding a fairly simple standard of ethics appropriate to the God-fearer status of his followers. It is not until around A.D. 56, with his letters to the Galatians, Corinthians, and Romans, that we begin to get a glimpse of Paul's full views about the implications of "his" gospel—as we have seen in previous chapters.

What apparently has changed in this time period is that delegates have visited Paul's congregations from James, including Peter himself, and they have begun to raise questions about some of the things they are hearing. We pick up these tensions particularly in Galatians and running through the Corinthian correspondence. There is an explicit challenge to Paul's apostleship; his emotional outburst against Peter and Barnabas at Antioch are our first hint at just how serious things could become.

One point that is extremely important but seldom noted is that although Paul calls himself an apostle, there is no indication that the Jerusalem leadership had ever given him that status. By authorizing his preaching to the Gentiles they were not thereby conferring on him any special apostolic authority. The book of Acts intends to imply that Paul and Barnabas were "apostles," simply because they were "sent out" as missionaries, but it is more likely that this designation, at least as used by the Jerusalem church, was reserved for the Twelve. The book of Acts indicates the same when Judas Iscariot, who had betrayed Jesus and killed himself, is formally replaced by the casting of lots by the Eleven, with a disciple named Matthias chosen (Acts 1:21–26). One of the requirements of such an apostle was that he had been with the group from the beginning—starting with the preaching of John the Baptizer and all through Jesus' lifetime. Paul clearly did not qualify. But as we have seen, in Paul's mind he was *over*qualified in this regard, since he was hearing directly from the heavenly Christ, while Peter and the others were relying on what they had learned from the "earthly" Jesus during his lifetime.

Things came to a confrontation sometime around A.D. 55–56. Our first evidence of the tension is in Paul's letter to the Galatians, but the full extent of Paul's break with the Jerusalem leadership comes out in 2 Corinthians 10–13, a section of the letter that seems to have been written independently of the whole as the situation Paul was dealing with at Corinth deteriorated and he came to feel he had lost all power with his followers.

Scholars agree that Paul is facing a group of outside opponents who have come to Corinth in his absence and tried to take over his congregation. They have been characterized in at least a dozen different ways, though most commonly they are thought to be some kind of Palestinian Jewish-Christian "Gnostics" who were boasting about their visions and revelations and their superior credentials as "apostles" while questioning Paul's legitimacy, power, and status.[7]

In the early nineteenth century, the German scholar Ferdinand Christian Baur, who is the "father" of critical studies of Paul, had proposed that Paul's opponents in 2 Corinthians 10–13 were none other than James, Peter, and the Jerusalem Twelve. His view has generally been abandoned since, though some would agree that whatever group was at Corinth claimed its authorization from the Jerusalem apostles. I believe that Baur was essentially correct.[8] What we find in these chapters is Paul's complete repudiation of the Jerusalem apostles and his determination to operate independently in the future, without regard to their approval or directives.

Paul is livid that these delegates from Jerusalem, including Peter, would dare to extend themselves into his territory and interfere with the community he had "fathered" by his own labor. As he tells the Corinthians, "even if I am not an apostle to others, at least I am to you; for you are the seal of my apostleship in the Lord" (1 Corinthians 9:2). His language clearly shows that others are questioning his apostolic claims. We can put together a sketch of Paul's opposition by collecting the responses and countercharges that he makes to defend himself and his apostleship.

> Are they Hebrews? So am I. Are they Israelites? So am I. Are they offspring of Abraham? So am I. Are they servants of Christ? I am a better one—I am talking like a madman—with far greater labors, far more imprisonments, with countless beatings, and often near death. (2 Corinthians 11:22–23)

> I ought to have been commended by you. For I was not at all inferior to these super-apostles, even though I am nothing. The signs of a true apostle were performed among you with utmost patience, with signs and wonders and mighty works. (2 Corinthians 12:11–12)

Here we can see that this rival group is appealing to its Jewish heritage, which Paul also could muster forth from his own background, but more important, the others are claiming to be "true" apostles, as opposed to Paul's role as "apostle to the Gentiles." Paul resorts to bitter sarcasm, calling them the "super-apostles" but asserting that he has labored harder, suffered more, has had more extraordinary revelations, and worked greater miracles than any of them. We have seen a less heated version of Paul's need to defend himself as "last but not least" when he compares his own apostleship with that of James, Peter, and the Twelve, declaring, "Last of all, as to one untimely born, he [Christ] appeared also to me. For I am the least of the apostles, unfit to be called an apostle . . . but I worked harder than any of them" (1 Corinthians 15:8–10).

Most telling as to the wider issues at stake is the language he uses to describe the threat to his flock:

> For if someone comes and preaches *another Jesus* than the one we preached, or if you receive a *different spirit* from the one you received, or if you accept a *different gospel* from the one you accepted, you submit to it readily enough. I am not in the least inferior to these super-apostles. (2 Corinthians 11:4–5)

This sounds almost identical to the way he opens his letter to the Galatians:

> I am astonished that you are so quickly deserting him who called you in the grace of Christ and turning to a *different gospel* . . . But even if we, or an angel from heaven, should preach to you a gospel contrary to that which we preached, let him be damned! (Galatians 1:6–8)

The entire letter to the Galatians makes clear the threat these apostles represent to Paul. They are observant of the Torah themselves, and though not requiring conversion on the part of Gentiles, they apparently present the option in a favorable light, and some of Paul's followers have responded positively.

Paul's most extreme characterization of these apostles shows the degree to which he has given up on any possible reconciliation of their views:

> For such men are false apostles, deceitful workmen, disguising themselves as apostles of Christ. And no wonder, for even Satan disguises himself as an angel of light. So it is no surprise if his servants, also, disguise themselves as servants of righteousness. Their end will correspond to their deeds. (2 Corinthians 11:13–15)

It is hard for us to imagine today that Paul might have the Jerusalem apostles in mind here—actually calling them servants of Satan. But this language should not surprise us because Paul has already written to the Galatians that anyone who preaches contrary to what he preaches is to be damned—even an angel from heaven! What he means here is not that Peter, James, and the Twelve are demonic or Satanic, but that *if* they are tearing down what he has built up as an apostle to the Gentiles, one empowered directly by Christ, they have served the cause of Satan, no matter what their association with Jesus might be.

We know that James, Peter, and the Twelve would have been appalled at what Paul says about the Torah and the revelation to Moses at Sinai. Although Paul's letters, other than Romans, are written directly to his intimate personal followers, it is likely that delegates from Jerusalem visiting his congregations, including Peter himself, had learned enough to realize the implications of Paul's gospel and his exalted claims to apostleship—namely the repudiation of the Jewish faith and its replacement with Paul's new covenant religion, in which there is neither Jew nor Gentile any longer.

It is quite telling that in his last letter to one of his churches, to his followers in Philippi, written when Paul was in prison in Rome,

Paul's language against his Jewish opponents is unbending, and if anything has become more bitter, even as he affirms once more his own status and place in the eyes of Christ. These are among the last words of Paul and they stand as testimony to all that he lived for and died for, and how he paved the way for a new religion called Christianity:

> Look out for the dogs, look out for the evildoers, look out for those who mutilate the flesh. For we are the true circumcision, who worship by the Spirit of God and glory in Christ Jesus and put no confidence in the flesh—though I myself have reason for confidence in the flesh also. If anyone else thinks he has reason for confidence in the flesh, I have more: circumcised on the eighth day, of the people of Israel, of the tribe of Benjamin, a Hebrew of Hebrews; as to the law, a Pharisee; as to zeal, a persecutor of the church; as to righteousness under the law, blameless. But whatever gain I had, I counted as loss for the sake of Christ. (Philippians 3:2–7)

At this point sometime in the early 60s A.D., Paul goes silent on us. We have nothing else directly from his hand. So far we have drawn our evidence of Paul's bitter and irrevocable repudiation of the Jerusalem leadership from his letters alone. Whether there was ever any direct confrontation between Paul and Peter after this point we cannot be sure. Strangely, the account in Acts also ends abruptly with Paul's imprisonment in Rome, as if nothing happened thereafter. Assuming that Luke-Acts was written at least as late as the end of the first century, we have a minimum of four decades of complete silence. Why are the deaths of Paul, Peter, and even James, all killed in the early 60s A.D., not heroically recounted in Acts to fill out the story of the beginnings of early Christianity? There has to be a reason for this silence. For our answer we have to turn to sources beyond the New Testament.

THE JESUS LEGACY

We have very few sources that tell us what happened with the Jewish-Christians who were connected to Jerusalem after the death of James in A.D. 62. As we have seen, the literary victory of Paul, whose ideas dominate the writings of the New Testament, is fairly complete. The Q source and the letter of James provide two exceptions. Among the earliest Christian writings by those usually called the "Apostolic Fathers," only the *Didache* lacks Paul's influence. The rest, including the letters of Clement of Rome, Ignatius, Polycarp, the Shepherd of Hermas, and Barnabas, are wholly in harmony with a Pauline perspective and decidedly anti-Jewish in outlook. In other words, Paul's gospel, so far as it was understood, won the day. Christians increasingly began to make the point explicitly that they were not Jewish and had nothing in common with Judaism. It was a victory of ideas as well as numbers since Gentiles quickly outnumbered Jews among the various Christian communities that began to spring up all over the Roman Empire into the second century A.D. Christian communities at Rome, Alexandria, Carthage, Ephesus, and Antioch, five central urban areas of the Roman Empire, began to dominate the Christian landscape. Greek language, philosophy, and culture prevailed in these Hellenistic–Roman Christian communities. The "Old Testament" was retained, but only in a Greek translation with the additional books of the "Apocrypha" added to what had been the Hebrew Bible.

There was also a political and military side to the triumph of Paul. Galilee, Judea, and Jerusalem were devastated by two successive revolts against Rome (A.D. 66–73 and 132–35). Both Vespasian and Hadrian, the emperors who presided successively over these two Roman victories, instituted harsh measures against Jews in the Land of Israel and throughout the empire. Hundreds of thousands had been killed or taken away into slavery. The homeland was devastated and the capital of Jerusalem with its magnificent Temple was in ruins. It was increasingly unpopular to be Jewish or to identify with Jewish causes.

Tradition tells us that the Jerusalem-based Jewish-Christians, led by Simon, the successor of James, also of the dynastic bloodline of Jesus' Davidic family, fled northeast into Transjordan, settling in areas around Pella and the district of Basan just before the outbreak of the First Jewish Revolt. We have no precise records of what happened to them, and we should probably not imagine them to be a solidly monolithic group with a central organization and agenda. What seems to have happened is that the movement scattered, and to some extent shattered, left without power or influence in the West, where Paul's Gentile churches were thriving. As a result, their Jewish-Christian perspectives played little to no part in influencing what went into the New Testament. By the second and third centuries A.D., remnants of their movement appear to be divided into various sects and factions, variously named in our sources Ebionites, Nazoreans, Elkesaites, Cerinthians, and Symmachians.[9] Unfortunately, most of what we know about these groups comes from orthodox Pauline Christian writers from the West who were eager to expose all forms of Jewish Christianity as heresy.

Despite their diversity there seem to be four general ideas that Jewish-Christian groups agreed upon: the eternal validity of the Torah of Moses, the acceptance of only the gospel of Matthew in Hebrew, the complete rejection of Paul as a heretic and apostate from the Torah, and the belief that Jesus was a human being, born of a mother and a father, chosen by God but not divine.[10] The best-known group, and the one that drew the most fire from orthodox Pauline circles, were the Ebionites. They most likely got their name from the Q teaching of Jesus: "Blessed are you poor ones [Hebrew: '*evyonim*]," a designation that appears dozens of times in the Psalms and Prophets as a description of God's true people in the last days. Irenaeus, one of our earliest sources on the Ebionites, describes them as follows:

They use the gospel according to Matthew only, and repudi-
ate the apostle Paul, maintaining that he was an apostate from
the Torah . . . they practice circumcision, persevere in those
customs which are enjoined by the Law, and are so Judaic in
their style of life that they even adore Jerusalem as if it were
the house of God. (*Against Heresies* 1.26.2)

The main issue that arises with regard to the Ebionites is
whether their ideas represent a largely unbroken perspective
and orientation stemming back to Jesus, James, and the original Jerusalem apostles, or whether they are a later sect of Jewish
Christianity that radicalized itself in the second and third centuries. Given what we have seen in Paul's own letters, including his
charge that the apostles who oppose him are "servants of Satan," it
is certainly plausible to assume that the Ebionites represent a link
to the Jerusalem apostles, at least in their main ideas. Their ideas
also seem to fit well with our other earlier Jewish-Christian sources
such as Q, the letter of James, and the *Didache*. Theirs was a thoroughly Jewish stance with a belief that Jesus was either a prophet
or the Messiah, heralding the imminent arrival of the kingdom of
God on earth.

A much more positive view of the Ebionite "gospel" is now
embedded in the fourth-century documents we call the *Pseudo-
Clementines*, which are made up of two major parts, the *Homilies*
and the *Recognitions*. A document embedded in the whole called
the *Kerygmata Petrou*, or the Preaching of Peter, is particularly
valuable in this regard. This document claims to be a letter written by Peter to James the brother of Jesus. Peter complains that
his letters have been interpolated and corrupted by those influenced by Paul so that they have become worthless. He urges
James not to pass along any of his teachings to the Gentiles, but
only to those members of the council of the Seventy whom Jesus
had appointed. Paul is sharply censored as one who put his own

testimony based on visions over the certainty of the direct teachings that the original apostles had from Jesus. The argument Peter makes is quite telling. He suggests that if people follow someone like Paul, who claims to have had visions of Jesus, how might one know he was not actually communicating with a demonic spirit impersonating Jesus? In contrast, if one goes by what Jesus actually taught to the original apostles, there is no possibility of such deception.

Scholars do not consider these materials to be authentic first-century documents, but they do appear to reflect later legendary versions of the very disputes that did occur during the lifetime of Paul, Peter, and James. They preserve for us some memory of the conflicts of which Paul's letters provide only dim and one-sided glimpses. What is particularly striking about the *Pseudo-Clementines* is the strong emphasis on testing everything by James: "Believe no teacher unless he brings from Jerusalem the testimonial of James the Lord's brother" (*Recognitions* 4:35).

Although the voices of these Jewish-Christians were gradually muted over the centuries as they largely disappeared from view, their perspectives, still embedded behind and between the lines of Paul's authentic letters, as well as in these scattered ancient sources, can still be heard.

The ultimate irony with regard to what Christianity became is the possibility that these voices that no longer speak might well represent something closer to the message of Jesus than do the teachings of Paul or Christianity itself. What one ultimately concludes regarding that issue still rests today, as it did in the first centuries of the Christian era, on what value one places on Paul's visionary experiences and his resulting claims to be directly communicating with Jesus. Trying to recover as best we can by historical methods what we can know about the life and teachings of Jesus and his earliest followers is one thing, whereas entering the world of Paul's theological interpretation of the cosmic heavenly "Christ" is quite another. The task of a historian is to offer as clear a view of Paul's own testimony in this regard as is possible from his own letters, while recovering to whatever extent possible those now silent voices who represented an earlier and alternative "Christianity before Paul."

APPENDIX

THE QUEST FOR THE HISTORICAL PAUL

What can we reliably know about Paul and how can we know it? As is the case with Jesus, this is not an easy question. Historians have been involved in what has been called the "Quest for the Historical Jesus" for the past 175 years, evaluating and sifting through our sources, trying to determine what we can reliably say about him.[1] As it happens the quest for the historical Paul began almost simultaneously, inaugurated by the German scholar Ferdinand Christian Baur.[2] Baur put his finger squarely on the problem: There are *four* different "Pauls" in the New Testament, not one, and each is quite distinct from the other. New Testament scholars today are generally agreed on this point.[3]

Thirteen of the New Testament's twenty-seven documents are letters with Paul's name as the author, and a fourteenth, the book of Acts, is mainly devoted to the story of Paul's life and career—making up over half the total.[4] The problem is, these fourteen texts fall into four distinct chronological tiers, giving us our four Pauls:

1. *Authentic or Early Paul:* 1 Thessalonians, Galatians, 1 and 2 Corinthians, Romans, Philippians, and Philemon (A.D. 50s–60s)

2. *Disputed Paul or Deutero-Pauline:* 2 Thessalonians, Ephesians, Colossians (A.D. 80–100)
3. *Pseudo-Paul or the Pastorals:* 1 and 2 Timothy, Titus (A.D. 80–100)
4. *Tendentious or Legendary Paul:* Acts of the Apostles (A.D. 90–130)

Though scholars differ about what historical use one might properly make of tiers 2, 3, or 4, there is almost universal agreement that a proper historical study of Paul should begin with the seven genuine letters, restricting one's analysis to what is most certainly coming from Paul's own hand. This approach might sound restrictive but it is really the only proper way to begin. The Deutero-Pauline letters and the Pastorals reflect a vocabulary, a development of ideas, and a social setting that belong to a later time.[5] We are not getting Paul as he was, but Paul's name used to lend authority to the ideas of later authors who intended for readers to believe their ideas come from Paul. In modern parlance we call such writings forgeries, but a more polite academic term is pseudonymous, meaning "falsely named."

Those more inclined to view this activity in a positive light point to a group of followers of Paul, some decades after his death, who wanted to honor him by continuing his legacy and using his name to defend views with which they assumed he would have surely agreed. A less charitable judgment is that these letters represent an attempt to deceive gullible readers by authors intent on passing on their own views as having the authority of Paul. Either way, this enterprise of writing letters in Paul's name has been enormously influential because Paul became such a towering figure of authority in the church.

The Pastorals (1 and 2 Timothy and Titus) are not included in our earliest extant collection of Paul's letters, the so-called Chester Beatty papyrus, which dates to the third century A.D.[6] Paul's apocalyptic urgency, so dominant in the earlier letters, is almost wholly absent in these later writings. Among the Deutero-Pauline tier, 2 Thessalonians was specifically written to calm those who were claiming that the day of judgment was imminent—the very thing Paul constantly proclaimed (2 Thessalonians 2:1–3).

In tiers 2 and 3 the domestic roles of husbands, wives, children, widows, masters, and slaves are specified with a level of detail uncharacteristic of Paul's ad hoc instructions in his earlier letters (Ephesians 5:21–6:9; Colossians 3:18–4:1; 1 Timothy 5:1–16). Specific rules are set down for the qualifications and appointment of bishops and deacons in each congregation (1 Timothy 3:1–13; Titus 1:5–9). There is a strong emphasis on following tradition, respecting the governmental authorities, handling wealth, and maintaining a respectable social order (2 Thessalonians 2:15; 3:6–15; 1 Timothy 2:1–4; 5:17–19; 6:6–10; Titus 3:1). The Pastorals, in particular, are essentially manuals for church officers, intended to enforce order and uniformity.

Some have argued that the passing of time and the changing of circumstances might account for the differences, but detailed studies of the commonly used vocabulary in Paul's undisputed letters, in contrast to the Deutero-Pauline and Pastoral letters, has settled the question for most scholars. I will make little use of these later documents in trying to reconstruct the "historical Paul."

The book of Acts, tier 4, presents a special problem in that it offers fascinating biographical background on Paul not found in his genuine letters as well as complete itineraries of his travels. The problem, as I mentioned in the introduction, is with its harmonizing theological agenda, which stresses the cozy relationship Paul had with the Jerusalem leaders of the church, and its overidealized portrait of Paul. Many historians are agreed that it merits the label "Use Sparingly with Extreme Caution." As a general working method I have adopted the following three principles:

1. Never accept anything in Acts over Paul's own account in his seven genuine letters.
2. Cautiously consider Acts if it agrees with Paul's letters and one can detect no obvious biases.
3. Consider the independent information that Acts provides of interest but not of interpretive historical use.

This last principle would include biographical information, the three accounts of Paul's conversion that the author provides, the various speeches of Paul, his itinerary, and other such details.[7]

Before applying these principles here is a skeletal outline of Paul's basic biographical data drawn *only* from his genuine letters that gives us a solid place to begin. Here is what we most surely know:

- Paul calls himself a Hebrew or Israelite, stating that he was born a Jew and circumcised on the eighth day, of the Jewish tribe of Benjamin (Philippians 3:5-6; 2 Corinthians 11:22).
- He was once a member of the sect of the Pharisees. He advanced in Judaism beyond many of his contemporaries, being extremely zealous for the traditions of his Jewish faith (Philippians 3:5; Galatians 1:14).
- He zealously persecuted the Jesus movement (Galatians 1:13; Philippians 3:6; 1 Corinthians 15:9).
- Sometime around A.D. 37 Paul had a visionary experience he describes as "seeing" Jesus and received from Jesus his gospel message as well as his call to be an apostle to the non-Jewish world (1 Corinthians 9:2; Galatians 1:11-2:2).
- He made only three trips to Jerusalem in the period covered by his genuine letters; one three years after his apostolic call, when he met Peter and James but none of the other apostles (around A.D. 40); the second fourteen years after his call (A.D. 50), when he appeared formally before the entire Jerusalem

leadership to account for his mission and gospel message to the Gentiles (Galatians 2:1–10); and a third, where he was apparently arrested and sent under guard to Rome around A.D. 56 (Romans 15:25–29).

- Paul claimed to experience many revelations from Jesus, including direct voice communications, as well as an extraordinary "ascent" into the highest level of heaven, entering paradise, where he saw and heard "things unutterable" (2 Corinthians 12:1–4).

- He had some type of physical disability that he was convinced had been sent by Satan to afflict him, but allowed by Christ so that he would not be overly proud of his extraordinary revelations (2 Corinthians 12:7–10).

- He claimed to have worked miraculous signs, wonders, and mighty works that verified his status as an apostle (2 Corinthians 12:12).

- He was unmarried, at least during his career as an apostle (1 Corinthians 7:8, 15; 9:5; Philippians 3:8).

- He experienced numerous occasions of physical persecution and deprivation including beatings, being stoned and left for dead, and shipwrecked (1 Corinthians 3:11–12; 2 Corinthians 11:23–27).

- He worked as a manual laborer to support himself on his travels (1 Corinthians 4:12; 1 Thessalonians 2:9; 1 Corinthians 9:6, 12, 15).

- He was imprisoned, probably in Rome, in the early 60s A.D. and refers to the possibility that he would be executed (Philippians 1:1–26).

This is certainly not all we would want but it is all we have, and considering that we have not a single line written by Jesus or any of his twelve apostles, having seven of Paul's genuine letters is a poverty of riches.[8]

The book of Acts provides the following independent bio-graphical information not found in the seven genuine letters:

- Paul's Hebrew name was Saul and he was born in Tarsus, a city in the Roman province of Cilicia, in southern Asia Minor, present-day Turkey (Acts 9:11, 30; 11:25; 21:39; 22:3).
- He came from a family of Pharisees and was educated in Jerusalem under the most famous rabbi of the time, Gamaliel. He also had a sister and a nephew that lived in Jerusalem in the 60s A.D. (Acts 22:3; 23:16).
- He was born a Roman citizen, which means his father also was a Roman citizen (Acts 16:37; 22:27–28; 23:27).
- He had some official status as a witness consenting to the death of Stephen, the first member of the Jesus movement executed after Jesus (Acts 7:54–8:1). He received an official commission from the high priest in Jerusalem to travel to Damascus in Syria to arrest, imprison, and even have executed any members of the Jesus movement who had fled the city under persecution. It was on the road to Damascus that he had his dramatic heavenly vision of Jesus, who commissioned him as the apostle to the Gentiles (Acts 9:1–19; 22:3–11; 26:12–18).
- He worked by trade as a "tentmaker," though the Greek word used probably refers to a "leather worker" (Acts 18:3).

So what should we make of this material from the book of Acts?

That Paul's Hebrew name was Saul we have no reason to doubt. Paul says he is of the tribe of Benjamin, and Saul, the first king of Israel, was also a Benjaminite, so one could see why a Jewish family would choose this particular name for a favored son (1 Samuel 9:21). Since Paul reports that he regularly did manual labor to support himself, and Jewish sons were normally taught some trade to supplement their studies, it is possible he was trained as a leather worker. There is an early rabbinic saying that "he who does not teach his son a trade teaches him banditry."[9]

Whether Paul was born in Tarsus, one has to doubt because Jerome, the fourth-century Christian writer, knew a different tradition. He says that Paul's parents were from Gischala, in Galilee, a Jewish town about twenty-five miles north of Nazareth, and that Paul was born there.[10] According to Jerome, when revolts broke out throughout Galilee following the death of Herod the Great in 4 B.C., Paul and his parents were rounded up and sent to Tarsus in Cilicia as part of a massive exile of the Jewish population by the Romans to rid the area of further potential trouble. Since Jerome certainly knew Paul's claim, according to the book of Acts, to have been born in Tarsus, it is very unlikely he would have contradicted that source without good evidence. Jerome's account also provides us with the only indication we have of Paul's approximate age. Like Jesus, he would have had to have been born before 4 B.C., though how many years earlier we cannot say. This fits rather nicely with Paul's statement in one of his last letters, to a Christian named Philemon, written around A.D. 60, where he refers to himself as an "old man" (Greek *presbytes*).[11]

Jerome's account casts serious doubt on the claim in Acts that Paul was born a Roman citizen. We have to question whether a native Galilean family, exiled from Gischala as a result of anti-Roman uprisings in the area, would have had Roman citizenship. We know that Gischala was a hotbed of revolutionary activity. John of Gischala was one of the most prominent leaders in the First Jewish Revolt against Rome (A.D. 66–70).[12] Paul also says that he was "beaten three times with rods" (2 Corinthians 11:25). This is a punishment administered by the Romans and was forbidden to one who had citizenship.[13] The earliest document we have from Paul is his letter 1 Thessalonians. It is intensely apocalyptic, with its entire orientation on preparing his group for the imminent arrival of Jesus in the clouds of heaven (1 Thessalonians 1:10; 2:19; 3:13; 4:13–18; 5:1-5, 23). One might imagine Paul the former Pharisee with no apocalyptic orientation whatsoever, but it is entirely possible, if Jerome is correct about his parents being exiled from Galilee in an effort to pacify the area, that Paul's apocalyptic orientation might have derived from his family and upbringing. Luke-Acts tends to mute any emphasis on an imminent arrival of the apocalypse, and that author characteristically tones down the apocalyptic themes of Mark, his main narrative source for his gospel.[14]

Acts is quite keen on emphasizing Paul's friendly relations with Roman officials as well as the protection they regularly offered Paul from his Jewish enemies, so claiming that Paul was a Roman citizen, and putting his birth in the Roman senatorial province of Cilicia, serves the author's purposes.

Acts' claim that Paul grew up in Jerusalem and was a student of the famous rabbi Gamaliel is also highly suspect. The book of Acts has an earlier scene, when the apostles Peter and John are arrested by the Jewish authorities, who are threatening to have them killed, in which Gamaliel stands up in the Sanhedrin court and speaks in their behalf, recommending their release (Acts 5:33–39). The story is surely fictitious and is part of the author's attempt to indicate to his Roman audience that reasonable-minded Jews, like noble Roman officials, did not condemn the Christians. It is likely that the author of Acts, in making Paul an honored student of Gamaliel, the most revered Pharisee of the day, wants to further advance this perspective. Throughout his account he constantly characterizes the Jewish enemies of Paul as irrational and rabid, in contrast to those "good" Jews who are calm, reasonable, and respond favorably to Paul (Acts 13:45; 18:12; 23:12).

Whether Paul even lived in Jerusalem before his visionary encounter with Christ can be questioned. In Acts it is a given, but Paul never indicates in any of his letters that Jerusalem was his home as a young man. He does mention twice a connection with Damascus, the capital of the Roman province of Syria (2 Corinthians 11:32; Galatians 1:17). Whether he was in Damascus, which is a hundred and fifty miles northeast of Jerusalem, in pursuit of Jesus' followers or for other reasons, we have no sure way of knowing. The account in Acts of Paul's conversion, repeated three times, that has Paul sent as an authorized delegate of the high priest in Jerusalem to arrest Christians in Damascus has so colored our assumptions about Paul that it is hard to focus on what we find in his letters.

Paul's connection to Jerusalem, or the lack thereof, has much to do with the oft-discussed question of whether Paul would have ever seen or heard Jesus, or could have been a witness to Jesus' crucifixion in A.D. 30. Since he never mentions seeing Jesus in any of his letters, and one would expect that had he been an eyewitness to the events of that Passover week he surely would have drawn upon such a vivid experience, it seems unlikely that he was a Jerusalem resident at that time.

Likewise, Paul's high-placed connections to the Jewish priestly class in Jerusalem can neither be confirmed nor denied. All he tells us is that he zealously persecuted the church of God and tried to destroy it (Galatians 1:12). Some translations have used the English word *violently*, but this is misleading and serves to reinforce the account in Acts that Paul was delivering people over to execution. The Greek word Paul uses (*huperbole*) means "excessively" or "zealously." We take Paul's word that he identified himself as a Pharisee, but there is nothing in his letters to indicate the kind of prominent connections that the author of Acts gives him.

OUTSIDE THE NEW TESTAMENT

Our earliest physical description of Paul comes from a late-second-century Christian writing *The Acts of Paul and Thecla*. It is a wildly embellished and legendary account of Paul's travels, his wondrously miraculous feats, and his formidable influence in persuading others to believe in Christ. The story centers on the beautiful and wealthy virgin Thecla, a girl so thoroughly mesmerized by Paul's preaching that she broke off her engagement to follow Paul and experienced many adventures. As Paul is first introduced, one of his disciples sees him coming down the road:

> And he saw Paul coming, a man small of stature, with a bald head and crooked legs, in a good state of body, with eyebrows meeting and nose somewhat hooked, full of friendliness; for now he appeared like a man, and now he had the face of an angel.[15]

We have no reason to believe this account is based on any historical recollection since *The Acts of Paul and Thecla* as a whole shows no trace of earlier sources or historical reference points. The somewhat unflattering portrait most likely stemmed from allusions in Paul's letters to his "bodily presence" being unimpressive and the subject of scorn, whereas his followers received him as an angel (2 Corinthians 10:10; Galatians 4:13–14).

It might come as a surprise, but outside our New Testament records we have very little additional historical information about Paul other than the valuable tradition that Jerome preserves for us that he was born in Galilee. The early Christian writers of the second century (usually referred to as the "Apostolic Fathers") mention his name fewer than a dozen times, holding him up as an example of heroic faith, but they relate nothing of historical interest. For example, Ignatius, the early-second-century bishop of Antioch, writes: "For neither I nor anyone like me can keep pace with the wisdom of the blessed and glorious Paul, who, when he was among you in the presence of the men of that time, accurately and reliably taught the word concerning the truth."[16] Some of the second- and third-century Christian writers know the tradition that both Peter and Paul ended up in Rome and were martyred during the reign of the emperor Nero—Paul was beheaded and Peter was crucified.[17] The apocryphal *Acts of Peter,* an extravagantly legendary account dating to the third or fourth century A.D., explains that Peter insisted on being crucified upside down so as to show his unworthiness to die in the same manner as Jesus.[18]

Ironically, it seems that we moderns, using our tools of critical historical research, are in a better position than the Christians of the second and third centuries to recover a more authentic Paul.

ACKNOWLEDGMENTS

My work on Paul and his pivotal role in the development of Christianity has now spanned more than four decades, leaving me indebted to countless teachers, students, and colleagues. I want to acknowledge my first teacher of Paul, the incomparable Abraham J. Malherbe, now a retired professor at Yale University, whom I first encountered at Abilene Christian College when I was a freshman in 1963. Malherbe, freshly come to us from Harvard, taught an entire course on the letter of 1 Thessalonians, and his impeccable guidance was my first taste of the academic study of Paul. A decade later, at the University of Chicago, I came under the spell of the young Jonathan Z. Smith, who opened for me the wider world of Hellenistic religions in the ancient Mediterranean world. I was a student of Christian origins but Smith showed me I had missed the forest for the trees in focusing almost entirely on the New Testament writings. My world was transformed as I began to understand the wider context in which Christianity grew and developed. I was honored as well as sobered to have Smith agree to guide me in my Ph.D. dissertation on Paul's mystical experiences. Working with this master teacher and scholar was a privilege but also a daunting challenge. The many hours he spent with me, patiently going through my early drafts of the dissertation chapters, are among the most treasured memories of my life. As I worked on the dissertation over the span of another decade I came to know Morton Smith of Columbia University, who graciously helped me with every aspect of my research on Paul. I will never forget the day he mailed me back an early draft of the dissertation with his annotations on every page, warning me with a phone call to be "sitting down" when I opened the package. His input was sharp and critical, but our dialogue over the course of two or three years contributed to my work in ways I could not have imagined.

My fellow students at Chicago, now lifelong colleagues, Eugene Gallagher, Jorunn Jacobsen Buckley, Arthur Droge, and Naomi Janowitz encouraged my work on Paul all these years and were a major factor in urging me to write this book for a wider audience. Beyond these I must thank my thousands of students at three universities over the course of my thirty years of teaching. The courses I have regularly taught on John the Baptizer, Jesus, James, and Paul have continued to shape my perspectives and never cease to fascinate my students as we "tinker with the foundations of Western civilization," always asking—how did we get here from there?

I thank my wife, Lori, who professes to know little of Paul but loves to listen to my passionate discourses as I pace about the house. It seems the only way I can really talk of Paul is when I am walking back and forth, spouting out some new insight. Finally I give my sincere gratitude to my ever-patient children, Eve and Seth, who have spent the past two years watching me struggle with "the Paul book," tolerating my hours away from the family far too many nights of a week.

Charlotte, North Carolina
November 29, 2010

NOTES

PREFACE: DISCOVERING PAUL

1. Some phrases of this confession of faith appear as early as Ignatius, an early-second-century Christian bishop (Ignatius, *Trallians* 9). Versions of the full "Apostles' Creed" are found in the late second century in the writings of Irenaeus (A.D. 130–202); see Joseph C. Ayer, *A Sourcebook for Ancient Church History* (New York: Charles Scribner's Sons, 1913), pp. 123–26. The standard version in English:

   I believe in God, the Father Almighty, Maker of heaven and earth, and in Jesus Christ, His only Son, Our Lord, Who was conceived by the Holy Ghost, Born of the Virgin Mary, Suffered under Pontius Pilate, Was crucified, died, and was buried. He descended into hell and on the third day He rose again from the dead. He ascended into heaven, and sits on the right hand of the Father Almighty, from whence He shall come to judge the living and the dead. I believe in the Holy Ghost, the holy Catholic Church, the communion of saints, the forgiveness of sins, the resurrection of the body, and the life everlasting. Amen.

2. My Greek professor was the late Dr. Paul Southern, who had learned his Greek from the incomparable A. T. Robertson. We were required to translate the original Greek text aloud without using any notes, and to parse any verb or explain any grammatical construction or vocabulary word on cue. Southern would often take the entire class period to probe the details of a sentence, phrase, or line.

3. *Things Unutterable: Paul's Ascent to Paradise in Its Greco-Roman, Judaic, and Early Christian Contexts* (Lanham, MD: University Press of America, 1986).

4. See my discussion on recovering this lost legacy in *The Jesus Dynasty* (New York: Simon & Schuster, 2006), pp. 305–17.

5. In *The Jesus Dynasty*, I investigate the historical Jesus and his original message and teachings.

6. The three other papal basilicas are St. Peter's Basilica, St. John Lateran, and St. Mary Major.

7. http://www.catholicnewsagency.com/news/st_paul_burial_place_confirmed/. Tradition has it that Paul's body was reburied in this sarcophagus in the late fourth century, with his head moved to the Lateran. The sarcophagus measures 8.4 x 4.1 x 3.2 feet.

8. The traditional date of Paul's death on the Catholic calendar is June 29, A.D. 67. Most scholars would put it a year or two earlier and A.D. 64 is a possibility, since we know of Nero's persecution of the Christians in Rome in the summer of that year following a fire that burned down a large portion of the city; see Tacitus *Annales* 15.44. The Church of the Martyrdom of St. Paul, at Tre Fontane, constructed in 1599, enclosed a fifth-century church containing a much older shrine (Ad Aquas Salvias) that venerated the stone column said to be the one over which Paul stretched his neck for the beheading. That column is visible today in a tiny alcove just to the left of the main altar enclosed by an iron gate, alongside three fountains. Legend has it that when Paul was executed, his decapitated head bounced three times, and each time a fountain sprang up as divine testimony to his greatness. The fountains are also incorporated inside the church today, just to the left of the stone column. The church is a small one with the deaths of both Peter and Paul depicted in vivid detail on paintings and carved frescoes. One hears the constant splashing of running water in its dimly lit interior. In 1867 excavations conducted at the site revealed the original mosaic floor of the church, the Roman-period street, and some coins from the time of Nero.

9. See Eusebius, *Church History* 2.25.5–7. Eusebius notes the general location on the Ostian Way. Later tradition explains that a wealthy Christian woman named Lucina offered the burial space. Other contradictory traditions have Peter and Paul killed at the same time and buried alongside one another at the site of St. Peter's Basilica. A highly embellished legendary account is found in the third-century *Acts of Paul* 11.

10. The pope's announcement coincided with the last day of the "Year of Saint Paul," which had run from June 29, 2008, through June 29, 2009, commemorating the two-thousandth anniversary of Paul's birth. Veneration of Paul during that year was declared an occasion of special "indulgence" for sins committed; see the pope's proclamation at the basilica: http://www.annopaolino.org/interno.asp?id=2&lang=eng

11. http://www.catholicnews.com/data/stories/cns/0903064.htm.

INTRODUCTION: PAUL AND JESUS

1. The only solid chronological peg we have in the letters of Paul is his reference in 2 Corinthians 11:32–33 to the period of his initial vision of Christ in the territory of Damascus during the reign of Nabatean ruler Aretas IV, who ruled the city between A.D. 37 and 39. This dating coincides with a valuable newly recovered early Christian document, the Syriac *Ascents of James*, which mentions Saul's journey to Damascus taking place seven years after the crucifixion. See Robert E. Van Voorst, *The Ascents of James* (Atlanta: Scholars Press, 1989), p. 59.

2. See Steve Mason, *Josephus, Judea, and Christian Origins: Methods and Categories* (Peabody, MA: Hendrickson, 2009), pp. 283–328. There is a summary of Mason's main argument at http://www.bibleinterp.com/articles/mason3.shtml.

3. Ibid., pp. 283–302.

4. Among these, in chronological order, were Judas the Galilean (4 B.C.); Simon of Perea (4 B.C.); Anthroges, called the "Shepherd king" (4 B.C.); an unnamed Samaritan (c. A.D. 36); Theudas; an unnamed figure Josephus calls the "Egyptian" (c. A.D. 56); Menahem son of Judas (A.D. 66); and John of Gischala (A.D. 66). See any index to the works of Josephus for the various references. Theudas and the "Egyptian" are also mentioned in the book of Acts, most probably based upon Josephus (Acts 5:36; 21:38); see Steve Mason, "Josephus and Luke-Acts," in *Josephus and the New Testament* (Peabody, MA: Hendrickson, 1992), pp. 185–229. In addition to the figures that Josephus mentions there was the "Teacher of Righteousness," mentioned often in the Dead Sea Scrolls (e.g., *Damascus Document* 1:11; 20:32; *1QpHab* 2:2). He is never named, though he apparently lived in the first century B.C., and like the others, was persecuted and killed for his claims. See the fascinating treatments by Michael O. Wise, *The First Messiah: Investigating the Savior Before Christ* (New York: Harper, 1999), and Israel Knohl, *The Messiah Before Jesus: The Suffering Servant of the Dead Sea Scrolls* (Berkeley: University of California Press, 2002).

5. Some of the major treatments of Paul that deal particularly with this issue of continuity and discontinuity with Jesus are: Bart Ehrman, *Jesus, Interrupted: Revealing the Hidden Contradictions in the Bible (and Why We Don't Know About Them)* (New York: HarperOne, 2009); Barrie Wilson, *How Jesus Became Christian* (New York: St. Martin's Press, 2008); Joseph Klausner, *From Jesus to Paul,* translated by William F. Stinespring (Boston: Beacon Press, 1943); Hugh J. Schonfield, *Those Incredible Christians* (New York: Bernard Geis Associates, 1968); Hyam Maccoby, *The Mythmaker:*

Paul and the Invention of Christianity (New York: Harper & Row, 1986); Paula Fredriksen, *From Jesus to Christ: The Origins of the New Testament Images of Jesus* (New Haven, CT: Yale University Press, 1988); Alan F. Segal, *Paul the Convert: The Apostasy and Apostolate of Saul the Pharisee* (New Haven, CT: Yale University Press, 1997); Gerd Lüdemann, *Paul: The Founder of Christianity* (Amherst, NY: Prometheus Books, 2001); L. Michael White, *From Jesus to Christianity: How Four Generations of Visionaries and Storytellers Created the New Testament and the Christian Faith* (San Francisco: HarperSanFrancisco, 2004); and N. T. Wright, *What Paul Really Said: Was Paul of Tarsus the Real Founder of Christianity?* (Grand Rapids, MI: Eerdmans, 1997); John Gager, *Reinventing Paul* (New York: Oxford University Press, 2000); John Dominic Crossan and Jonathan L. Reed, *In Search of Paul: How Jesus's Apostle Opposed Rome's Empire with God's Kingdom* (San Francisco: HarperSanFrancisco, 2004); and Garry Wills, *What Paul Meant* (New York: Penguin, 2006).

6. See in particular Richard I. Pervo, *Dating Acts: Between the Evangelists and the Apologists* (Santa Rosa, CA: Polebridge Press, 2006), which convincingly demonstrates that the author of Acts is writing in the early second century, much later than the traditional date of A.D. 80–85. Either way, early or later, the anonymous work is not written by Paul's otherwise obscure companion but shows every evidence of being a pseudonymous literary production typical of the times. See A. J. Droge, "Did 'Luke' Write Anonymously? Lingering at the Threshold," *Die Apostelgeschichte im Kontext antiker und frühchristlicher Historiographie*, edited by J. Frey, C. K. Rothschild, and J. Schröter, BZNW 162 (Berlin: de Gruyter, 2009), pp. 495–518.

7. See Wilson, *How Jesus Became Christian,* and Maccoby, *The Mythmaker.*

8. Paul's first seven letters, in chronological order, are most likely: 1 Thessalonians, Galatians, 1 and 2 Corinthians, Romans, Philippians, and Philemon. The other six, 2 Thessalonians, Colossians, Ephesians, and certainly 1 and 2 Timothy and Titus, are thought by most scholars to be either heavily interpolated or written decades after his death, making them less reliable for reconstructing an authentic "historical" Paul. See Bart Ehrman, "In the Wake of the Apostle: the Deutero-Pauline and Pastoral Epistles," chap. 23 in *The New Testament: A Historical Introduction to the Early Christian Writings,* 4th ed. (New York: Oxford University Press, 2008), pp. 272–394.

9. It is possible that Paul was once married since he says he advanced within Judaism beyond his peers. Jewish men his age would normally marry; not to marry would be considered abnormal. In his letters he speaks of the "loss of all things" and also refers to a situation where an "unbelieving wife"

might leave one who has joined his movement, so it is possible he is alluding to his own personal situation. He says the brother or sister, so abandoned, should not feel obligated to heed Jesus' teaching that there can be no divorce for any cause (Philippians 3:7; 1 Corinthians 7:12-16).

10. The thirteen letters attributed to Paul make up approximately 32,500 of 138,000 total words. See Steve Mason, "Methods and Categories," at http://www.bibleinterp.com/articles/mason3.shtml.

CHAPTER 1: CHRISTIANITY BEFORE PAUL

1. According to Luke, Jesus began his public career when he was around thirty years old (Luke 3:23). Before that we have the single story of Jesus as the "precocious child" (Luke 2:41-52). Josephus, the first-century Jewish historian, makes a similar claim about his own childhood brilliance: "Moreover, when I was a child, and about fourteen years of age, I was commended by all for the love I had to learning; on which account the high priests and principal men of the city came then frequently to me together, in order to know my opinion about the accurate understanding of points of the law" (*Life* 9).

2. John Dominic Crossan calls the first twenty years the "dark age" of early Christianity. See *The Birth of Christianity* (San Francisco: HarperSanFrancisco, 1998), p. ix. See also James G. Crossley, *Why Christianity Happened: A Sociohistorical Account of Christian Origins (26-50 C.E.)* (Louisville, KY: Westminster John Knox Press, 2006).

3. Galatians 1:19; 2:9; Acts 21:18-26.

4. See Mark 1:19 and 3:17. These two brothers, known for their fiery, impetuous personalities, were nicknamed by Jesus "the sons of Thunder." See Mark 10:35; Luke 9:53-54. Along with Peter, the brothers James and John are often singled out as a privileged threesome of inner intimates among the Twelve (Mark 5:37; 9:2; 14:33). According to the book of Acts this James was beheaded around A.D. 40 by Herod Agrippa I, grandson of Herod the Great (Acts 12:1-2).

5. Robert Eisenman, *James the Brother of Jesus: The Key to Unlocking the Secrets of Early Christianity and the Dead Sea Scrolls* (New York: Viking Penguin, 1997); John Painter, *Just James: The Brother of Jesus in History and Tradition* (Columbia: University of South Carolina Press, 1997); Bruce Chilton and Craig A. Evans, eds., *James the Just and Christian Origins*, Supplements to Novum Testamentum (Leiden: Brill, 1999); Richard Bauckham, *James: Wisdom of James, Disciple of Jesus the Sage* (London: Routledge, 1999); Bruce Chilton and Jacob Neusner, eds., *The Brother of Jesus: James the Just and His Mission* (Louisville, KY: Westminster John Knox Press, 2001); Hershel

Shanks and Ben Witherington III, *The Brother of Jesus: The Dramatic Story & Meaning of the First Archaeological Link to Jesus & His Family* (New York: HarperOne, 2003); and Jeffrey J. Bütz, *The Brother of Jesus and the Lost Teachings of Christianity* (Rochester, VT: Inner Traditions, 2005).

6. See my account in *The Jesus Dynasty,* pp. 14–20.

7. No one has questioned the authenticity of the ossuary itself and critics disagree as to which parts might be genuine and which might have been forged. Hershel Shanks offers an insider's up-to-date summary of the current state of affairs regarding the ossuary inscription and considers the case for its authenticity to be a strong one. See Hershel Shanks, *Freeing the Dead Sea Scrolls: And Other Adventures of an Archaeology Outsider* (New York: Continuum, 2010). The original case defending the authenticity is detailed in Shanks and Witherington, *The Brother of Jesus.* For the perspective of scholars critical of authenticity, see Ryan Byrne and Bernadette McNary-Zak, eds., *Resurrecting the Brother of Jesus: The James Ossuary Controversy and the Quest for Religious Relics* (Chapel Hill: University of North Carolina Press, 2009). The latest summary of evidence is at http://www.bibleinterp.com/articles/authjam358012.shtml.

8. See Jerome, *Against Helvidius,* who defends the Catholic doctrine of the *perpetus virginitate* (perpetual virginity) of Mary. Joseph, her faithful husband, also lived a celibate life.

9. Epiphanius, *Panarion* 29.3.8 to 29.4.4.

10. See the discussion and references in *The Jesus Dynasty,* pp. 73–81.

11. Scholars call this period "late Second Temple Judaism" (200 B.C. to A.D. 73). The variations within Jewish groups and sects of this time were many, far more than the standard breakdown of Josephus into Pharisees, Sadducees, Essenes, and Zealots. The book of Acts indicates that the Jesus movement was known in some circles as the Nazarenes, presumably meaning followers of Jesus of Nazareth as the Messiah (Acts 24:5). Whether this was a name they chose to use or one given to them by others, we don't know. One of the best histories of the period is Shaye J. D. Cohen, *From the Maccabees to the Mishnah,* 2nd ed. (Louisville, KY: Westminster John Knox Press, 2006). It is noteworthy that George W. E. Nickelsburg and Michael E. Stone include a significant number of texts from the New Testament in their edited collection of documents, *Early Judaism: Texts and Documents on Faith and Piety,* 2nd ed. (Minneapolis: Augsburg Fortress Press, 2009).

12. See Steve Mason, "Jews, Judaeans, Judaizing, Judaism: Problems of Categorization in Ancient History," in *Journal for the Study of Judaism* 38 (2007): 457–512, and the most helpful distinctions made by Daniel Boyarin, "Rethinking Jewish Christianity: An Argument for Dismantling a Dubious

Category (to which is Appended a Correction of my *Border Lines*)," in *Jewish Quarterly Review* 99:1 (2009): 7–36.

13. See my arguments in *The Jesus Dynasty* that this Mary, mother of James and Joses, is clearly Jesus' mother (pp. 77–81).

14. There were two Jewish revolts in the homeland of Judea and Galilee against Rome. The first, lasting from A.D. 66 to 73, and ending with the last stand at the fortress Masada, resulted in the destruction of the city of Jerusalem and its Temple. It began during the last year of the reign of Nero and was brought to a conclusion by the new emperor, Vespasian, and his son Titus, who became emperor in A.D. 69. The second, associated with the messianic leader Bar Kosiba (also known today as Bar Kochba), lasted from A.D. 132 to 136, during the reign of Hadrian. Both cumulatively resulted in anti-Jewish legislation that restricted Jewish rights and freedom, especially in the homeland. See Louis Feldman, *Jew and Gentile in the Ancient World* (Princeton, NJ: Princeton University Press, 1993).

15. See my arguments in *The Jesus Dynasty*, pp. 243–54, that James functions as a messianic successor of Jesus, ruling over the Council of Twelve that Jesus has set up as a provisionary revolutionary government in preparation for the apocalyptic Kingdom that had drawn near.

16. *Sanhedrin* 56–60.

17. See the innovative and insightful work of April D. DeConick, *Thomasine Traditions in Antiquity: The Social and Cultural World of the Gospel of Thomas*, edited with J. Asgeirsson and R. Uro, Nag Hammadi and Manichaean Studies (Leiden: Brill, 2005); *Recovering the Original Gospel of Thomas: A History of the Gospel and Its Growth*, Supplements to the *Journal of the Study of the New Testament* 286 (London: T. & T. Clark, 2005), and *The Original Gospel of Thomas in Translation: A Commentary and New English Translation of the Complete Gospel*, Supplements to the *Journal of the Study of the New Testament* (London: T. & T. Clark, 2006).

18. This idea is found often in ancient Jewish sources (e.g., *2 Baruch* 15:7).

19. Quoted by Eusebius, *Church History* 2.1.3.

20. Ibid., 2.1.4.

21. Ibid., 2.1.2. Translations of Eusebius are by Kirsopp Lake in the Loeb Classical Library edition.

22. Ibid., 2.23.4.

23. *A Greek-English Lexicon of the New Testament and Other Early Christian Literature*, 3rd ed., s.v. "Diadexomai," p. 227.

24. Robert E. Van Voorst, *The Ascents of James: History and Theology of a Jewish-Christian Community*, SBL Dissertation Series 112 (Atlanta: Scholars Press:

1989). Van Voorst has isolated this source from *Recognitions* 1.33–71 and demonstrated its antiquity.

25. Syriac *Recognitions* 1.43.3.

26. Josephus, *Antiquities* 20.200–1.

27. Hegesippus's account is preserved in extensive quotations by Eusebius, *Church History* 2.23.3–18.

28. See James M. Robinson and Helmut Koester, *Trajectories Through Early Christianity* (Philadelphia: Fortress Press, 1971), pp. 158–204; Paul Nadim Tarazi, *The New Testament: Introduction: Paul and Mark* (Yonkers, NY: St. Vladimir's Seminary Press, 1999).

29. See Bruce Metzger, *The Canon of the New Testament* (Oxford: Clarendon Press, 1987), pp. 191–201.

30. Eusebius, *Church History* 2.23.24–25.

31. See Peter H. Davids, "Palestinian Traditions in the Epistle of James," in *James the Just and Christian Origins,* eds. Bruce Chilton and Craig A. Evans (Leiden: Brill, 1999), pp. 33–57.

32. For a restored copy of the Q source see www.religiousstudies.uncc.edu/jdtabor/Qluke.html.

33. Pronounced: *díd-a-kay.*

34. Several English translations are in the public domain and are available on the Web at http://www.earlychristianwritings.com/didache.html. I have used here the new translation by Bart Ehrman, *The Apostolic Fathers,* Loeb Classical Library 24, vol. 1 (Cambridge, MA: Harvard University Press, 2003), pp. 417–43. The Loeb edition has a critical Greek text on facing pages with the English translation.

CHAPTER 2: RETHINKING RESURRECTION OF THE DEAD

1. Shimon Gibson, *The Final Days of Jesus: The Archaeological Evidence* (New York: HarperOne, 2009), p. 165, in his chapter called "Who Moved the Stone?"

2. The gospel of Mark, considered by most scholars to be the earliest of our four New Testament gospels, is usually dated between A.D. 75 and 80. I put it at least as late as A.D. 80, and perhaps even a bit later. See John Kloppenborg, "*Evocatio Deorum* and the Dating of Mark," *Journal of Biblical Literature* 124:3 (2005): 419–50, for a discussion of the various proposals and arguments. Luke and John are generally thought to be the latest of our four gospels and recently a number of scholars have begun to put them into the early second century A.D. There is a papyrus fragment (John Rylands Library, Manchester, catalogued as P51), the oldest of any

New Testament writing, containing a few lines from the gospel of John that some experts have dated on paleographic grounds alone to the early second century. The early dating is quite suspect. See Brent Nongbri, "The Use and Abuse of P52: Papyrological Pitfalls in the Dating of the Fourth Gospel," *Harvard Theological Review* 98 (2005): 23–48. Since all four authors of our gospels are anonymous, despite the personal names attached to these works by editors, and no explicit dates are given in any of these texts, one has to judge by internal evidence, particularly the relationship of the authors to the catastrophe of the first Jewish revolt, A.D. 66–73, when Jerusalem was destroyed by the Romans and Judea and Galilee were brutally subjugated. David Trobisch has presented a convincing case for the production of an edited edition of the first New Testament in the mid-second century A.D., possibly by Polycarp; see *The First Edition of the New Testament* (New York: Oxford University Press, 2000).

3. James D. Tabor, "What the Bible Really Says About Death, Afterlife, and the Future," in *What the Bible Really Says,* edited by Morton Smith and Joseph Hoffmann (New York: Harper & Row, 1990), pp. 33–51, also available at http://www.religiousstudies.uncc.edu/jdtabor/future.html.

4. The most extensive treatment of these issues is that of Alan F. Segal, *Life After Death: The History of the Afterlife in Western Religion* (New York: Doubleday, 2004).

5. Plato, *Phaedo* 65C, translation by Harold North Fowler, *Plato,* Loeb Classical Library (Cambridge, MA: Harvard University Press, 1914).

6. See Arthur J. Droge and James D. Tabor, "The Death of Socrates and Its Legacy," chap. 2 in *A Noble Death: Suicide and Martyrdom Among Christians and Jews in Antiquity* (New York: HarperCollins, 1992).

7. Plato, *Phaedo* 107A.

8. Translation by C. W. Keyes, Cicero, *De Re Publica,* Loeb Classical Library (Cambridge, MA: Harvard University Press, 1928).

9. See Droge and Tabor, *A Noble Death,* chap. 4, "Acquiring Life in a Single Moment," pp. 85–112.

10. Segal, *Life After Death,* pp. 120–45.

11. Two possible exceptions are Enoch, whose death is not recorded with the explanation that "God took him," and Elijah, who ascends to heaven in a heavenly chariot, presumably escaping death, though this is not explicitly stated (Genesis 5:24; 2 Kings 2:11–12). See Segal, *Life After Death,* pp. 154–57.

12. Ezekiel's vision of the valley of dry bones is usually understood to be meta-phorical, symbolizing the national regeneration of the people of Israel from Exile (Ezekiel 37:1–14). Isaiah 26:19 is sometimes cited as an early reference

to a general resurrection but properly translated it says, "Your dead shall live, my carcass shall arise," so the referents are unclear and the context suggests a symbolic rather than a literal meaning. There are a number of "near death" references, but in each case they refer to escaping death by being rescued from Sheol (Jonah 2:2–6; Psalms 88:1–6). For a thorough discussion of these and related passages in the Hebrew Bible see Segal, *Life After Death,* pp. 255–61.

13. Unfortunately this passage has often been mistranslated with a Christian slant, now made immortal by the chorus of Handel's *Messiah:* "I know that my Redeemer lives," referring to Christ. What Job is saying has nothing to do with his own hope in life after death or resurrection, but quite the opposite. He says plainly that he *wishes* that after his flesh has decayed, if his case is permanently inscribed with an iron pen on a rock, someone would come along, read it, and vindicate him.

14. See Josephus, *Jewish War* 2.119–66.

15. The classic discussion of the differences between the two approaches to death, that of Socrates and Jesus, is the groundbreaking lecture by Oscar Cullman, now published in *Immortality and Resurrection: Death in the Western World: Two Conflicting Currents of Thought,* edited by Krister Stendahl (New York: Macmillan, 1965).

16. *Jewish War* 2.163, translation by H. St. J. Thackeray, *Josephus* (Cambridge, MA: Harvard University Press, 1927).

17. Celsus, *On the True Doctrine,* translated by Joseph Hoffmann (New York: Oxford University Press, 1987), p. 110.

18. N. T. Wright's assertion that the Revised Standard Version and most other modern translations have mistranslated the Greek words *psuchikos* and *pneumatikos* as "physical" and "spiritual" is not convincing. See Craig A. Evans and N. T. Wright, *Jesus, the Final Days: What Really Happened?* edited by Troy A. Miller (Louisville, KY: Westminster John Knox Press, 2009), pp. 86–89. Wright insists that the resurrection body, according to Paul, though transformed, glorified, and immortal, is nonetheless a *material* body, but with significant new properties. He calls it "transphysicality." It is certainly correct that Paul's idea of a spiritual body is nothing like a ghost or disembodied spirit, but it is hardly material or physical, any more than God or the angels are "material" in Paul's thinking. The Greek word *pneumatikos,* related to the noun "spirit" or "wind" (*pneuma*), is precisely the opposite of the material. For a "body" to have substantiality does not mean it has to be "material." What Wright misses is Paul's analogy of the body as old and new clothing, with death as the "naked" state. It is not that the old clothing is somehow transformed into a new heavenly garb, but that the old

is discarded, returns to dust, and the "unclothed" ones who have died (Paul prefers "fallen asleep") awaken and put on new immortal clothing. See N. T. Wright, *The Resurrection of the Son of God* (Minneapolis: Fortress Press, 2003), pp. 312–61, for his complete argument.

19. The verb "to see" here is passive and literally means "he was seen," in the sense of sighted by this or that person.

20. Mark 6:14–29; *Jewish Antiquities* 18.116–19.

21. See http://www.haaretz.com/magazine/week-s-end/in-three-days-you-shall-live-1.218552 for the main news story published in Israel's leading newspaper, *Haaretz*.

22. Israel Knohl, *Messiahs and Resurrection in 'The Gabriel Revelation'* (London: Continuum, 2009), has published the most complete study with text, translation, and commentary. I am following here his main line of interpretation.

23. *Jewish War* 2.57–59.

CHAPTER 3: READING THE GOSPELS IN THE LIGHT OF PAUL

1. Evans and Wright, in *Jesus, the Final Days*, attempt to argue on historical grounds that the conclusion that Jesus emerged from the tomb bodily is the only rational explanation of our evidence. The debate by William Lane Craig and Gerd Lüdemann, *Jesus' Resurrection: Fact or Figment*, edited by Paul Copan and Ronald K. Tacelli (Downers Grove, IL: InterVarsity Press, 2000), rehearses in a fairly exhaustive manner the standard arguments pro and con.

2. Tertullian, *De Spectaculis* 30. The gospel of John mentions that the tomb of Jesus was in a garden and presupposes an unnamed gardener, most likely giving rise to this apocryphal story (John 19:41; 20:15). In a fanciful seventh-century text, pseudonymously attributed to the apostle Bartholomew, the gardener's name is Philogenes. See J. K. Elliott, *The Apocryphal New Testament* (Oxford: Oxford University Press, 1993), pp. 669–70. A medieval Jewish text, *The Toledot Yeshu*, elaborates the tale with even further embellishments.

3. Hugh J. Schonfield, *The Passover Plot* (New York: Bernard Geis Associates, 1965). Michael Baigent most recently published this theory in new dress; see *The Jesus Papers: Exposing the Greatest Cover-Up in History* (San Francisco: HarperSanFrancisco, 2006).

4. See John Dominic Crossan, *The Historical Jesus: Life of a Mediterranean Jewish Peasant* (San Francisco: HarperSanFrancisco, 1991), pp. 354–94.

5. Geza Vermes, *The Resurrection: History and Myth* (New York: Doubleday, 2008), pp. 141–48.

6. Though Mark, followed by Matthew and Luke, seem to put the crucifixion on the afternoon following a Passover meal the night before (Mark 14:12–16; Matthew 26:17–19; Luke 22:7–13), it remains unclear that the "Last Supper" was in fact a Passover meal. John's chronology is more precise and he notes explicitly that this final meal was "before the Passover" and that the Jewish authorities were rushing to crucify Jesus before sundown on the day of preparation for Passover so as to observe the meal that evening (John 13:1; 18:28; 19:14). See my more detailed discussion in *The Jesus Dynasty*, pp. 198–204.

7. Josephus, *Jewish War* 4.317, and the Mishnah *Sanhedrin* 6.4.

8. Matthew is the only gospel that says the tomb belonged to Joseph (Matthew 27:60). This is unlikely since the other gospels make no such connection and Mark and John specify this burial spot was temporary, chosen for its proximity to the place where the Romans crucified Jesus. Matthew is interested in showing how Jesus fulfilled prophecies of the Hebrew Bible and there is a text in Isaiah that predicts a messianic figure would be buried "with a rich man," so most scholars are convinced that he likely added this detail for that reason (Isaiah 53:9).

9. For the possibility that such a Jesus family tomb has been discovered in Jerusalem see *The Jesus Dynasty*, pp. 22–33 (also the Epilogue in the paperback edition published in 2007, pp. 319–30), as well as Simcha Jacobovici and Charles Pellegrino, *The Jesus Family Tomb: The Evidence Behind the Discovery No One Wanted to Find* (New York: HarperOne, 2008), and James D. Tabor and Simcha Jacobovici, *The Jesus Discovery: The New Archaeological Find That Reveals the Birth of Christianity* (New York: Simon & Schuster, 2012).

10. For reasons to identify the woman called "Mary the mother of James" as Jesus' mother see my arguments in *The Jesus Dynasty*, pp. 73–81.

11. For a more detailed discussion of these additional endings of Mark see *The Jesus Dynasty*, pp. 230–31.

12. See the discussion in Raymond Brown, *The Virginal Conception and the Bodily Resurrection of Jesus* (New York: Paulist Press, 1973), pp. 120–23.

13. See chapter 14, "Dead but Twice Buried," pp. 223–40.

14. An edited e-mail response from Jerome Murphy-O'Connor, professor of New Testament, Ecole Biblique, Jerusalem, quoted with his permission.

15. Jane Schaberg and others have argued that this special appearance to Mary Magdalene narrated by John preserves for us an early tradition that Mary Magdalene was the first witness to Jesus' resurrection. See *The Resurrection of Mary Magdalene: Legends, Apocrypha, and the Christian Testament* (New York: Continuum, 2002). Matthew says that Jesus met the "women," includ-

ing Mary Magdalene, as they were running from the tomb. The longer ending of Mark, though not likely original to Mark, nonetheless echoes the tradition that "he appeared first to Mary Magdalene" (Matthew 28:9–10; Mark 16:9–12).

16. Eusebius, *Church History* 4.12.

17. *Gospel of Peter* 14 [58], translation from J. K. Elliott, *The Apocryphal New Testament*, pp. 157–58.

18. See R. H. Stein, "Is the Transfiguration (Mark 9:2–8) a Misplaced Resurrection Account?," *Journal of Biblical Literature* 95 (1976): 79–96.

19. The tradition that Judas was replaced with Matthias, to fill out the apostolic council to twelve, as Jesus had established, is put seven weeks after Jesus' death, when the Eleven would have already returned to Galilee. The official list of the Twelve, over the next decades, was an important foundation of the movement and was seen to have lasting, eschatological significance based on the promise of Jesus (Luke 22:30; Revelation 21:14). Some ancient manuscript copies of 1 Corinthians amend Paul's reference to the "Twelve" to read "Eleven," in an attempt to harmonize with Luke (24:9, 33) where Jesus appears the same day to the "Eleven," not the "Twelve," since Judas was dead (compare Matthew 28:16; longer Mark 16:14).

20. See Robert L. Wilken, *The Christians as the Romans Saw Them* (New Haven, CT: Yale University Press, 1984).

21. See Lucian, *The Passing of Peregrinus*; Justin Martyr, *Dialogue with Trypho*; and Origen, *Contra Celsum*.

22. The philosopher Philostratus published a *Life of Apollonius* with the support of the Syrian empress Julia Domna, wife of Septimius Severus, around A.D. 220, though much like Luke he claims to be relying on eyewitness accounts and earlier sources. See Philostratus, *Life of Apollonius* 1.2, translated by C. P. Jones, edited by G. W. Bowersock (Baltimore: Penguin, 1970).

23. C. P. Jones, "An Epigram on Apollonius of Tyana," *Journal of Hellenic Studies* 100 (1980): 190–94.

24. See *Augustan History*, Alexander 29.2.

CHAPTER 4: LAST BUT NOT LEAST

1. See my discussion in *Things Unutterable*, pp. 69–97.

2. If Paul's initial vision of Christ took place around A.D. 37, his three years in Arabia would have ended around A.D. 40–41. Fourteen years later takes one to A.D. 54–55, which corresponds closely to when his Corinthians correspondence was written. See Morton Enslin, *Reapproaching Paul* (Philadelphia: Westminster Press, 1972), pp. 53–55.

3. See the many studies listed by Bruce Metzger, *Index to Periodical Literature on the Apostle Paul* (Grand Rapids, MI: Eerdmans, 1960), pp. 15–16.

4. See the arguments of Robert M. Price, "Punished in Paradise," *Journal for the Study of the New Testament* 7 (1980): 33–40. Given the self-reported experiences of celibate monks and priests who struggle with sexual thoughts that they attribute to demons, it is possible Paul refers to such temptations, or perhaps even a literal physical condition such as periodic priapism.

5. For example, in the Dead Sea Scrolls, see *Testimonia* (4Q175, compare 4Q558) in Geza Vermes, ed., *The Complete Dead Sea Scrolls in English*, 4th ed. (New York: Penguin, 1998), pp. 495–96.

6. Rabbis Hillel and Shammai were the two most renowned Torah scholars of their generation (traditionally 50 B.C. to A.D. 20). These sayings are recorded in the *Mishnah*, one of the earliest collections of rabbinic materials.

7. Philo, *De Opificio Mundi* 128; *De Vita Contemplativa* 30–31; *Quod Omnis Probus Liber Sit* 80–83; Luke 4:16–17; Acts 9:20; 13:15; 15:21; *Corpus Inscriptionum Iudaicarum* 1404; Josephus, *Wars* 2.289–92. There has been considerable debate among scholars as to what activities, liturgical and otherwise, might have taken place in Jewish synagogues or houses of study during the Roman period and some have discounted the references in Luke-Acts as having any historical value for the first century practice. For an overview of the history of this discussion, see an online article by Anders Runesson that puts things in a proper balance: http://www.bibleinterp.com/articles/Runesson-1st-Century_Synagogue_1.shtml.

8. See *Damascus Document* 6:19; Luke 22:28–30.

9. Paul uses a Greek translation of Isaiah that has "the nations" or Gentiles, in the plural, in both Isaiah 49:7 and 8, whereas the Hebrew text has "nation" in the singular—as if to address the Israelites.

10. The common English translation of 1 Thessalonians 4:14 seems to imply the dead are *already* with Christ, but then Paul goes on to say they will "meet" in the air, which makes no sense. A proper translation makes things clear: "For since we believe that Jesus died and rose again, even so, through Jesus, God will bring [from the dead] along with him, those who have fallen asleep."

11. See Albert Schweitzer, *The Mysticism of Paul the Apostle*, translated by William Montgomery (London: A. & C. Black, 1931), pp. 136–37, as well as Arthur Droge, "MORI LUCRUM: Paul and Ancient Theories of Suicide," *Novum Testamentum* 30 (1988): 263–86.

12. The itinerary proposed in the later letters of 1 and 2 Timothy and Titus—where Paul is released from prison, continues his missionary work, and ends up imprisoned a second time in Rome, where he is executed—is not reliable.

CHAPTER 5: A COSMIC FAMILY AND A HEAVENLY KINGDOM

1. For a photo, transcription, and translation of this and many other similar letters from the period, see Adolf Deissmann, *Light from the Ancient East,* translated by Lionel R. M. Strachan (Grand Rapids, MI: Baker Book House, 1978), pp. 178–83.

2. Romans 11:25; 16:25; 1 Corinthians 2:1, 7; 1 Corinthians 4:1, 15:51.

3. See Deissmann, *Light from the Ancient East,* pp. 366–67.

4. Steve Mason is the one who has pointed this out. See his discussion in *Josephus, Judea, and Christian Origins: Methods and Categories* (Peabody, MA: Hendrickson, 2009), pp. 283–328. There is a summary of Mason's main argument at http://www.bibleinterp.com/articles/mason3.shtml.

5. See Ra'anan S. Boustan and Annette Yoshiko Reed, eds., *Heavenly Realms and Earth Realities in Late Antique Religions* (Cambridge, U.K.: Cambridge University Press, 2004).

6. Many modern Christian Evangelicals, influenced by the interpretations of nineteenth-century biblical scholar John Nelson Darby, base their view of a "secret rapture" of the church before the Second Coming of Christ on this passage in Paul.

7. Although Luke is following a passage in Mark 12:24–25 here as his source, these particular descriptions of the nature of the resurrection he adds to Mark's narrative, as one can see with a side-by-side comparison.

8. Isaiah 61:1 is the core text where Yahweh "anoints" by the Spirit the one who is to bring "Good News." Jesus quotes this text in Luke 4:18–21, applying it to himself as the Messiah. The Dead Sea Scrolls also quote Isaiah 61:1 and refer to this figure as the "Anointed one of the Spirit." See "The Heavenly Prince Melchizedek," 11Q13 in Vermes, ed., *The Complete Dead Sea Scrolls in English,* pp. 500–1.

9. The Greek word I have translated here "son-ship" (*hiothesios*) appears in some English translations as "adoption." This is misleading since it can imply in English that there is no "natural" relationship between the parent and the child, only a legal one. Paul believes that the select group is truly made up of *children* of God, begotten by his Spirit, every bit as much as Jesus became a child of God.

10. One of the better studies is by James G. Dunn, *Christology in the Making* (Philadelphia: Westminster, 1980).

11. Some scholars have argued that Paul is not referring to Jesus' preexistence here but rather to his choice, as a human being created in the image of God, to "empty" himself and become an obedient servant, providing a model for the glorification process. See Charles Talbert, "The Problem of Pre-Existence in Phil. 2:6-11," *Journal of Biblical Literature* 86 (1967): 141–53. The schol-

arly discussion of the passage is extensive. See Ralph P. Martin, *Carmen Christi: Philippians ii.5–11 in Recent Interpretation and in the Setting of Early Christian Worship*, 2nd ed. (Grand Rapids, MI: Eerdmans, 1983).

12. There was ample development of these kinds of speculative cosmological ideas within various forms of mystical Judaism at the time and one can assume Paul would have been aware of these. See Schonfield, "The Christology of Paul," in *Those Incredible Christians*, pp. 227–41.

13. See my discussion of Jesus and John the Baptizer and their proclamation of the Kingdom in *The Jesus Dynasty*, pp. 125–67.

14. See Leviticus 23:9–10.

CHAPTER 6: A MYSTICAL UNION WITH CHRIST

1. Only once in the Hebrew Bible does the idea of believing or trusting in Moses occur, but it is as an agent of God, when the Israelites at the crossing of the Red Sea "believed in Yahweh, and in his servant Moses" (Exodus 14:31).

2. Outside of Paul's letters (58 times), or letters attributed to Paul (27 times), the phrase "in Christ" occurs only once in the book of Acts, where the reference is to *faith in* Christ (Acts 24:24), and three times in the letter known as 1 Peter, where Paul's ideas are directly echoed by the author (1 Peter 3:15; 5:10, 14).

3. The great classic study is Albert Schweitzer, *The Mysticism of Paul the Apostle*, translated by William Montgomery (London: A. & C. Black, 1931). Schweitzer successfully argued that one does not need to go to "pagan" Greco-Roman religions to find close parallels to Paul's mysticism. Paul's thinking is rooted in Jewish apocalyptic traditions of the late Second Temple period (300 B.C. to A.D. 70).

4. Romans 3:22, 26; Galatians 2:16; 3:22.

5. The most direct reference is 1 Corinthians 9:14: "In the same way the Lord commanded that those who proclaim the gospel should get their living by the gospel." One can assume that passage could be connected to Luke 10:17: "The laborer is worthy of his hire." It is possible, but not certain, that he knows Jesus' teaching forbidding divorce (1 Corinthians 7:10), but when he says he has something "from the Lord," it can just as likely mean he is claiming a subsequent revelation from the heavenly Christ. That is surely the case in 1 Corinthians 11:23–26, where he relates the scene of the Lord's Supper. Paul teaches that loving one's neighbor fulfills the Torah, but since this saying was common among rabbis of his day, not only Jesus, we can't say he is referring to Jesus (Galatians 5:14; Romans 13:10). The book of Acts quotes Paul as

quoting Jesus once: "Remembering the words of the Lord Jesus, how he said, 'It is more blessed to give than to receive'" (Acts 20:23). Ironically, this does not appear to be a direct quotation but an allusion, perhaps to Luke 6:38.

6. See Margaret Barker, *The Great Angel: A Study of Israel's Second God* (Louisville, KY: Westminster John Knox Press, 2002), and Alan F. Segal, *Two Powers in Heaven: Early Rabbinical Reports About Christianity and Gnosticism* (Leiden: Brill, 2002).

7. The literal term in Hebrew, "messenger-Yahweh," is usually translated as "the angel of Yahweh," but this is not the best choice for English since "angel" in English has its own set of connotations quite different from Hebrew. In Hebrew the phrase used, *mal'ak Yahweh*, means a manifestation of Yahweh and this figure speaks and acts *as* Yahweh in the first person, appearing and departing, sometimes in a flame of fire (see Genesis 16:10; 18:33; 22:11; Exodus 3:2; Judges 13:20). There are a few passages where these "two Yahwehs" are mentioned in a single verse: "Then Yahweh [below] rained on Sodom and Gomorrah brimstone and fire from Yahweh [above] from heaven" (Genesis 19:24).

8. See Schonfield, "The Christology of John," in *Those Incredible Christians*, pp. 243–55.

9. See David B. Capes, *Old Testament Yahweh Texts in Paul's Christology*, WUZT 2.47 (Tübingen: J. C. B. Mohr/Paul Siebeck, 1992) for ways that Paul applied texts of the Hebrew Bible about Yahweh directly to Jesus.

10. Josephus, *Antiquities* 18.117–19.

11. They had to do with ritual purity after contact with such contaminants as blood, a corpse, disease, or bodily discharges (Leviticus 14:8–9; 15:1–33; 19:13). Running water from a lake or stream was preferred though ritual pools or baths called *mikveh* are commonly found in Jewish homes and public buildings during this period.

12. *Community Rule* 3.1–10, in Vermes, ed., *The Dead Sea Scrolls in English*, pp. 100–1.

13. See my discussion in *The Jesus Dynasty*, pp. 134–37.

14. See Richard E. Demaris, "Corinthian Religion and Baptism for the Dead (1 Corinthians 15:29): Insights from Archaeology and Anthropology," *Journal of Biblical Literature* 114 (1995): 661–82.

15. The author of Acts records one such riverside baptism (Acts 16:13–15).

16. Naked baptism was considered essential and is specified in all of our sources. Presumably, the sexes were segregated even if male attendants officiated, but it is possible that women attended to women. We are not sure how this practice was carried out to ensure modesty. In Judaism to this day men and women who visit the *mikveh* or ritual bath remove all clothing.

When male witnesses are present in the case of women, they stand out of sight. See Jonathan Z. Smith, "Garments of Shame," in *Map Is Not Territory* (Leiden: Brill, 1978), pp. 1–23.

17. Paul never mentions the "laying on of hands" in his letters but the author of the books of Acts seems to know of the practice, tracing it back to Paul (Acts 19:6). It is also mentioned twice in later letters attributed to Paul (1 Timothy 4:14; 2 Timothy 1:6). The book of Hebrews, which seems to have some connection to Pauline ideas, mentions "baptisms and the laying on of hands" in conjunction with one another (Hebrews 6:2).

18. See Romans 16:16; 1 Corinthians 16:20; 2 Corinthians 13:12; 1 Thessalonians 5:26.

19. The idea of two distinct forms of the Eucharist, one from Paul and the other from the Jerusalem church, was effectively argued by Hans Lietzmann in 1926. Needless to say it stirred up a whirlwind of controversy, though overall I find it quite convincing. For an updated discussion see R. H. Fuller, "The Double Origin of the Eucharist," *Biblical Research* 8 (1963): 60–72.

20. Translation from Ehrman, *The Apostolic Fathers*, vol. 1, p. 431.

21. See Bruce Metzger, *The Text of the New Testament*, 3rd ed. (Oxford: Oxford University Press, 1992), pp. 156–85, for a discussion of various New Testament manuscript traditions. The Western Text (Codex Bezae, designated D) has a number of significant omissions, particularly in Luke, that some scholars have argued are more authentic but the example of Luke 19b–20 seems to be a clear attempt by the textual editors to remove the difficulty of the two cups. It is more likely that Luke's original text had both than that a later manuscript tradition would have added the second cup. Additions and omissions are almost always in the service of harmonization, that is, when the scribes see difficulties they wish to help resolve with the text they are copying.

22. See *The Messianic Rule* 2.10–20 (1QSa), in Vermes, ed., *The Dead Sea Scrolls in English*, pp. 159–60.

23. See Preserved Smith, *A Short History of Christian Theophagy* (Chicago: Open Court, 1922). Parallels have been suggested with Attis the Phrygian god, Mithras, and particularly Dionysus, where an animal was torn apart and eaten raw.

24. Dennis Edwin Smith, *From Symposium to Eucharist: The Banquet in the Early Christian World* (Minneapolis: Augsburg Fortress Press, 2003).

25. See the discussion and references in Morton Smith, *Clement of Alexandria and a Secret Gospel of Mark* (Cambridge, MA: Harvard University Press, 1973), pp. 217–19.

26. Bruce Chilton has suggested that Jesus did indeed refer to "body" and

"blood"; not to his own, but to that of the Passover sacrifice that he was rejecting as part of a corrupt Temple system: "This is my body"—the bread; "This is my blood"—the wine, so no need for the literal flesh-and-blood sacrifice of a lamb. As attractive as I find this alternative, it seems to me unlikely since the juxtaposition of the terms bread/body and wine/blood comes from Paul and has no independent source. See Bruce Chilton and Craig A. Evans, *Jesus in Context: Temple, Purity, and Restoration* (Leiden: Brill, 1997), pp. 59–89.

27. See Sydney E. Ahlstrom, *A Religious History of the American People* (New Haven, CT: Yale University Press, 2004), pp. 385–510.

28. On this point see Schweitzer, *The Mysticism of Paul the Apostle*, pp. 18–24.

29. In Galatians 4:3–4, Paul refers to the astral spirits who enslave humankind but are defeated by Christ.

30. See Robert Wilken, *The Christians as the Romans Saw Them*, pp. 16–20.

CHAPTER 7: ALREADY BUT NOT YET

1. For a good effort at putting a positive face on Paul's views of women see Garry Wills, *What Paul Meant* (New York: Penguin, 2006), pp. 89–104. Wills agrees that Paul, as a man of his culture and time, could not wholly escape the sexism common in both Jewish and Greco-Roman culture, but Wills concludes that Paul taken overall defends women's equality. What Wills has failed to take into account, in my view, is the inherent and unavoidable contradiction between Paul's "already but not yet" stance on all of these related gender issues. An evangelical Christian attempt at the same task is Brian J. Dodd, *The Problem with Paul* (Downers Grove, IL: InterVarsity Press, 1996).

2. See Cynthia L. Thompson, "Hairstyles, Head-coverings, and St. Paul: Portraits from Roman Corinth," *Biblical Archaeologist* 51:2 (June 1988): 99–115.

3. This prohibition against braided hair, put up above the neck and ears, shows up elsewhere in the New Testament: "Women should adorn themselves in respectable apparel, with modesty and self-control, not with braided hair" (2 Timothy 2:9); "Do not let your adorning be external—the braiding of hair" (1 Peter 3:3).

4. This theme of humankind falling into corruption through these "fallen" angels is a common one in Jewish texts of the period; see *Jubilees* 5:1–6, *1 Enoch* 15:1–12. It also shows up in a few New Testament texts: 2 Peter 2:4; Jude 6. The emphasis is that these angels *left* their proper place in the created order. There are several other possible interpretations, among them

the fascinating proposal of Jason BeDuhn that Paul is speaking of the creation of the sexes, divided into male and female, as the inferior work of angels, when God had originally intended Humankind/Adam to be an androgynous unified being: "'Because of the Angels': Unveiling Paul's Anthropology in 1 Corinthians 11," *Journal of Biblical Literature* 118:2 (1999): 295–320. BeDuhn offers a very thorough review of the abundance of scholarly literature attempting to interpret this difficult verse. In the end I remain convinced that the lustful gaze of the angels is what Paul has in mind.

5. The Dead Sea Scrolls sect shared this idea that the holy angels were present when the group assembled. See Joseph A. Fitzmyer, "A Feature of Qumran Angelology and the Angels of I Cor. xi. 10," *New Testament Studies* 4 (1957): 48–58. Fitzmyer does not share the view that Paul's reference is to lustful angels, but simply to the holiness of angels present in the assembly who would be offended by any kind of immodesty on the part of women. My argument is that Paul's cosmos is as thick with negative spiritual forces as with positive, and he mentions in this same context both the "discerning of spirits" and the likelihood that some are being "moved" by demonic activity posing as the Spirit of Christ (see 1 Corinthians 12:1–4).

6. See Borg and Crossan, *The First Paul*, pp. 55–57.

7. See the footnote in the Revised Standard Version.

8. Thomas C. Oden, *First and Second Timothy and Titus* (Louisville, KY: John Knox Press, 1989), 101.

9. Sandra R. Joshel, *Slavery in the Roman World* (Cambridge, U.K.: Cambridge University Press, 2010).

10. See S. Scott Bartchy, "Slavery (Greco-Roman)," in *Anchor Bible Dictionary* (New York: Doubleday, 1992).

11. Anthony Everitt, *Cicero: The Life and Times of Rome's Greatest Politician* (New York: Random House, 2003), pp. 121, 175–77, 241–47, 319–24.

12. The Revised Standard Version, as well as many others, translates this problematic phrase "avail yourself of the opportunity," which is surely less offensive than the more literal reading. S. Scott Bartchy supports this, translating more freely: "Were you a slave when you were called? Don't worry about it. But if, indeed, you become manumitted, by all means [as a freedman] live according to [God's calling]." See *MALLON CHRESAI: First-Century Slavery and 1 Corinthians 7:21*, Society of Biblical Literature Dissertation Series 11 (Atlanta: Scholars Press, 1973). The New Revised Standard Version returns to something closer to my understanding: "Even if you can gain your freedom, make use of your present condition now more than ever."

CHAPTER 8: THE TORAH OF CHRIST

1. See Julie Galambush, *The Reluctant Parting: How the New Testament's Jewish Writers Created a Christian Book* (San Francisco: HarperSanFrancisco, 2005); Amy-Jill Levine, *The Misunderstood Jew: The Church and the Scandal of the Jewish Jesus* (San Francisco: HarperSanFrancisco, 2007); Barrie Wilson, *How Jesus Became Christian* (New York: St. Martin's Press, 2008); James D. G. Dunn, ed., *Jews and Christians: The Parting of the Ways* (Grand Rapids, MI: Eerdmans, 1999).

2. The polemics of Christians against Jews are early and amazingly bitter; see William Nicholls, *Christian Antisemitism: A History of Hate* (New York: Jason Aronson, 1995).

3. See the discussion by Shaye J. D. Cohen, "Judaism without Circumcision and 'Judaism' without 'Circumcision' in Ignatius," *Harvard Theological Review* 95:4 (2002): 395–415, as well as the study by Thomas A. Robinson, *Ignatius of Antioch and the Parting of the Ways: Early Jewish-Christian Relations* (Peabody, MA: Hendrickson, 2009).

4. See Louis Feldman, *Jew and Gentile in the Ancient World* (Princeton, NJ: Princeton University Press, 1993).

5. One of the classic Jewish treatises on the relationship of Israel and the nations of the world is that of the nineteenth-century Italian Rabbi Elijah Benamozegh, *Israel and Humanity* (*Israël et l'Humanité*), translated and edited by Maxwell Luria (New York: Paulist Press, 1994).

6. See Acts 15:19–21 plus references in Acts 10:1–2; 13:16, 26, 43, 50; 16:14; 17:4, 17; 18:7, as well as Luke 7:1–9. See the discussion, "The Godfearers: Did They Exist?," which includes "The God-Fearers: A Literary and Theological Invention," by Robert S. MacLennan and A. Thomas Kraabel; "Jews and God-Fearers in the Holy City of Aphrodite," by Robert F. Tannenbaum; and "The Omnipresence of the God-Fearers," by Louis H. Feldman, in *Biblical Archaeology Review* 12:5 (September/October 1986): 44–63.

7. Males, whatever their age, were required to undergo circumcision, and both males and females were immersed in a *mikveh* or Jewish ritual bath. See Louis H. Feldman, "Conversion to Judaism in Classical Judaism," *Hebrew Union College Annual* 74 (2003): 115–56; Shaye J. D. Cohen, *The Beginnings of Jewishness* (Berkeley: University of California Press, 1999), pp. 219–21; and Joseph R. Rosenbloom, *Conversion to Judaism: From the Biblical Period to the Present* (Cincinnati: Hebrew Union College Press, 1979).

8. The Talmud says that the twelfth petition of this prayer, the *Birkat HaMinim*, was added in the late first century by the rabbis, directed against Christians (*notzerim*) who were giving Jesus divine status. See *Berachot* 28b and William Horbury, "The Benediction of the 'Minim' and Early Jewish-

Christian Controversy," *Journal of Theological Studies* 33:1 (1982): 19–61.

9. Larry Hurtado and others have more recently advanced the argument that such worship of Jesus as divine originated not with Paul but among Jesus' earliest Jewish followers, in response to faith in his resurrection and ascension to heaven. See Larry W. Hurtado, *Lord Jesus Christ: Devotion to Jesus in Earliest Christianity* (Grand Rapids, MI: Eerdmans, 2005). Hurtado refers to this as "binitarian devotion," as it includes always God the Father, but now with Jesus as Lord at the right hand of God. The latest contribution to this debate is James D. G. Dunn, *Did the Early Christians Worship Jesus? The New Testament Evidence* (Louisville, KY: Westminster John Knox Press, 2010).

10. Paul's phrase "under the Torah of Christ" is literally "in (the) law of Christ," meaning within its jurisdiction, just as one who is Jewish is "in (the) law of Moses" while Gentiles are "outside" that law.

11. *Jubilees* 7:20–28; Acts 15:19–20; *Babylonian Talmud Sanhedrin* 56a–56b.

12. The Apocrypha contains ten books, all dating to the two centuries before the time of Jesus, that are included in Catholic Bibles and the ancient Greek Old Testament (Septuagint) but excluded from the Hebrew Bible or Christian Old Testament.

CHAPTER 9: THE "BATTLE OF THE APOSTLES"

1. An impressive visual website of St. Peter's Basilica with photos and descriptions is http://www.stpetersbasilica.org.

2. In the gospel of John there is an allusion to Peter's death (John 21:18–19), and the pseudo-Pauline text of 2 Timothy 4:6–8 seems to know of Paul's death. In both cases nothing that specific is related as to time, place, or manner of execution.

3. Irenaeus, *Against Heresies* 3.1.1; 3.3.2.

4. See Raymond E. Brown and John P. Meier, *Antioch and Rome: New Testament Cradles of Catholic Christianity* (New York: Paulist Press, 2004), p. 98.

5. Tacitus, the Roman historian, is our best source for this persecution. He is the first Roman writer to mention "Christus" ("Chrestus") and his execution in Judea under Pontius Pilate. His account gives one insight into the attitude of the ruling class in Rome in the early second century A.D. toward this newly emerging eastern cult called "Christianity": "But all human efforts, all the lavish gifts of the emperor, and the propitiations of the gods, did not banish the sinister belief that the conflagration was the result of an order. Consequently, to get rid of the report, Nero fastened the guilt

and inflicted the most exquisite tortures on a class *hated for their abominations,* called Christians by the populace. Christus, from whom the name had its origin, suffered the extreme penalty during the reign of Tiberius at the hands of one of our procurators, Pontius Pilatus, and *a most mischievous superstition,* thus checked for the moment, again broke out not only in Judaea, the first source of the evil, but even in Rome, where all things hideous and shameful from every part of the world find their centre and become popular. Accordingly, an arrest was first made of all who pleaded guilty; then, upon their information, an immense multitude was convicted, not so much of the crime of firing the city, as of *hatred against mankind.* Mockery of every sort was added to their deaths. Covered with the skins of beasts, they were torn by dogs and perished, or were nailed to crosses, or were doomed to the flames and burnt, to serve as a nightly illumination, when daylight had expired. Nero offered his gardens for the spectacle, and was exhibiting a show in the circus, while he mingled with the people in the dress of a charioteer or stood aloft on a cart. Hence, even for criminals who deserved extreme and exemplary punishment, there arose a feeling of compassion; for it was not, as it seemed, for the public good, but to glut one man's cruelty, that they were being destroyed." Tacitus, *Annales* 15.44, translation by Alfred John Church and William Jackson Brodribb, *Complete Works of Tacitus* (New York: Modern Library, 1942), pp. 380–81.

6. Suetonius, *Lives of the Twelve Caesars: Claudius* 25.4 and Acts 18:1–3.

7. John J. Gunther surveys the views of thirty-nine scholars who have proposed thirteen categories of identification. See *St. Paul's Opponents and Their Background: A Study of Apocalyptic and Jewish Sectarian Teachings* (Leiden: Brill, 1973).

8. See Jeffrey J. Bütz, *The Brother of Jesus,* pp. 154–61, which offers a persuasive reconsideration of the correctness of F. C. Baur's essential position.

9. A. F. J. Klijn and G. J. Reinink, *Patristic Evidence for Jewish Christian Sects,* Supplements to *Novum Testamentum* 36 (Leiden: Brill, 1973).

10. See Hans-Joachim Schoeps, *Jewish Christianity,* translated by Douglas R. A. Hare (Philadelphia: Fortress Press, 1969), for a summary of the basic Ebionite sources that survive and a discussion of their contents.

APPENDIX: THE QUEST FOR THE HISTORICAL PAUL

1. The Quest was given both its history and its name by Albert Schweitzer, whose groundbreaking book, published in 1906 with the nondescript German title *Von Reimarus zu Wrede* (From Reimarus to Wrede), was given the more provocative title in English, *The Quest of the Historical Jesus,*

translated by William Montgomery (London: A. & C. Black, 1910).

2. The beginning of the modern Jesus Quest is usually dated to around 1835 with the publication of David Strauss's *Life of Jesus*. The full work, *Das Leben Jesu kritisch bearbeitet* (Tübingen, 1835–36), was published in English as *The Life of Jesus, Critically Examined*, 3 vols. (London, 1846), translated by George Eliot, the pen name of British novelist Mary Ann Evans. Baur's major work, *Paulus, der Apostel Jesu Christi, sein Leben und Wirken, seine Briefe und seine Lehre* (Paul the Apostle of Jesus Christ: His Life and Works, His Letters and His Teaching), was published in 1845. Strauss was a student of Baur at the University of Tübingen.

3. Most recently, Marcus Borg and John Dominic Crossan, *The First Paul: Reclaiming the Radical Visionary Behind the Church's Conservative Icon* (New York: HarperOne, 2009). A more conservative, but nonetheless critical treatment relying more on the letters of Paul than the book of Acts is that of Jerome Murphy-O'Connor, *Paul: A Critical Life* (New York: Oxford University Press, 1996).

4. An English copy of the New Testament, Revised Standard Version, with text only and no notes or references, runs 284 pages total. The thirteen letters attributed to Paul, plus the book of Acts, add up to 109 pages of the total—just over one-third.

5. See Bart Ehrman's summary analysis "In the Wake of the Apostle: The Deutero-Pauline and Pastoral Epistles," in *The New Testament: A Historical Introduction to the Early Christian Writings*, 4th ed. (New York: Oxford University Press, 2008), pp. 272–394.

6. "Chester Beatty Papyri," in *Anchor Bible Dictionary*, vol. 1 (New York: Doubleday, 1992), pp. 901–3.

7. Not only was the composition of such speeches common in Greek literary histories: it was in fact expected. Thucydides, in his *History* of the Peloponnesian war, says that he composed speeches according to "what was called for in each situation" (1.22.2). Josephus, a contemporary of the author of Acts, is a prime example; see Henry Cadbury, *The Making of Luke-Acts* (New York: Macmillan, 1927), and Arthur J. Droge and James D. Tabor, *A Noble Death: Suicide and Martyrdom Among Christians and Jews in Antiquity* (New York: HarperCollins, 1992), pp. 53–112.

8. The letters of James and Jude might be exceptions, though many scholars question whether these two brothers of Jesus were part of the Twelve and others question the authenticity of the letters themselves. Few scholars consider the letters of 1 and 2 Peter as written by Peter. 1 Peter, in particular, is surprisingly "Pauline" in tone and content and fits nothing we know of Peter based on more reliable sources—including Paul's genuine letters. The

letters of John are not from John the fisherman, one of the Twelve, but from a later John, sometimes referred to as "John the Elder," who lived in Asia Minor (see Eusebius, *Church History* 3.39.4–7).

9. *Pirke Avot* 2.3.

10. Jerome, *De Virus Illustribus* (PL 23, 646).

11. See Murphy-O'Connor, *Paul: A Critical Life*, pp. 1–5. The translation "ambassador," found in the Revised Standard Version, is conjectural, with no manuscript support. It assumes the misspelling of the Greek word "ambassador" (*presbeutes*) as "elder" (*presbytes*), but "elder" is the reading in all our manuscripts. The New Revised Standard Version and New Jerusalem Bible correctly have "elder."

12. Josephus, *Jewish War* 7.263–65. Josephus mentions John of Gischala often in his history of the revolt.

13. See *Digest* 48.6–7, a compendium of Roman law in *The Digest of Justinian*, edited by T. Mommsen, translated by A. Watson (Philadelphia: Pennsylvania State University Press, 1985).

14. A comparison of Mark 13, sometimes called the "Synoptic Apocalypse," or the "Little Apocalypse," with Luke 21, which is the author's rewriting of Mark, shows how the "end of the age" is indefinitely extended and no longer tied to the Jewish-Roman war of A.D. 66–70.

15. Translation by Wilhelm Schneemelcher, in Edgar Hennecke's *New Testament Apocrypha*, edited by William Schneemelcher, translated by R. McL. Wilson, vol. 2 (Philadelphia: Westminster Press, 1965), p. 353.

16. Ignatius, *Philippians* 3:2.

17. See Eusebius, *Church History* 2.14.5–6 and 3.1.2. Eusebius says he is relying on Origen, an early-third-century Christian theologian.

18. An expanded legendary account is found in the apocryphal *Acts of Peter* 37–38.

INDEX

"An exciting, extraordinary, exceptional discovery. See for yourself the first archaeological evidence ever for early Christian belief in resurrection."

— Barrie Wilson, Professor of Religious Studies, York University, Toronto, and author of *How Jesus Became Christian*

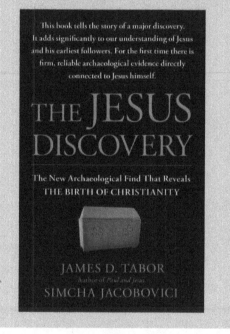

The fascinating story behind a major archaeological discovery—the oldest known depiction of a Christian symbol—that revolutionizes our understanding of Jesus and early Christianity.

Pick up or download your copy today! SIMON & SCHUSTER A CBS COMPANY